THE SPIRIT OF
CHINESE PHILOSOPHY

by

FUNG YU-LAN, Ph.D.

Professor of Philosophy, Tsinghua University

translated by

E. R. HUGHES, M.A.

Reader in Chinese Philosophy, Oxford University

GREENWOOD PRESS, PUBLISHERS
WESTPORT, CONNECTICUT

Originally published in 1947
by Kegan Paul, Trench, Trubner & Co., Ltd., London

First Greenwood Reprinting 1970

SBN 8371-2816-1

CONTENTS

AUTHOR'S PREFACE TO THE ENGLISH EDITION

My country's war with Japan broke out in 1937. Since that time, I have given a good part of my time to a series of books, which I have called a " series written at a *time of national rebirth* ". In these writings, it seems to me, there has taken shape—more solidly than was the case in my mind previously—a system of thought to which I have given the name of The New Li Hsüeh. The significance of this name will become clear to the reader as he peruses this book.

In this series, four of the books are particularly relevant to this system of thought in its philosophical aspect : the first, *Hsin Li Hsüeh* (Commercial Press, Shanghai, 1939), which deals with the metaphysical aspects of the system : the second, *Hsin Yüan Jen* (Commercial Press, 1943), referred to in this book also as *A New Treatise on the Nature of Man*, which deals with the ethical implications of the system : the third, this present book, entitled *Hsin Yüan Tao*, which deals with the historical background to the system. The fourth one, now in preparation, will be entitled *Hsin Chih Yen*, and will deal with the methodology of the system.

The *Hsin Yüan Tao*, treating as it does of the developments in the main stream of Chinese philosophy, may be taken as a concise history of Chinese philosophy, though not in the strict sense. At any rate, it certainly can be taken as a supplement to my two-volume History of Chinese Philosophy, the first volume of which has been translated by Dr. Derk Bodde of Pennsylvania University (Henry Vetch, Peiping, 1937 : Allen and Unwin, London). I have put in this book all my new ideas in regard to Chinese philosophy which have arisen since the publication of my History ten years ago.

I wish to take this opportunity of expressing my thanks to my friend, Mr. E. R. Hughes, of Oxford University, for the pains which he has taken in making this English rendering. In this connection it should be noted that whilst in many passages the resources of the English language have proved fairly adequate to the demands made on them, yet in other passages the translator and I sadly agreed that there seemed no way of rendering the full sense of the original. This applies particularly to passages quoted from the ancient writers, and is an inevitable drawback to a translation, whatever the languages concerned.

My thanks are also due to the China Philosophy Society, and to the Translation and Compilation Bureau, in Chungking, for the interest, encouragement and support which they gave so that my book might appear in an English form, and particularly to the China Philosophy Society for the honour which it has done me in making this book the first of its *Library of Chinese Philosophy*, and the first to be put before the English reading public.

FUNG YU-LAN.

KUNMING,
September, 1944.

TRANSLATOR'S PREFACE

In most cases there is no need for a translator to intrude himself alongside the author of the original version. In this case, however, certain exceptional circumstances stare me in the face, so that I must ask the reader's indulgence.

In the first place, there is plainly a rapidly growing number of people in Britain who want to know the truth about China, and in pursuit of this aim wish to study what the Chinese have to say about themselves. Here your true scholar and scientist in China finds himself in a difficulty. In facing a foreign audience, it is so easy to err in painting the picture too brightly or too darkly ; therefore the better the scholar he is the less he can be persuaded to discharge this duty. To overcome this difficulty, the only thing to be done is to take what a man has written for his own people and translate it. This is the *raison d'être* of this translation of Dr. Fung's most recent book. In other words, what seemed most needed in Britain was what a teacher had to say, a teacher to whom his fellow-countrymen are looking for teaching at this time when the integrity of their national life has been so sharply assailed. As the Author's Preface shows, the " War of Resistance " has had a searching effect on him, bringing to the surface what lay deep in him, and causing him to write and write. This philosopher, at any rate, was not living in an ivory tower and letting the world go by (as indeed I saw in 1943, when his eldest son went off to the war on the Salween Front).

Further, one utterance by a thinker and teacher, however outstanding and representative he may be, is not enough. What a thoughtful Englishman is wanting along this line is a succession of utterances, so that he may come to feel the movement in the thinker's mind, may go away from him after one bout and come back to him a year or so later to consider a second, and then later a third, utterance straight from the living pen. Then this thoughtful Englishman can begin to place him, and in placing him get an insight into the " Great Tradition " which he has inherited and which to the extent of his powers he is helping to consolidate, or it may be in some measure to break down.

Here I think Dr. Fung is particularly valuable to us. To

begin with, his boyhood, spent in his home province of Honan, the seat of China's first cultural advance, came at the time when the Boxer Incident and its aftermath stirred China's scholars in the deep places of their souls, as they had not been stirred for fourteen centuries. As in those earlier days they had to see themselves afresh against the background of an Indian and Western-Asian " West " with its Buddhist challenge, so in these later days they had to do the same in the face of a European West. This time for many hundreds of young men the challenge entailed going to the West and giving the most formative years of their youth to the intensive study of Western culture, either its institutions and law, its history and traditional philosophies, or its later phases in the natural sciences. What this meant is only now to be understood and even so only in part. Where there has been a movement of the mind outward, it will be followed by a movement of the mind inward, and that the movement of a new mind, critically alert in a fashion previously impossible. The fruits of this process take time to mature, but when they have matured, as far as they can within a generation, they have a significance which is not merely personal. Nor is that significance to be judged solely by a criterion of mechanical logical perfection.

Thus, for example, some readers may perhaps feel dubious over the kind of relation which Dr. Fung sees between metaphysical propositions and formal propositions (vid. c. iii and elsewhere). I have my own doubts, though reading Mr. Austin Farrer's *Finite and Infinite* I get some light on the problem. (Cf. R. G. Collingwood's *The Idea of Nature*, e.g. pt. ii, c. 3, and his emphasis on Hegel's " That is as far as consciousness has gone ".) Again, by way of example, I, with my deeply rooted theistic mind, am not sure that I grasp the significance of Dr. Fung's " the sublime " and " the beyond ". They tend to elude me, just as my theism makes him suspect an unwarranted anthropomorphic twist to my mind.

However, it is not for a translator to enlarge on his own opinions. The main point is that the reader should appreciate *The Spirit of Chinese Philosophy* as one of the fruits of the new ferment in China. For Dr. Fung, as for his scholar contemporaries, now in their fifties and sixties, the " Great Tradition " of the European West had to be explored ; this on its own merits as part of China's world heritage. An appreciation of this in many of China's best scholars will give the right approach to the " new *li hsüeh* ", with its roots in the Sung *li hsüeh* (dogma of the ideal pattern), and its new appreciation of Western categories of thought.

There is one other matter. The author's position is, for all its courageous idealism (in the popular sense), none the less fundamentally realistic (in the philosophical sense). I trace a Chinese characteristic here. It is that a great deal of Western eighteenth-century idealistic philosophizing seems to the good Chinese mind rather otiose, serving no great purpose. And yet, as this book shows clearly enough, the fundamental problems on which Bishop Berkeley and others busied themselves with such nervous energy were familiar to Chinese thinkers from classical times. May we not say that they accepted the idealist dilemma and preserved their composure over it, in spite of the cutting edge which Buddhist epistemology gave to the controversy? They would, I expect, have thought Dr. Johnson rather silly really when he stubbed his foot against a stone; and yet predominantly they remained realists, and from that angle went on to ask the question for the human race, what there was in the universe on which it could rely and what on which it could not. Not an unsensible course to pursue!

Alongside of this lay the tendency to explore the ethical implications to every kind of philosophical problem. Now, to assume from this, as too often has been done in Western circles, that Chinese philosophy has only been concerned with the ethical and has not tried to explore the metaphysical bases to ethics, is about as absurd as it could be. It merely shows that we are ignorant of the involved history of Chinese thought. Here again, Dr. Fung's book is valuable to us. It shows how his mind moves naturally and easily to and fro between pure philosophy and applied. This may make us catch our breath, but again it is, after all, the sensible procedure for a realist, and a mystical realist at that. For one thing, it would appear that it saves the study of philosophy from the excessive intellectualization which we tend to suffer from in the West.

In conclusion, the reader may well ask why this book has been translated first and not the earlier ones in the series to which Dr. Fung refers. The answer is, because the *Hsin Li Hsüeh* seemed to me too long and too technical for the non-professional philosopher, whilst this book, although not a history of Chinese thought, does work out its theme on a historical basis, and for that reason alone meets our need. Also, I confess that I was attracted by the ink being hardly dry on the author's manuscript.

As I have said above, I had the feeling that what my fellow countrymen wanted was something which is palpably alive to-day and not a vintage of twenty or even ten years back. There is also a real advantage in a significant book being published in the two languages at the same time. The thinker thus submits his philosophizing to foreign and home criticism at the same time. The less of a time-lag there is, the better it is for everybody concerned. By this means, we can get started with the Socratic method on a grand scale, the really critical method on the scale which printing has made possible and which the breaking down of the distance-barrier between East and West makes it imperative that we should employ.

SUMMARY OF CHAPTER III IN DR. FUNG'S *HSIN YÜAN JEN* (CHUNGKING, 1943)

Man's life is distinguishable into spheres of different grade : (1) the unselfconscious, natural sphere ; (2) the utilitarian sphere ; (3) the moral sphere ; (4) the transcendent sphere.

(1) A man may be nothing more than a creature of unquestioning natural instincts. He may be without thought of the existence of the universe or of society, without thought even of his own existence. Unreflectively, he follows his natural tendency, or his personal habits, or the customs of the society in which he lives. He just acts as he does without understanding why he acts so, and indeed without being conscious that his actions are what they are. This sphere of human life is the sphere of human innocence.

(2) Next, a man may be aware of himself as distinct from other men, and thus distinguishing himself, seek exclusively his own greatest advantage, concentrate on increasing his personal property or improving his position, on getting a good reputation, whether in the immediate future or after his death. This sphere of human life is that of egoistic " profit ".

(3) Next, it is possible for an individual to be aware of something above himself, namely society, and to be aware that society is a whole of which he is a part. Action in this sphere is exclusively for the good of the man's society ; in so acting he discharges his " duty " to his society. He devotes himself to his society, rejoicing in his society's joy and sorrowing over its sorrow. This kind of action is moral action, and this sphere of human life is the " moral " sphere.

(4) Lastly, it is possible for an individual to be aware of something above society, namely the universe ; to realize that whereas society is a whole, the universe is the Great Whole. The action of such an individual will be exclusively for the sake of the universe, he will devote himself to the Great Whole, rejoicing in its joy, but not sorrowing over its sorrow because the Great Whole has nothing over which it can sorrow. This sphere of human life is the " transcendent " sphere.

To be aware of the existence of the Great Whole is what the *Hsin Yüan Jen* terms " knowledge of Heaven ". To do one's duty by the Great Whole is what it terms " service of Heaven ". To rejoice in the Great Whole is what it terms " rejoicing in Heaven ". To identify oneself with the Great Whole is what it terms " identification with Heaven ".

Of the four spheres, the natural sphere and the utilitarian sphere are the outcome of things being left as they are, the moral sphere and the sphere of Heaven-and-Earth are the product of cultivation. The first two spheres are the gift of Nature, the other two are the creation of man's spirit. The first two spheres the *Hsin Yüan Jen* affirms to be lower, the other two higher. This is because these two spheres, the moral and the transcendent, owe their existence to a deeper understanding of man's life, and to a higher state of self-consciousness in man with regard to his own actions. In other words, these two spheres owe their existence to higher knowledge.

The possession of this knowledge is that whereby man is distinguished from the other animals. According to the old tradition of Chinese philosophy, the function of philosophy was to enable men to reach these higher spheres. The sphere of Heaven-and-Earth may be described as the sphere of philosophy, for it is self-evidently the product of philosophy. The moral sphere is also the product of philosophy. Mere conformity with moral rules is not the same thing as morality. The matter is not simply one of transgressing certain recognized moral rules or of nourishing certain recognized moral habits. If it were so, men in a state of unselfconscious innocence or egoistic profit-seekers might lay claim to being moral men. If men are to be in possession of the moral sphere, they need to be in possession of an understanding of the moral rules, to have a consciousness of the nature of their own actions, namely, that they are real actions according to moral principles and practised as such. We may borrow the words of a great teacher of the Chan School (in Chinese Buddhism) : " Knowledge—this one word—is the fountain-head of all mysteries." Thus philosophy is the branch of learning whereby man is enabled to attain to this knowledge.

THE SPIRIT OF CHINESE PHILOSOPHY

INTRODUCTION

There are all kinds and conditions of men. With regard to any one of these kinds, there is the highest form of achievement of which the members of that kind are capable. Take, for example, the men engaged in the practical administration of political affairs. The highest form of achievement in that class is that of the great statesman. So also in the field of art, the highest form of achievement of which artists are capable is that of the great artist. Although there are all these different classes of men, yet all the members of them also belong to the class *homo*. Of the members of this all-embracing class, the men who achieve the highest of which man is capable reach the stature of being sages. This amounts to saying that the highest achievement of man *qua* man is in what we call the transcendent sphere.[1]

If men wish to attain to the transcendent sphere do they necessarily have to leave that general life in society which men enjoy in common, or even to divorce themselves from life ? This is a problem. For the philosopher who deals with the transcendent sphere, the easiest tendency is to say " This is necessary." The Buddha said that life itself is the root and fountain-head of the misery of life. Plato also said that the body is the prison of the soul. And some of the Taoists have said, " Life is an excrescence, a tumour, and death is to be taken as the breaking of the tumour." Here is a view which entails separation from what may be said to be the net of the matter-corrupted world. If the highest sphere is to be reached, that entails separation from the manner of living common to our fellows in general. Indeed, separation from life entirely is entailed. Only so can the final liberation be obtained. This kind of philosophy is what is generally known as " other-worldly philosophy ". The life of which this other-worldly philosophy speaks is a sublime one, but it is incompatible with the manner of life maintained in common among men. This manner of life in society is what the Chinese philosophical tradition calls men's relations in their daily functioning,

---

[1] In speaking here of a " sphere " the author is using the terminology of his earlier work, the *Hsin Yüan Jen* (*A New Treatise on the Nature of Man*). In the third chapter of this he distinguishes between four spheres of living of which man is capable. The essence of this third chapter is to be seen in the Summary above.

and this is incompatible with the other-worldly philosophical theory as to the highest life of all. We speak of the other-worldly philosophy as sublime but not concerned with the mean of common activity.

There are some philosophies which emphasize men's relations in their daily functioning. They speak about this and about morality but they either are unable to—or at any rate do not—speak of the highest life of all. These philosophies are what are generally described as " this-worldly " ; and in truth they are not worthy to be called philosophies. We may describe them as concerned with performing the common task, but not attaining to the sublime. From the point of view of a this-worldly philosophy, an other-worldly philosophy is too idealistic, of no practical use, negative ; it is what is known as steeped in emptiness. From the point of view of an other-worldly philosophy, a this-worldly philosophy is too empirical, too superficial : it may be positive, but it is like the quick walking of a man who has taken the wrong road ; the quicker he walks the more he deviates from the right road.

There are many people who say that Chinese philosophy is a this-worldly philosophy. This opinion cannot be said to be either wholly right or wholly wrong.

On a superficial view these words are not wholly wrong, because on that view Chinese philosophy, irrespective of its different schools of thought, directly or indirectly concerns itself with government and ethics. It appears to emphasize society not the universe, the daily functioning of human relations and not hell and heaven, man's present life and not his life in a world to come. Mencius said, " The sage is the acme in human relations," and the sentence taken literally means that the sage is the morally perfect man in society. This ideal man being of this world, it seems that what Chinese philosophy calls a sage is a very different order of person from the Buddha in Buddhism and the saint in the Christian religion.

This, however, is only the superficial view of the question. Chinese philosophy cannot be understood in this over-simple way. So far as the main tenets of its tradition are concerned, if we understand them, they cannot be said to be wholly this-worldly, just as, of course, they cannot be said to be wholly other-worldly. We may use a newly coined expression and say that this philosophy is world-transcending. The meaning of this is that it is both of this world and of the other world.

Chinese philosophy has one main tradition, one main stream of thought. This tradition is that it aims at a particular kind of highest life. But this kind of highest life, high though it is, is not divorced from the daily functioning of human relations. Thus it is both of this world and of the other world, and we maintain that it " both attains to the sublime and yet performs the common tasks ".[1] What Chinese philosophy aims at is the highest of realms, one which transcends the daily functioning of human relations, although it also comes within the scope of this daily functioning. That is : " It is not divorced from daily regular activity, yet it goes straight to what was before the heavens." The first of these two expressions represents the this-worldly side, the second the other-worldly side. That is to say that, both sides being present, Chinese philosophy is what we describe it to be, namely world-transcending. Because it is of this world it is concerned with common activity : because it is other-worldly it reaches up to the sublime : its attention is directed to both worlds, its concern is with both worlds.

Having this kind of spirit, it is at one and the same time both extremely idealistic and extremely realistic, extremely practical, though not in a shallow way. So also it is positive, but not in the sense of a man taking the wrong road and the faster he walks the more he deviates from the right road.

This-worldliness and other-worldliness stand in contrast to each other as do idealism and realism ; and this is the antithesis between what we describe as the sublime and common activity. In ancient Chinese philosophy the antithesis was made between what was called " the inner " and " the outer ", " the root," and " the branches " and " the fine " and " the coarse " ; and after the Han era there was the contrast between what was called " the abstruse " and " the daily task", the contrast between abandoning the world and being in the world, between the active and the contemplative, between the essence and its functioning. All these contrasts are perhaps the same as the contrast between the sublime and the common, or (at any rate) these contrasts are of the same kind. In a world-transcending philosophy and its accompanying manner of life all these contrasts do not continue to be antithetical. This does not mean that, to put it shortly, they are abolished, but that according to the world-transcending

---

[1] These words quoted here and elsewhere in this book are borrowed from the *Chung Yung* : " borrowed " in the sense that the meaning we attach to them is not necessarily the same as the meaning they have in the original. (F. Y. L.)

view-point they are made to become a whole. The sublime and the common still exist with all their differences, but they are synthesized into one whole. How can this be done? This is one problem which Chinese philosophy attempts to solve, and herein lies the spirit of that philosophy, whilst in the solution it gives lies the contribution which it makes to the study of philosophy.

The philosophers of China hold that the highest life of all, that at which philosophy aims, is both this-worldly and other-worldly; and that the men who are in possession of this highest life are the sages. The life of the sage is a transcendent one, and the spiritual achievement of the Chinese sages corresponds to the saint's achievement in Buddhism and the West. They all come under the same head. But to transcend the world does not mean to be divorced from the world, and therefore the Chinese sage is not the kind of sage who is so sublime that he is not concerned about the business of the world. His character is described as one of sageness in its essence and kingliness in its manifestation. That is to say that in his inner sageness he accomplishes spiritual cultivation, in his outward kingliness he functions in society. It is not necessary that a sage should be the actual head of the government in his society. With regard to practical politics, for the most part the sage certainly has no opportunity to be such; and when the statement is made " sage within and king without " it only means that he who has the noblest spirit should theoretically be king. As to whether he actually had or had not the opportunity to be king, that is immaterial.

Since the character of the sage is one of sageness within and kingliness without, philosophy, according to the Chinese tradition, is a branch of learning which exists to enable men to possess this kind of character. Therefore what philosophy discusses is what the philosophers of China describe as the Tao (Way) of " sageness within and kingliness without ".

In China, whatever the school of thought, all Chinese philosophy maintains this Tao in one way or another. But not every school satisfies the criterion of both attaining to the sublime and performing the common task. There are some schools which over-emphasize the sublime, some which over-emphasize the common. This means that some of the philosophies in China are near to being other-worldly, others near to being this-worldly. In the history of Chinese philosophy, from first to last, the more influential philosophers have been those who have attempted to synthesize the two sides, the sublime and the common.

With regard to this problem it may be said that "the later arrivals take the higher place": in other words that there has been a progressive development in Chinese philosophy. It is this progressive course which is traced in this book, the different theories of each important school being considered in historic order. Also the criterion of "attainment to the sublime and concern for the common" is used, with a view to deciding the value of each of the schools.

This task of ours is very like that undertaken in the *T'ien Hsia Chapter*, in the *Chuang Tzŭ Book*, in relation to the pre-Ch'in philosophy. We cannot be sure who the author of this chapter was, for there is no record; but the way in which he accomplished his task was admirable. He is one of the finest historians of ancient philosophy, as also one of the finest critics and appraisers. In his chapter he uses the expression "sageness within and kingliness without", and denotes this principle as "the Tao method", i.e. the method which enables men to know the whole truth. He holds that among the philosophers of his time not one obtained "the Tao method" as a whole. Each only obtained one part of it, or one aspect. Since each only partially apprehended the Tao method, therefore what each had to say was "only the words of one school" and did not constitute an expression of the Tao: it was but one method with its limitations.

Since the Tao is the principle of "sageness within and kingliness without", it is also, from the point of view of its comprehensive use by man as a method, "the attainment of the sublime and the performance of the common task." This is what the *T'ien Hsia* Chapter emphasizes. We find there "the man who is not divorced from the absolute, is a heavenly man: the man who is not divorced from the essential is a spirit man; the man not divorced from the true is a complete man. Make Heaven absolute; make spiritual quality the root; make the Tao the door which reveals this in changing (life). The man who does this is to be called a sage". Kuo Hsiang (died A.D. 312) in commenting on this passage said, "These four designations differ in the author's speech, but at bottom they are equivalent to one person." These four kinds of men are all men living in the sphere of the highest life of all, the transcendent realm. "Heavenly man," "spirit man," and "complete man" denote but one man, only expressed in different fashion. But the sage is not the same as the other three. He has all the qualities which the others have, but he has also something which they have not.

The sage " makes Heaven absolute ", and thus he " is not divorced from the absolute ". He makes moral power fundamental, and thus he " is not divorced from the essence ".[1] He makes the Tao the door, and thus he is not divorced from the true.[2] This is what the heavenly man and the other two possess. But the sage also has the ability to deal adequately with life in all its variety. In this respect the sage has what the others have not. He is able to attend to the sublime, yet to be concerned with common activity. The others can attend to the sublime to the extreme, but it is very doubtful whether they can also deal with common activity. Following on these statements comes one about the noble-minded man. The words are " he makes human-heartedness his form of doing favour, and righteousness his form of reasoning (activity), makes music his form of harmonizing, in sweet compelling fashion being kind and human-hearted ". This kind of man lives in the high moral sphere ; and can deal with common activity, but cannot attend to the sublime.

The *T'ien Hsia Chapter* appears to take this criterion of attainment to the sublime and the performance of the common task as its criterion in criticizing the views of the philosophers of that era. At least we can say that, according to Kuo Hsiang's interpretation, something very like this was the actual meaning in the *T'ien Hsia Chapter*. In the succeeding passage we find " The men of old, how complete they were ! They were the mates of the spirits,[3] imbued with Heaven and Earth, nourishing well all creatures, harmonizing the society of man, bringing the dew of their grace to all the clans, clear as to the fundamental numbers, linking them to the less important measures in a far-reaching and all-embracing fashion, including in their operations the small and the great, the fine and the coarse ". The reference in " the men of old " is to the sages. The sages were able to synthesize the antitheses between the root and the branches, between the small and the great, the fine and the coarse. The sages were able to be mates to the spirits and be imbued with Heaven and Earth, and they were also able to nourish well all creatures and harmonize

---

[1] In a later passage of the *T'ien Hsia Chapter* there come the words " consider the fundamental as the fine essence, and material things as the coarse ". (F. Y. L.)

[2] In the *Lao Tzŭ Book* comes the statement, " Taking the entity of the Tao within, it is a fine essence, and this essence is very true, and within this truth is reality." Chuang Tzŭ said, " The Tao has truth and reality and is non-active and without form." (F. Y. L.)

[3] *shen ming*, lit. spirit lights. The term occurs frequently enough in early literature, but it is not clear whether it has a distinctive meaning from plain *shen*. The spirits designated are not spirits of the dead but spirits in the sense of Lares and Penates. (E. R. H.)

the society of man. In the first part of the passage the reference is to the spiritual power of sageness within ; in the second part to the achievement of kingliness without. The expression " spirits " denotes the spiritual aspect of the universe. If there are such men with the character adequate for being sage within and kingly without, they are able to " perfect the excellence of heaven and earth and assume the appearance of spirits ". In an earlier passage we find " Where did the spirits descend from and where was their light produced ? There was the birth of the sage and the completing process of the king, all this originating from the One ! " : words which put the sage-kings and the spirits on the same level. Thus the truth about " the One " is the Tao method, and the Tao method is then the fundamental principle of sageness within and kingliness without. The Confucian scholars originally regarded the recording of " the men of old " as their task, but unfortunately what they wrote is somewhat of the nature of " numbering and measuring ", i.e. deals with unimportant details in the sacred books. In the *T'ien Hsia Chapter* we find " What is intelligible in numbers and measurements, this the historians who follow the old traditions still have. What is in the sacred books, the *Odes*, *History* and *Rituals* and *Music*, this the scholars of Tsou and Lu, the teachers in their awe-inspiring (robes) for the most part could understand." To this Kuo Hsiang's comment is, " They could be clear about the visible consequences. But what about that whereby the consequences came to be ? " Therefore, according to the *T'ien Hsia Chapter's* interpretation, the Confucian philosophers were not in accord with the criterion of the sublime.

The other schools were not impartial or comprehensive, but consisted of " tortuous-minded scholars ". Their theories did not represent the whole principle of sageness within and kingliness without, but over-emphasized one aspect. None the less, the Tao method is in these theories. " They had heard the rumour of this aspect and delighted in it." Further down the *T'ien Hsia Chapter* records Mo Tzŭ's theories and in conclusion says, " Mo Tzŭ truly loved the world. In his search for the good of the world, even if he was unsuccessful, he still went on in spite of getting worn out. Nevertheless, he was a man of great natural talents." That is all the critic can say of him. Kuo Hsiang comments on this : " he had not the spiritual power (of the Tao)," that is to say, he did not make dwelling in the sublime part of the criterion.

The *T'ien Hsia Chapter* also records Sung K'eng and Yin Wen's theories and says of them, " they took the cessation of war to be the achievement without and the reduction of desire to small proportions as the quality within : in matters small and great, fine and coarse, they just practised to this point and stopped there." Kuo's comment is, " they were unable to reach the sphere of abstraction and ferry over into the beyond." They knew the distinction between the within and the without, the small and the great, the fine and the coarse, but " they went only to this point and no further ". They also did not make dwelling in the sublime part of the criterion.

The *T'ien Hsia Chapter* also records the theories of P'eng Meng, T'ien P'ien, and Shen Tao. It says of them, " they did not know the Tao ; though in a general way they had heard something about it." Kuo's comment is, " they definitely came short." They were able to view creation from the point of view of the Tao. They knew that, " for everything there is that of which it is capable and that of which it is not capable." Therefore they said, " Selection involves exclusion ; instruction involves incompleteness ; the Tao omits nothing." That in the terminology of the *Hsin Yüan Jen* meant that they " knew Heaven ", but they regarded the formation of character as consisting in " being like creatures without knowledge ". For them that was sufficient ; and there was no use for sages, since " a clod of earth does not miss the Tao ". They hoped to abolish the distinctions of knowledge to such a degree that, as we say in the *Hsin Yüan Jen* about identification with Heaven, they did not know that the men in that sphere of living, being without knowledge (i.e. mundane knowledge), yet have self-conciousness and are not like senseless creatures. Thus Peng Meng, T'ien P'ien, and Shen Tao are of " the sublime ", but not of the wholly sublime.

The *T'ien Hsia Chapter* also records the theories of Kuan Yin and Lao Tan. " They built their system on the principle of the permanence of non-being and being, and centred it upon the idea of super-oneness. Their outward expression was weakness and humility. Pure emptiness that yet did not destroy objective things was for them reality. They regarded the fundamental as the essence, and things as coarse . . . and dwelt quietly alone with the spirits. They did indeed attain to the measure of the wholly sublime. On the other hand, they were always tolerant towards things, and not aggressive towards men." They may be described as able to deal with common activity.

The *T'ien Hsia Chapter* also records Chuang Tzǔ's idea. " Above he roamed with the Creator. Below he made friends of those who, without beginning or end, are beyond life and death. In regard to the fundamental he was comprehensive and great, profound and free. In regard to the essential, he may be called the harmonious adapter to higher things." He attained to the wholly sublime. On the other hand, " he came and went alone with the spirit of Heaven and Earth, but had no sense of pride in his superiority to all things. . . . He did not condemn either right or wrong, so he was able to get along with ordinary people. . . . He also may be described as able to deal with common activity."

The *T'ien Hsia Chapter* appraises Lao Tan and Chuang Chou, but when recording their theories it says, " One aspect of the Tao method of the ancients was there, and Kuan Yin, Lao Tan, and Chuang Chou heard the rumour of that aspect and delighted in it." From this we can say of Lao Tan and Chuang Chou that they were not impartial, nor inclusive. The *T'ien Hsia Chapter* may consider their theories as an important part or aspect of the Tao method, but they still form only one part or one aspect. On this point we are not in a position to come to a definite conclusion, although we may disregard the author of the *T'ien Hsia Chapter* and come to our own conclusion. We may say that these theories do not wholly agree with the criterion of attainment to the sublime and the performance of the common task. Therefore we only say that Lao Tan and Chuang Chou may be described as able to deal with common activity. Since there is a chapter later (vid. c. 4) in which is given an exposition of Lao Tan's and Chuang Chou's views, there is no need to say more here.

CHAPTER I

CONFUCIUS (551–479 B.C.) AND MENCIUS (372–289 B.C.)

As the *T'ien Hsia Chapter* put it " the scholar gentlemen (*shih*) of Tsou and Lu only had understanding (of the old books), the *Odes*, the *History*, the *Rituals* and *Music* " and in them " the details of number and measurement ". As applied to the ordinary scholar (*Ju*) the criticism was right. The term " *ju* " originally denoted a particular profession, namely, the men who helped with expert advice on the rituals and regularly gave teaching on them. They had a practical knowledge of these matters, including the forms of the traditional music, as dealt with in certain accepted handbooks. That being the nature of their expertise, what Kuo Hsiang said of them was quite true, that they only knew " the surviving traces of the men of old " and did not understand " that in these survivals which caused them to survive ".

This criticism, however, cannot be used of Confucius and Mencius. They were Ju, but they were also creators of a school of Ju philosophy. The ordinary Ju who as a class existed before Confucius and Mencius, were by no means the same as the Ju philosophers (*Ju Chia*). Whereas the former were in society the expert readers and writers in regard to the old traditions, the latter constituted a new school of learning. Confucius and Mencius also expounded the rituals and music and the " men of old ", but what they had to say was not merely a " reflection of the light of the men of old " but " a development of that light ". Confucius said, " I am a transmitter and not a creator, I believe in the past and love it " (vid. *Lun Yü, Bk. VII*). This is what the ordinary ju had all along been doing, but Confucius in speaking thus really meant that by transmitting he created. Because he created by transmitting, he was not merely an ordinary Ju, but the creator of a Ju philosophy.

The Ju philosophers expounded *jen* (human-heartedness) and *yi* (righteousness) and became known for this in later generations. According to Classical Chinese terminology, where human-heartedness and righteousness are used separately, each has its own meaning ; but where they are used together, the combination denotes what to-day we call " principled morality ". The *Lao Tzŭ Book* says, " Away with *jen* and have done with *yi*," by which is meant not merely that these two virtues were not wanted, but that no kind of morality was wanted. In later generations it would be said that a certain man was " highly *jen* and *yi* ", by which was meant that he was a man of high moral quality. And the same with regard to a man who was called " not-*jen* and not-*yi* " : the meaning was that he was an immoral person. Thus the significance of the name which the Ju philosophers gained by expounding *jen* and *yi* is equivalent to the name " moral philosophers ".

These Ju philosophers were not merely preachers of the rules or precepts of morality, calling men to keep and remember them blindly. They really understood that whereby morality is morality, viz. that element in moral action which makes it moral. To use the terminology of the *Hsin Yüan Jen*, they really understood how life in the moral sphere differs alike from the life in the utilitarian sphere and the life in the unselfconsciously natural sphere.

We now proceed first to deal with the chief teachings of these Ju philosophers, namely human-heartedness, righteousness, the ritual-observing disposition and wisdom. In later days these four, with the addition of " reliability " (trustworthiness) became " the Five Constant Virtues ". But Mencius only spoke of " four buds ", namely human-heartedness, righteousness, the ritual-observing disposition, and wisdom ; and although Mencius was the first to systematize them, these four were what Confucius constantly expounded.

Let us take first the meaning of righteousness. Mencius said, " Human-heartedness represents the human heart, righteousness the human way " (vid. *Bk. VI, A*). Righteousness is the road in which men ought to walk, is what is described as " what ought to be so and is so not for any utilitarian end ".[1] The meaning of this " ought to be so " implies an obligation. But when we speak of an obligation in this connection we need to distinguish it from one in the utilitarian sense. The two senses are different. The utilitarian obligation is conditional, relative not absolute. For instance, we say that a man ought to study hygiene. This " ought " exists because hygiene is a means to health. Good health is the ultimate aim of hygiene, and hence hygiene " ought " to be pursued only in so far as a man desires health, this kind of end. But if a man does not wish to be healthy, then the pursuit of hygienic conditions of living does not contain any " ought " for

[1] A phrase by Ch'en Ch'un, a disciple of Confucius. (F. Y. L.)

him. This kind of " ought " has real imperative force to it, but this force is not apart from utilitarian ends.

Righteousness is a moral obligation, and this kind of obligation is an unconditional one. That is to say it has real imperative force apart from any utilitarian ends. Because it is unconditional, therefore it is absolute. This then is the kind of obligation which is implied by righteousness ; and righteousness is that element in moral action by which action becomes moral action. If a man's actions are to be moral, it is necessary that he should unconditionally do those things which he feels to be obligatory. That is to say, he cannot do those things as the means to achieve his personal ends ; for then they would not be unconditioned. His action depends on the will to seek this end ; it is this end which makes the action obligatory and without this will the action ceases to be obligatory. Thus, since the moral obligation is an unconditional one, it follows in the case of a conditioned action that although it is obligatory for the man concerned, and although it may happen to be in accordance with righteousness, yet it is not a righteous action.[1]

Now, this does not mean that any man in doing what is morally obligatory for him, is acting blindly or at random. What is obligatory for him also has a fixed end, and with all his heart and all his strength he seeks to attain this end. What he does not do is to take the attainment of this end to be the means to any utilitarian end. For instance, take a man with a certain task to perform, one which as a moral man he sincerely performs. All the actions which are obligatory in relation to this task he performs with all his might in order to achieve success. Speaking from this aspect, these actions have an end, but if they are done in sincerity the reason for them is necessarily only that it is obligatory for him to act so, not because he wishes by so doing to obtain either some reward from above or the praise of his fellows. This is the meaning of an " unconditional obligation ". It is thus only when a man does unconditionally what it is obligatory for him to do that his action becomes a moral one. Only then is the sphere in which he lives the moral sphere. To use the Ju philosophers' language, an action taken

[1] To the Western philosophical reader the connection of this train of thought with Kant's " categorical imperative " and " hypothetical imperative " is obvious. If it be wondered why Dr. Fung does not make this clear, it should be remembered that he is writing for his fellow-countrymen who are in the great majority of cases unfamiliar with Kant's philosophy. Also Dr. Fung might wish not to borrow any extraneous authority to an argument originating in his Chinese tradition. Cf. p.16. (E. R. H.)

for a personal utilitarian end is with a view to profit (*li*), whilst the action taken irrespective of utilitarian ends is a righteous action. This is what the Ju philosophers described as the distinction between profit and righteousness. They laid special emphasis on this point. Confucius said, " The noble-minded man comprehends righteousness, the low-minded man comprehends profit." (*Lun Yü, Bk. IV.*) Mencius said, " The cock crows and gets up : the man who does good betimes is a disciple of Shun (the sage emperor). The cock crows and gets up, and his ' betimes ' is for the sake of profit, so that he is a disciple of Chih (the great robber). If you want to know the difference between Shun and Chih, it lies between profit and goodness." (*Mencius, Bk. VII, A.*)

The difference between these two is what we have described in the *Hsin Yüan Jen* as the distinction between the utilitarian life and the moral life. If a man's actions be ones which are not irrespective of utilitarian ends, they still may be in accord with morality, but they are not moral actions. The life he lives is the utilitarian life, not the moral life.

In a later generation Tung Chung-shu (2nd century B.C.) said, " Let him rectify his idea of rightness and not scheme for profit for himself : let him understand the right way and not success for himself." These words of his have the same significance as those of Confucius and Mencius given above. But there are some people who misunderstand them. For instance Yen Hsi-chai (1635–1704) said, " Is there any farmer in the world who tills his fields without scheming for a harvest ? Is there any fisherman who lets down his net and does not count on getting fish ? " This point of view, disallowing any material end, is the same as Lao Tzŭ's with its root principle of ' non-being ' and the Buddha's with its root principle of ' emptiness '. " This criticism is entirely beside the point. The question is for what reason the field is tilled, for what end the fish is caught. If a man does it for his own profit, his action cannot be a moral one. Nevertheless, although it is not a moral action, it does not necessarily follow that it is an immoral action. It is possible for it to be an amoral action.

The Ju philosophers, in speaking of " righteousness ", some-times made the point that in certain circumstances the best method of transacting a certain piece of business is the righteous method. In the *Chung Yung* there occur the words, " Righteousness is the right and proper." We ask about a certain piece of business, how rightly to transact it, or what is the right, i.e. the best method of transacting it. Any kind of business in any kind of circumstances has its right method of transaction, and that is the best method for transacting it in those circumstances. Here, when we speak of " the best ", there are two possible meanings : (1) the best from the standpoint of morality, (2) the best from the standpoint of profit ; i.e. the largest possible profit for the man who transacts that particular business, whilst from the moral angle the result should be the greatest possible moral achievement for the man who transacts it. And then we say " in certain circumstances ", because the rightness in " the right " and " proper " has also the meaning of " the right defined in relation to the circumstances ". This is why Mencius said, " A great man is not bent on having his words believed nor on making his actions effective. He takes his stand on righteousness, nothing else." (*Mencius, Bk. IV, B.*)

What we are saying here about righteousness in action is rather like what the Ju philosophers described as " the mean ". There is, however, a difference. The term " hitting the mean " [1] is used equally with righteousness to describe the transacting of any business. But in itself the concept " hitting the mean " is exclusively an amoral one, neither moral nor immoral, and therefore to be distinguished from the concept of " righteousness ". For instance, in ordinary circumstances eating is an amoral business. A man takes a meal and eats neither too much nor too little : he neither goes beyond the mark, nor falls short of it. This may be described as in accord with the mean, but it cannot be described as in accord with righteousness. Righteousness does not come into the question at all.

So far in the above two paragraphs we have given only a formal exposition of " righteousness " ; for there is no reference to what kind of business is the subject of an unconditioned obligation. Nor is there any reference to what—from the moral standpoint—is " the best method ". We may say that the Ju philosophers maintained that anything which conduces to the benefit of society or of others, this is an unconditioned obligation. And any action which in any way conduces to such benefit, this is from the moral standpoint the best method of transacting any business.

[1] Cf. the Western " Golden Mean ". The Chinese concept of " the mean " has more markedly than the Western popular concept the idea of action which is positively central, exactly right, in contrast to the exaggerations of too much or too little. (E. R. H.)

We only say " we *may* say that the Ju philosophers maintained . . . ", for in this matter they were not entirely explicit. But their meaning was like this; and we have to understand this meaning before we can understand their distinction between righteousness and profit.

There are critics who say that these philosophers laid emphasis on the distinction between righteousness and profit, but that they constantly fell into inconsistencies over it. As the *Lun Yü* has it, " When the Master went to Wei, Jan Yu was driver of his carriage. The Master said, ' What a big population ! ' Jan Yu said, ' When the numbers have increased, what next requires to be done ? ' The reply was, ' Enrich them.' When Jan Yu asked what further still required to be done, the reply was ' Give them good teaching '." (*Lun Yü, Bk. XIII.*)   Confucius thus laid emphasis on the wealth and numbers of the people. Is not this an emphasis on " profit " for the people ? Also in *Mencius* we find " Mencius had an audience of King Hui Liang who said to him, ' You have counted a thousand miles as not too far to come here. Surely you have some way of profiting my country.' Mencius replied, ' Sire, why must you say profiting ? There is human-heartedness and righteousness, nothing more.' " Thus Mencius took the king to be wrong in speaking of profit. Yet he proposed to the king what we modern people speak of as " an economic policy ", so that men might be able to wear silk and eat meat ; that in the nourishment of their lives and the burial of their dead they might have no sense of dissatisfaction. Thus surely Mencius himself also was concerned with profit!

The reason why this question is raised here in connection with Confucius and Mencius is that such questioners do not clearly understand the distinction made by the Ju philosophers between righteousness and profit. They do not know that profit here indicates private profit. The actions which are directed to obtaining private profit are profit-seeking actions. But, if the profit which is sought is not the private profit of an individual but the public profit of society or of others, then these actions are not profit-seeking but righteous. The public profit of society or of others is then the unconditioned obligation of every individual in society. To seek, without any conditions attached, the profit of society or of others, is the aim of a righteous action. Righteousness is the moral value in this kind of action. All actions which have moral value are moral actions. And all such actions are righteous actions. They imply righteousness because all actions with moral value of necessity (logically) take unconditionally as their objective the profit of other men. E.g., a filial son unconditionally seeks the profit of his parents, and a kind father of necessity unconditionally seeks the profit of his son. Unconditionally to seek to benefit the parents or the sons is the objective in their actions. Filial duty or parental kindness are the moral values in their actions. Therefore what is called " profit ", if it be profit for the individual, is the direct opposite to righteousness. But if what is called " profit " is the public profit of society, other men's profit, then not only are profit and righteousness not opposed to each other, but profit is even the content of righteousness. The Ju philosophers made a sharp distinction between righteousness and profit, but there were also times when they took righteousness and profit to have an intimate connection. E.g., in the amplification of the *Yi Scripture* under the Ch'ien hexagram there are these words : " Profit is the harmonizing element in righteousness." The reason for this lies in what we are saying. In a later generation Ch'eng Yi (1033–1107) said, " Righteousness compared with profit is just something public compared with something private." (*Erh Ch'eng Yi Shu, Bk. XVII.*) To seek private profit, my own profit, is to be profit-seeking : to seek public profit, the profit of other men, is to act righteously.

Turning to the other Ju virtue, *jen*, Mencius said, " *Jen* is (the expression of) the human heart " (*Bk. VI, A.*) In the *Chung Yung* it is said, " the *jen* man is one who is a man." Ch'eng Yi said, " Unselfishness impregnated with fellow-feeling, this is *jen*." (*Erh Ch'eng Yi Shu, Bk. XVII.*) Any transaction which is done unconditionally as a benefit to society or some other man, this is a righteous action. But if, when a man acts in this way, it is not only because of the unconditional obligation but also because of an honest love and sense of fellow-feeling with society and other men—if he has what we call sympathy—then not only is the action a righteous action, it is also a *jen* action. That is why it is said, " *Jen* is (the expression of) the human heart," and " To be human-hearted is to be a man ". Mencius also said, " A sense of fellow-feeling is the bud of *jen*."

Righteousness includes *jen* ; a *jen* action is most certainly a righteous action. But while *jen* implies righteousness, for an action to be righteous does not necessarily entail that it is a *jen* action. The Ju philosophers' unconditioned obligation bears some resemblance to the western philosopher, Kant's position. But although in speaking of " the categorical imperative " Kant did justice to the concept of righteousness, he did not do justice to the extra concept of *jen*.

A *jen* man is sure to have good ability in considering others. Because of what he desires for himself, he can consider other men and know what they desire. Because of what he does not desire, he can consider others and know what they do not desire. Thus through knowing other men's desires by his own desires, in wanting to become a solid man in society, he makes other men solid ; in wanting success for himself, he makes other men successful. (*Lun Yü, Bk. VI.*) " I treat the aged in my family properly and extend this to the aged in other men's families ; treat the young in my family properly and extend this to the young in other men's families." (*Mencius, Bk. I, A.*) This is what is called (in China) *chung*. Because of what I do not desire, I know what others do not desire, and therefore " what I do not desire for myself I do not apply to others ". (*Lun Yü, Bk. XV.*) This is called *shu*. The combination of *chung* and *shu* is what is known as the great way of *chung* and *shu*. The great teacher of the Sung era, Chu Hsi, explained this as follows : " To do one's very best, this is *chung*, to extend this beyond oneself is *shu*." But it is better to say, " To do one's very best for the sake of others is *chung* " ; i.e. *chung* like *shu* involves extending oneself to include others. *Chung* is the positive aspect of extending oneself to include one's fellow men, *shu* is the negative aspect. As is said in the *Lun Yü*, " *Chung* and *shu* both mean being very able to find illustrations near at hand." Add to this Mencius' statement " able in extending the scope of his actions ". Chu Hsi's comment here is, " To illustrate is to compare. The near at hand is in one's own person as illustrating other men and thereby knowing what they desire." This is exactly what is known as " *chung* ". Men can also take what they do not desire, to illustrate what other men do not desire. This in truth is what is called *shu*. Thus, " to extend the scope of one's actions " to include others, this is the starting point of the practice of *jen*. Therefore Confucius said, " To be able to find illustrations near at hand, this, and nothing else, is the method of *jen*." (*Lun Yü, Bk. VI.*) *Jen* is the very centre of Confucius' philosophy, and *chung* and *shu* are the starting points of *jen*. Hence Confucius said, " My Tao is to thread together into one," and Tseng Tzŭ could explain this by saying, " The Master's Tao is *chung* plus *shu*, and nothing more nor less." (*Lun Yü, Bk. IV.*)

Thirdly, *li* (ritual) is the standard of conduct which man

B

has fixed, judging it to be the representative of righteousness. Above we have said that the content of righteousness is the benefit of others. The content of *li* also is benefit to others. Thus in the *Record of Rites* (*Ch'ü Li*), we find, " Ritual is humbling oneself to pay respect to others ; putting others first and oneself second." Also, as we have said above, righteousness is in some ways the mean, so that the statement might be made that righteousness is the moral mean in the moral aspect of action. Therefore the Ju philosophers used the concept of the mean to explain the nature of ritual action. In the *Chung Ni Yen Chü* there is the following : " The Master said, ' It is the ritual which determines the mean.' " Again, as we have said above, " Righteousness is the right-and-proper," and this right-and-proper is " the delimitation of the mean according to the circumstances ". According to the Ju philosophers ritual is " variable " ; it varies according to the occasion. Thus in the *Li Ch'i* of the *Record of Rites*, we find " The occasion is for ritual of very great importance " ; and in the *Yo Chi*, " The times of the Sage Emperors differed from each other, therefore their music was not the same ; the three Sage Kings lived in different eras, and their rituals were also different."

Lastly, in *chih* (wisdom) lies the understanding of human-heartedness and righteousness and ritual conduct. A man must have an understanding of *jen* before he can do *jen* acts ; and the same applies to righteousness and ritual conduct, specially with regard to the last, if a man is not to toe the line blindly. If he has not this understanding, his actions may be in accord with *jen* and *yi*, but speaking strictly they are not acts of *jen* and *yi* ; at the most they can only be in accord, and even so only in the sense everywhere attached to blindly toeing the line. The man without understanding in this matter only follows his nature or what he has been taught. Although his actions may be in accord with morality, that is all they are : they are not moral acts. The life he lives is not the moral life, but only the unselfconsciously natural life. If he wants to live the higher life, he must logically rely on knowledge. Confucius said, " If knowledge gets it but *jen* cannot maintain it, then even if a man gets it, he is sure to lose it." (*Lun Yü, Bk. XV.*) To use the language of the *Hsin Yüan Jen*, understanding can enable men to reach the higher sphere, but it cannot enable them to abide in it. Understanding alone is not sufficient, but without understanding man cannot even reach the higher sphere.

According to this, *jen* and *yi* and *li* and *chih* on the surface are all on the same footing. Actually, however, *jen* and *yi* are on a different level from *li* and *chih*. Mencius would appear to have been conscious of this, for he said, " The central reality of *jen* is to serve one's parents, of *yi* to obey one's elder brother. The central reality of *chih* is knowing these•two things. The central reality of *li* lies in a cultured restraint in relation to these two things." (*Bk. IV, A.*) Here we have an illustration that *li* and *chih* are not on the same level as *jen* and *yi*.

Thus the Ju philosophers in the stress they laid on the distinction between righteousness and profit quite clearly achieved a recognition of the difference between the utilitarian sphere and the moral sphere. The sphere· in which the profit-seeking man lives is the utilitarian sphere of profit, whilst the sphere in which the man who does righteously lives is the moral sphere. Their placing of wisdom along with the three other great moral powers quite clearly shows that the difference between the unself-consciously natural sphere and the other higher spheres was amply recognized by them. Confucius said, " The common people can be made to obey, but they cannot be made to know." (*Lun Yü, Bk. VIII.*) Mencius said, " To act without being clear why, to practise without enquiring into, all their life to follow and not to know the principle involved, this applies to the mass of men." (*Bk. VII, A.*) The life of the man who follows without knowing why, is indeed the unselfconsciously natural life.

None the less, the Ju philosophers did not make a clear distinction between the moral life and the transcendent life. For this they were constantly criticized by the Taoist philosophers ; and there was good ground for this criticism. But when the Taoists regarded the Confucianist views as entirely restricted to *jen* and *yi* and as making the moral sphere the highest of all, this attitude was wrong. Although the Confucianists were continually speaking of *jen* and *yi*, their outlook was not restricted to *jen* and *yi* : the highest life of which they spoke was not merely the moral life. This can be discerned in the words which Confucius and Mencius used in stating the sphere in which they lived. We have only to think of Confucius' words : " At fifteen I set my heart on learning . . . " and Mencius' discussion of the nourishment of the great morale,[1] and work

---

[1] The " great morale " is the famous " *hao jan chih ch'i*," which Legge translated " vast-flowing passion nature ". Dr. Fung's objection to this is that " passion nature " inevitably suggests something which is near to being, if not actually being, evilly passionate and out of control. (E. R. H.)

out the meaning as we follow the text in these passages. We shall then see the sphere in which Confucius and Mencius lived.

Thus Confucius said, " At fifteen I set my heart on learning ; at thirty I took my stand ; at forty I had no doubts ; at fifty I was conscious of the decrees of Heaven ; at sixty I was already obedient to these decrees ; at seventy I just followed my heart's desire, without overstepping the boundaries (of the right)." This is Confucius, in his own words, speaking of the changes which took place during his lifetime in his relation to the spheres in which he lived. When he mentions " at thirty " and " at forty ", etc., these represent the main stages through which he passed ; and the words should probably not be taken as literally denoting one change every ten years.

The " learning " to which he refers is not what is commonly now thought of as learning. Confucius said, " To hear the Tao in the morning and then at night to die, that would be all right." (*Lun Yü, Bk. IV.*) Also he said, " If a gentleman sets his heart on the Way and is ashamed of bad clothes and bad food, he is not worthy to talk with." (*Lun Yü, Bk. IV.*) He also said, " Set your heart on the Tao." (*Lun Yü, Bk. VII.*) Thus in speaking of setting his heart on learning, this was in reference to learning the Tao (i.e. the Great Way for man). The ordinary meaning of learning is to increase one's store of knowledge, whilst the Tao is that whereby men are lifted on to a higher level of life. Lao Tzŭ said, " To get learning is daily to increase, to get the Tao is daily to decrease." Here his reference is to the common meaning of learning, and for him this was antithetical to the Tao. Although for Confucius and the Confucianists after him the learning of Tao was hardly a daily decreasing, yet this learning was to them also different to ordinary learning.

In the introduction we have maintained that the unselfconsciously natural life and the utilitarian life are gifts of nature, the moral life and the transcendent life are the creation of man's spirit. Now, if we want to get these two higher forms of life, we need first to understand a certain principle. That principle is what is called " the Tao ". For men in this world, hearing the Tao is the most important thing of all. This is why Confucius said, " To hear the Tao in the morning and at night to die, that is all right." " The people of the younger generation are able to command respect, but how do you know whether their future will be like the present ? " If after the age of forty or fifty, a man is still without hearing the Tao, there is nothing to be respected in him. (*Lun Yü, Bk. IX.*)

" At thirty I took my stand." Confucius also said, " Take your stand on the rituals " (*Lun Yü, Bk. VIII*) ; and also, " not to know the rituals is to have no means of standing firmly." (*Bk. XX.*) As we have said above, the rituals embody a certain standard of action set up to represent righteousness and to represent the moral mean. " To be able to stand firmly " is to be able to will to obey the rituals. If a man can do this, then it is possible " to subdue one's self and recover the ritual disposition ". The recovery of this disposition amounts to this. " Do not look at anything which is counter to the rituals, do not hear anything which is counter to them, do not speak anything which is counter to them, do not move in any way which goes counter to them." (*Lun Yü, Bk. XII.*) To subdue oneself is to subdue the selfishness in one's self. For the man living in the utilitarian sphere his actions are all for the sake of his personal profit. This kind of person is then a selfish man. To act morally one must first subdue this selfishness. That is why, when Yen Yüan asked Confucius about *jen*, he replied, " Subdue one's self and recover the ritual disposition ; this is human-heartedness."

" At forty I had no more doubts." Confucius said, " The wise man has no doubts." (*Bk. XIV.*) We said above that wisdom was understanding in relation to *jen* and *yi* and *li*. Now Confucius " at thirty took his stand ", that is to say that in action he could obey the dictates of the rituals, these being representative of righteousness. Thus his actions would be in accord with righteousness. But such acts as we have seen are not necessarily righteous acts. There must be the further step, namely, to wisdom, before there is a perfect understanding of human-heartedness and righteousness and ritual conduct. With such an understanding the result is an end to doubts.

It is only then when a man has this undoubting knowledge that he can begin in all truth to act human-heartedly and righteously. The sphere in which he lives only then begins to be the moral sphere. This was the point which Confucius had reached in learning the Tao ; he came into possession of the moral sphere.

Confucius said, " There are men who have set their hearts on learning, but the learning on which they have set their hearts may not be that of the Tao. There are men who, although they have set their hearts on learning the Tao, may not be able to stand firm [i.e. to have subdued themselves and recovered the ritual disposition]. There are men who may be able to stand firm, but may not be able to weigh things in relation to the occasion " [i.e. to have a perfect understanding regarding ritual]. (*Lun Yü, Bk. IX.*) If there is not this understanding, then a man does not know that " for rituals the particular circumstances are of very great importance ". If this be the case, then it is like what Mencius said, " To lay hold of the mean without taking into account the occasion, is like grasping one thing only." (*Mencius, Bk. VII, A.*) " To grasp one thing only " is to maintain one dead standard, one rigid method, in the face of varying changes. Mencius also said, " A great man's words are not necessarily to be trusted, nor his actions obviously straightforward ; but he does what righteousness demands." This, then, is what is described as " the weighing things in relation to occasions ". Only the man who has reached the point of knowing without doubting can do this. This saying by Confucius also refers to the level of progress achieved in learning the Tao. It is after the same pattern as the explanation we have given, so that these two passages illustrate each other.

" At fifty I was conscious of Heaven's decrees." *Jen* and *yi* and *li* are matters connected with society. Confucius, having reached the stage he did, also knew that above society there was " *T'ien* " (Heaven). Thus the sphere in which he lived was one transcending the moral sphere. The heavenly decrees of which he spoke may be interpreted as changes of things in the universe, changes which are beyond the limit of men's power, changes about which human strength can do nothing. This is the meaning of the later Ju philosophers. Heavenly decrees may also be explained as the commandments of God. This looks rather like the meaning Confucius gave to the expression. Assuming this to be right, then his consciousness of Heaven's decrees is something like what we have described in the *Hsin Yüan Jen* as " knowing Heaven ".

" At sixty I was already obedient to these decrees." With regard to this sentence, people formerly made literary interpretations of the text without being able to explain it satisfactorily. The " *erh* " should not be interpreted as meaning " ear " but as " *erh yi* " which means " already ". The text I surmise originally to have been " *erh yi* ", which when spoken quickly becomes " *erh* ". Later generations of copyists did not know that the " *erh* " was equal to " *erh yi* ". Seeing that in the sentence above and below there is an " *erh* ", they put another " *erh* ", and thus the text became " *erh erh shun* ". Thus the way was opened for the later scholars to interpret " *erh* " as meaning ear, an interpretation which is very difficult to understand.[1] Since, in the previous sentence, Confucius has spoken of understanding Heaven's decrees, the meaning here is, " I was already obedient to Heaven's decrees." This is something like what we have described in the *Hsin Yüan Jen* as " serving Heaven ".

" At seventy I followed my heart's desire and did not overstep the boundaries of the right." In the *Hsin Yüan Jen* we said that the man who lived in the moral sphere and did moral acts did so by deliberately choosing, and that he needed to make an effort himself. The man living in the transcendent sphere does not necessarily act by deliberate choice or with a great exertion of himself. This does not mean that it is because he has good habits, but because he has a lofty understanding. Confucius, with his following of his heart's desire without overstepping the bounds, would appear to have had this lofty understanding and so " without forcing himself he hit the mark ". This is something like what we called in the *Hsin Yüan Jen* " rejoicing in Heaven ".

In the *Hsin Yüan Jen* we spoke of the universe, i.e. " the Great Whole ", " the essence," " the world of the essence " and " the Tao " : concepts which are all philosophical concepts. Any man who can perfectly understand these concepts can " know Heaven ", and after he knows Heaven, he can serve Heaven, and after that can rejoice in Heaven, and last of all become identified with Heaven. What is called Heaven is the universe or the Great Whole. Above we have said that to know Heaven's decrees is as if a man knows Heaven ; obeying Heaven's decrees is as if he served Heaven ; following his heart's desire and not overstepping the bounds is as if he rejoiced in Heaven. We say " as if " because Confucius' " Heaven " is " as if " there were a " Heaven with a Ruler, not the universe, the Great Whole ". Assuming this to be really so, then the final sphere to which Confucius attained was also an " as if " kind of sphere.

Mencius has written himself of his own (highest) sphere of living, as we find in the discussion on the " *hao jan chih ch'i* ".[2]

---

[1] I owe this suggestion to my colleague. Professor Shen Yo-ting. (F. Y. L.)

[2] *Ch'i*, original meaning vapour or gas, later used in both physical, metaphysical, psychological, and physiological senses. For Mencius' special meaning, vid. p. 24. This section previous generations have for the most part been unable to explain. The interpretation given here is to be found in detail in an article published in the *Tsing Hua Learned Journal*, but the outline is given above.

" Kung-sun Ch'ou asked his Master [i.e. Mencius] what he specialized in.   Mencius replied, ' I know the right and the wrong in what people say, and I am skilful in cultivating the *hao jan chih ch'i*.'   The questioner then asked what this was, and Mencius replied : ' It is difficult to express. It is *ch'i*, immensely great, immensely strong.   If it be directly cultivated without handicap, then it pervades all Heaven and Earth.   It is the *ch'i* which is achieved by the combination of righteousness with the Tao, and without it there would be starvation.   It is the product of accumulated righteousness, not of a righteousness which has been snatched [lit. got by surprise attack].   (For) if a man be dissatisfied with his conduct, then starvation [1] will set in.   I maintain that Kao Tzŭ did not know righteousness, because he externalized it.   There must be something done, and that without stopping.   The mind must not forget, nor must it give artificial assistance.' "

Hao jan chih ch'i is a special term of Mencius' own.   He himself confessed that this idea was hard to explain, and men after him for the most part have given literary explanations which do not interpret the phrase satisfactorily.   The context of this discussion includes a previous discussion on Pe Kung Yu and Meng Shih She, two warriors, and their cultivation of their valour.   Their method of doing this consisted in " maintaining their *ch'i* ".   From this we can learn that the *ch'i* in this passage is the morale as in valour, as when people speak of the high morale of an army.   Now, in speaking of himself as skilled in cultivating his *hao jan chih ch'i*, this *ch'i* is of the same nature as the *ch'i*, morale, in the two warriors.   The difference lies in the addition of *hao jan* which means great to a supreme degree.   Now what makes it on a vast scale ?   The morale which the two warriors cultivated is only a matter between one man and another, but the supreme morale is a matter between man and the universe.   The morale of valour can honourably establish a man in society without fear or favour.   So also the supreme morale can honourably establish a man in the universe without fear or favour.   This supreme morale can make men like this.   That is why it is said " This morale in itself, how immensely great, how immensely strong it is ! Cultivated without handicap it pervades all Heaven and Earth."

The morale of the warriors still needed cultivating, if it was to be obtained.   The cultivation of their valour was the cultivation of their morale.   All the more does the supreme morale need

[1] Malnutrition which leads to starvation. (E. R. H.)

cultivation, if it is to be obtained. That being so, the method of cultivation is, according to Mencius, one of combining righteousness and the Tao, without which combination in a man he is in a state of malnutrition. The Tao here mentioned is the same Tao as that which Confucius had in mind when he said " Set your heart on the Tao ", and it represents the principle through the existence of which men are enabled to attain to the highest sphere of life. Thus there are two aspects to this method. One is the understanding of a principle called the Tao, whilst the other is the energetic doing of the deeds which man ought to do in the universe, i.e. accumulating righteousness. The combination is described as " a marriage " between righteousness and the Tao. That one of the two aspects should be neglected would not do at all. If there should be an accumulation of righteousness but no understanding of the Tao, this would be " un-seeing, unquestioning ", or " throughout life obeying and not knowing the reason why ". If there should be understanding of the Tao and no accumulation of righteousness, the state of affairs would be that described in the saying about a man's *jen* being uncertain owing to its being unintelligent : " although it be gained, it will be lost." Unless the method in both these respects gets to work, the *ch'i* in man becomes starved.

Once there is understanding of the Tao and long accumulation of righteousness, the supreme morale bursts into existence entirely naturally. The least bit of forcing causes failure. As has been said, " it is the creation of accumulated righteousness, and not of righteousness snatched (*hsi*)." [1] And in a later passage Mencius said " Therefore I say that Kao Tzŭ does not know righteousness, and it is because he externalizes it ". Kao Tzŭ took a concept of righteousness from outside himself and with it forced his mind to be calm. Mencius regarded righteous action as a natural growth of the mind. Act righteously over a long period, and the *hao jan chih ch'i* naturally emerges from the centre of your being.

If a man feels dissatisfied with his conduct, there results a state of starvation. In the *Tso Chuan* we find the saying that the army with a good cause is invigorated : without a good cause it is enervated. People constantly say " when one's cause is good, one's morale is high ". If the cause is bad, then the morale is low ; and the same applies to the common idea about valour. It applies also to *hao jan chih ch'i* with the result that the man who

---

[1] Chu Hsi said, " *Hsi* has the meaning of *hsi* in connection with soldiers, viz. got by surprise attack " (*Yü Lei*, chüan 52).

cultivates this morale needs at all times to understand the Tao and to accumulate righteousness, not allowing one thing in his mind to be out of tune. This is what comes in the quotation above, " Something must be done without stopping.[1] The mind must not forget." Without stopping means the same as the mind on no account forgetting. The task of the man who cultivates *hao jan chih ch'i* is just that. He needs at all times to understand the Tao and to keep on accumulating righteousness ; thus his *hao jan chih ch'i* will naturally emerge. He must not be in haste to arrive, nor take special measures to that end. The man who takes such measures is what Mencius described as giving artificial assistance to things to grow.[2] Thus the main element in the work of cultivating is that there should be neither forgetting nor giving of artificial assistance.

The sphere in which the man who has the supreme morale lives is the transcendent sphere. In another passage Mencius said, " To dwell in the wide house of the world of men, to stand in the correct position in it, and to follow the great Way (Tao) of it, having obtained one's ambition, to practise one's principles for the good of the people ; when that ambition is disappointed, to practise them alone ; when riches and honour cannot make one dissipated, when poverty and mean station cannot make one swerve, and power and force cannot make one bend ; these are the characteristics of the great man." (*Bk. III, B.*) If we compare this " great man " with the man who has *hao jan chih ch'i*, we can see that the sphere in which the " great man " lives is not as high as the sphere in which the other lives. This " great man ", living as he does in the wide house of the world of men, and standing in the correct position in it and practising the great Tao of it, cannot be said not to be a great man. But we still cannot say that he is the greatest kind of man. Riches and honour do not make him dissipated, poverty and mean station do not make him swerve, power and force do not make him bend. Such a man cannot be said not to be strong, but he has not got the highest kind of strength.

The question is what we mean by the greatest kind of man and the highest kind of strength. Whilst the greatness and

[1] The *cheng* character must be taken as *chih* to stop : *vide* Chiao Hsun's (eighteenth-century) interpretation in his commentary on Mencius. (F. Y. L.)

[2] The peasants of Sung State were famous at that time for their simplicity. The story is told of one of them coming home from the fields and complaining of weariness because he had been helping the corn to grow. When his son went to look, he found the plants half out of the ground and dying. (E. R. H.)

strength of the " great man " is in relation to society, the greatness and strength of the man with *hao jan chih ch'i* is in relation to the universe. The wide house the " great man " lives in is that of the world of men ; the position he stands in is in the world of men ; the Tao he follows is the Tao of the world of men. The *ch'i* of the man who has the supreme kind of *ch'i* (morale), being cultivated by righteousness, pervades all Heaven and Earth. Here is the difference between the meaning of *t'ien hsia* (the world of man) and *T'ien Ti* (Heaven and Earth or the Universe). We can say order the country and bring peace to the world, but we cannot say order the country and bring peace to Heaven and Earth. We can say as we do in China the world at peace or the world in confusion, but we cannot say Heaven and Earth at peace or Heaven and Earth in confusion. The world of men denotes the great whole of man's society. Heaven and Earth denote the great whole of the universe. The sphere in which the " great man " lives is the moral sphere, whilst the sphere in which the man with *hao jan chih ch'i* lives is the transcendent sphere. The sphere of the first is limited, the sphere of the second, although his body is only seven feet (Chinese) tall, is yet one which transcends all limitations and rises to the infinite.

Having reached this position, success naturally adds nothing to him, neither does a poverty-stricken dwelling detract from him ; quite naturally neither can riches and honour make him dissipated, nor poverty and mean station make him swerve, nor majesty and force make him bend. But these features in him are different from what they are in the man living in the moral sphere. Chu Hsi said, " The adjective ' enlightened ' fails to describe the *hao jan chih ch'i*. Once we speak of it, we get the idea of wideness, greatness, endurance and strength, like a great river in its vast on-coming flow. The kind of men whom riches and honour, poverty and mean station, majesty and force, cannot make to swerve or bend, all are on a lower level. They are not to be spoken of in this connection." (*Yü Lei*, chüan 52.) These words of Chu Hsi's are indeed on a parallel with the ideas expressed above. The man who has reached this position may be described as being identified with Heaven. Mencius' words, " pervading Heaven and Earth " and " above and below along with Heaven and Earth flowing on " (*Bk. VII, A*) may be said to express the idea of identification with Heaven.

Thus then, taking what has been said above, we may say that the sphere of which Mencius spoke is a higher one than that

CHAPTER II

THE PHILOSOPHERS YANG CHU AND MO TI

Mencius said, " I know the right and the wrong in what people say, and I am skilful at cultivating my great morale." Kung Sun Ch'ou asked him in what way he knew this, and he answered, " I know what is concealed in flattering statements. I know what is the beguilement in licentious statements. I know what is the incompatibility in heretical statements. I know where the weakness lies in excuses. What people say is born in the mind ; the injury thereby done appears in government. The words are spread abroad in government ; the injury they do is in public affairs. If a sage should again arise, he would bear out my words." (*Bk. II, A.*)

At that time it was the theories of Yang Chu and Mo Ti which Mencius regarded as the most insidious and pernicious. He said, " The whole world is filled with the sayings of Yang Chu and Mo Ti. The doctrines held everywhere, if they are not close to those of Yang Chu, are close to those of Mo Ti. Yang's principle of ' Each for himself ' amounts to making the sovereign of no account. Mo Ti's principle of ' Universal love ' amounts to a man making his father of no account. To have no father and no sovereign is to be a beast of the field." " Unless these doctrines be stopped, Confucius' doctrines cannot shine forth. These pernicious opinions mislead the people and block the way of human-heartedness and righteousness." Also " I am frightened about this and want to protect the doctrines of the sages of the past. Reject Yang and Mo, and cast out these depraved ideas, so that they have no way to flourish."

Mencius held that the one great task of his life was to cast out Yang and Mo, that his merit in opposing them might be compared with (the sage king) Yü's merit in controlling the floods and bringing peace to the world, and Chou Kung dealing with the barbarians and driving away the wild beasts so that the people were at rest, and Confucius who by his writing of the Spring and Autumn Annals put fear into the hearts of anarchy-producing ministers and rebellious sons. (*Bk. III, B.*)

That it was possible for the theories of Yang to stand in the way of human-heartedness and righteousness, is quite clear. As we said in Chapter I, the content of *jen* and *yi* is " for the other man ", whilst Yang Chu proposed the principle of " for myself ". Mencius said, " Though he might have benefited the whole world by plucking out a single hair, he would not have done it." (*Bk. VII, A.*) Also Han Fei said of Yang " a man who despised things and prized life " ; also, " His policy was not to enter a city which was in danger, not to remain in the army ; and for the great profit of the world he would not give a hair from his shin." (*Han Fei Tzŭ Hsien Hsüeh*, chüan 19.) This despising of things and prizing of life describes the Yang Chu school. As for the remark about the profit of the world and a hair from his shin there are two interpretations. One is that to get the profit of the whole world for himself he would not give up one hair, and this illustrates his contempt for things and his value of life. The other interpretation is that he would not give up a hair in order to profit the whole world, and this illustrates his principle of " all for myself ". Whichever interpretation is right, these were the two convictions he had, namely, value life and be all for one's self : convictions which were quite incompatible with the convictions held by the Confucianists, namely " sacrifice yourself to become *jen* " and " give up your life to uphold *yi* ".

Thus Yang Chu's school was an early form of Taoism. Taoism came from recluses. We get a glimpse of such in the *Lun Yü*, for Confucius met a number of them ; and since he had the wish to save the world, they did not approve. According to them, Confucius was " a man who knew that that cannot be done and yet he does it " (*Bk. XIV.*) " They exhorted him saying ' Stop, stop ! '. Those who take part in governing are in danger " (*Bk. XVIII*); and " The world everywhere is in the same disturbed condition. Who can change it ? " (*Ibid.*) They called themselves " the men who shunned the world ", and " only took care of themselves ". Thus with regard to society they had no constructive attitude and amongst them there were men who could state their line of reasoning, by which they proved the rightness of their conduct. These, then, were the early kind of Taoists, and Yang Chu was their leader.

The main tenets which Yang Chu held can be found in outline in *Lao Tzŭ*, *Chuang Tzŭ* and the *Lü Shih Ch'un Ch'iu*.[1] In the *Lao Tzŭ Book* there is " Which is dearer, one's reputation or one's self ? Which is the most, one's self or one's property ? " (c. 44).

---

[1] This book was composed by a group of scholars about 250 B.C. It is the first book in Chinese literature which can be dated with accuracy to within a year or two. (E. R. H.)

This is the same line of reasoning as that of " despising things and valuing life ". In the *Chuang Tzŭ Book* (Zang Sheng chapter)it is said, " When you do something good, beware of reputation : when you do something bad, beware of punishment. To follow the in-between road is your constant principle. Then you can guard your body, nourish your parents, and complete the tale of your years " (ch. 3). This also is the same line of reasoning as that of despising material things and valuing life. Should a man's wickedness reach a certain point, he will come to it that he receives society's reprimand and punishment ; and this is not in accord with prizing life. But should a man be too good, to the point where he obtains a fine reputation, this also is not in accord with the principle of valuing life. " The trees on the mountains are their own enemies, the leaping fire the cause of its own quenching. Cinnamon is edible, therefore the cinnamon tree is cut down. The Ch'i oil is useful, therefore the tree is gashed." (*Chuang Tzŭ Book*, ch. 4.) " The size of the tree attracts the wind " ; this is the harm coming from having great ability or a great name. Therefore the man who is skilful at nourishing his life does not do too much evil, neither must he do too much good, but just live in between good and evil : as is said, " Follow the in-between road as your constant principle ". This is also the tenor of the chapters on " Value Yourself ", " Life as the Root ", and " Prize Life " which come in the *Lü Shih Chun Chiu*.

This is the first step towards the development in the direction of the Taoist theories. Men who prize their life need to avoid injuring themselves and should not let other men or other things injure them. How is one to do this ? Yang Chu apparently had but one method, and the key word was " shun ". " Shun the world," " Shun being famous," " Shun being punished " : altogether make shunning the ultimate objective. But there is no end to the chances and changes in human affairs : harm is something that is inescapable. A great part of the *Lao Tzŭ Book* is a setting forth of general rules governing the changes of things in the universe. The man who knows these, if he can respond to them in conduct, can obtain freedom from injury. This was the second development in the Taoist theories. But because human affairs change endlessly, and amongst these the unseen complications are too many, therefore the doctrines which are set forth in the *Lao Tzŭ Book* were still unable to guarantee sure and certain avoidance of injury to man. Thus in that book we find words which make a third line of defence : " The chief source of trouble arises from my having a body. When the time comes and I have no body, what troubles will there be still remaining ? " (c. 13). These are the words of a thoroughly understanding man. Chuang Chou followed this up by setting up the doctrine of unifying others with himself and equalizing life and death. In other words he did not regard profit as profit and loss as loss. Thus physical harm is not truly injury. This was the third stage of development in the Taoist theories.

These developments in Taoism can be illustrated by quoting a passage in the *Chuang Tzŭ Book* where he tells a story. " Master Chuang was walking among the hills when he saw a great tree covered with most luxuriant foliage. A wood-cutter stood by it and did not cut it down. Master Chuang asked him his reason and he replied, ' It is no use.' Master Chuang said, ' Because this tree has no exceptional qualities, it is able to complete its allotted term of years.' The Master went away from the hills and spent the night in a friend's house. The friend was accordingly delighted and ordered a servant to kill and prepare a goose. The servant asked which goose he should kill, the one that cackled or the one that did not. His master replied ' Kill the one that cannot cackle '. The next day a disciple put the question to the Master : ' Yesterday the tree on the mountain was able to complete its allotted term because it had no special qualities. Now, because it had no special qualities, this goose of ours has died. What do you, sir, make of this ? ' The Master laughed and said, ' My way lies between having special qualities and not having them, and this being in between seems to be right, but is not. That is why those who practise this method are unable to avoid trouble completely. If there could be assumption of the Tao and its spiritual power and immersion in it, this would not happen.' " (ch. 20.) Also, " Being immersed in the Great Ancestor of things, he regarded other things as things but he was not regarded by other things as a thing. What is there which can trouble him ? " In this story the first part describes Yang Chu's theory of making life secure and shunning injury, whilst the second part illustrates Chuang Chou's theory in the same connection.

Having special qualities corresponds to doing something good in the sense of the passage quoted above (vid. *Chuang Tzŭ Book*, ch. 3) ; having no special qualities corresponds to doing something bad in the same connection. The state of being between having special qualities and not having them corresponds to the

" following the in-between path as your constant principle ". According to this story, if men cannot " take death and life to be just one item (and not separate items) and possibility and impossibility to be one connected chain " (ch. 5), in our human world, no matter in what way we do our best to shun trouble, the upshot is that we cannot guarantee any way of entirely avoiding it. Whether a man has special qualities or not, or is in the in-between condition, there is no guarantee that he will only receive good fortune and not receive bad fortune. If you are a perfect man, then " whether you are alive or whether you are dead will have no effect on you, and all the more is this so in relation to profit and loss " (ch. 2). To have reached this sphere of living is really to be able " to avoid trouble ". This then is what is described as " to regard things as things but not be regarded by other things as a thing " ; which is to say that the men in this kind of sphere are in regard to everything self-propelling and not propelled from without.

With regard to the man who assumes the Tao and its spiritual power and roams freely in it as also " in the beginning of things ", his sphere of living is the transcendent sphere. With regard to the man who calculates in relation to having special qualities or not having them in order to fly to profit and flee from loss, his sphere of living is the utilitarian one. The early Taoists only recognized this sphere : the later Taoists recognized the transcendent one. Between the earlier Taoists and the later is clearly a thread of development. We may say that the early Taoists were selfish ; but in the last resort, their selfishness has turned and sacrificed itself ; just like a man committing suicide ; he has blotted himself out. In this connection, the Buddhist's motive in seeking to be liberated from the misery of life and death and so becoming a monk, this motive also is a selfish one. The outcome, however, for him later is life in the transcendent sphere. This is selfishness wiping out selfishness.

So far as the early Taoists are concerned, they were selfish. Their principle was to encourage selfishness. They " prized life ", that is to say, prized their own lives ; as they put it, " for myself." Therefore their idea was not in accord with the criterion of attaining to the sublime. Their sphere of living was the utilitarian one and may be said " to have blocked the way to *jen* and *yi* ". As Tzŭ Lu said of them, " they want to make themselves clean, but they throw into confusion the great relationships of life " (*Lun Yü, Bk. XVIII*) ; or to use Mencius' words, " Yang's

' for myself' amounts to having no sovereign." " For myself," is the same as wanting to make myself clean, and " having no sovereign " is the same as " throwing into confusion the great relationships of life ". To use our modern terms, if men are for the sake of themselves only, then there is no society. For there not to be a society is something impossible to contemplate.

It is entirely obvious that Yang's theory blocked the way to *jen* and *yi*, because the Confucian emphasis on *jen* and *yi* contained an emphasis on " the other man ". On the other hand, since Mo Ti's universal love really aimed at benefiting others, why was it criticized as blocking the way to *jen* and *yi* ? In replying to this question it is necessary to explain how the Confucianists and Mohists were in some ways basically different.

Their difference can from several points of view be quite easily discerned. The Mohists criticized the Confucianists as follows : " The Ju principles ruin the whole of society in four ways. They hold that Heaven has no discernment and that the spirits of the dead are not really spirits, with the result that Heaven and the spirits are not pleased. This is enough to ruin society. Also they insist on elaborate funerals and make mourning last a long time, duplicate the coffins, making an inner and an outer, and the number of robes for the corpse very numerous, whilst the funeral processions are like the mass removal of a population. The three years of weeping, the getting others to help him [i.e. the chief mourner] to stand up, the leaning on a stick to enable him to walk, the ear hearing nothing and the eye seeing nothing, this is enough to ruin society. Also the playing of lutes, the singing, the beating of drums and the practising of music, this is enough to ruin society. Also, the view that there is fate, that riches and poverty, long life and an untimely death, good order and anarchy, and times of peace and times of danger are pre-determined, and it is impossible to worsen or improve them, so that when those in high places act on this theory they do not attend to their administrative duties, and when those beneath them act on this theory they do not attend to their business : this is enough to ruin society." (*Kung Meng.*)

The idea of fate which the Mohists denounced was not what the Confucianists held. They did not believe that men's poverty and riches and all the other conditions in life were pre-determined, and that it was impossible to worsen or improve them. When Confucius spoke of " fate ", he may have meant Heaven-determined. When Mencius and Hsün Ch'ing spoke of fate, they certainly only meant that there are certain changes in the universe through which men pass and which are beyond the limited control of man's strength ; and these are something about which man can do nothing. But what the Ju were convinced of was that man should do his best while awaiting his lot, not that he should stop exerting himself and be merely dependent on fate. None the less, the Mohists were persuaded that what they denounced was really what the Confucianists believed. Apart from this point, the issue very much expresses the differences between the Confucianists and the Mohists.

Whether the Mohists were right or wrong we need not discuss here, though it should be said that the Mohist criticism was limited for the most part to these aspects. For instance, in the chapter entitled *Anti-Confucianism* in the *Mo Tzŭ Book* they denounce the Confucianists on these grounds : " They enhance the beauty of ritual and music, wherewith they debauch people. They lengthen the period of mourning and make weeping hypocritical, whereby people deceive their parents. They establish a fate and cause people to slip into poverty, whilst they themselves live luxuriously. They go counter to the basic industry of farming, abandoning their business and doing everything lazily." Also, " those with long life cannot exhaust the learning required for their studies, even young men with the vigour of youth cannot practise all their ceremonial duties. Even those who have amassed wealth cannot afford music. They enhance the beauty of wicked arts and thereby lead their sovereign astray. They make a great business of music, and thereby debauch the innocent people. Their doctrines cannot meet the needs of the age, their learning cannot educate the people." These criticisms are of the same character as those quoted from the *Kung Meng* chapter.

With regard to the Confucianists' central thought of *jen* and *yi*, the Mohists had no criticism to make, for at bottom they also were advocates of *jen* and *yi*. Yet it is possible that they did criticize the Confucianists and this in three ways. Tzŭ Hsia's disciples asked Mo Ti whether men of breeding engaged in duelling. Mo Ti replied that they did not. The disciples then said " Even dogs and pigs fight, why should not a knight engage in duelling ? " Mo Ti said, " What a distressing situation ! In regard to what you say, you are named after T'ing and Wen,[1] in regard to what you do, you are illustrated by dogs and pigs.

---

[1] Two of the sage-emperors who built up a civilized way of living in society. (E. R. H.)

Very distressing ! " (*Keng Chu.*) The inference to be drawn from this is that the Mohists could say of the Confucianists that their speech and their actions did not tally. They might have much to say on *jen* and *yi*, but they did not actually put these principles into practice.

Again, the Mohists said, " Duke Yeh Tzŭ Kao asked Chung Ni (Confucius) about government : ' How will the man skilful in governing act ? ' Chung Ni said, ' Those who are skilful in governing, cause distant people to come near and old things to become new.' Our Master, Mo, heard about this and said that Duke Yeh was not to the point in his question, and Chung Ni was not to the point in his answer. Of course, Duke Yeh knew that those who are skilful in governing cause distant people to come near and old things to become new. What he (really) asked was how to do it. Since a man here was not told what he did not know, but was told what he did know, therefore Duke Yeh was not to the point in his question. Confucius, also, was not to the point in his reply." (*Keng Chu.*) The inference to be drawn from this illustration is that the Confucianists could talk about *jen* and *yi*, but they did not know how they should practise *jen* and *yi*.

Again, the Mohists also said, " Our Master, Mo, asked the Ju why they made music. Their reply was, ' Music is for music's sake.' Our Master Mo replied, ' You have not answered my question. Now if I ask you why a house is built and you reply " In winter, to get shelter from the cold, in summer, to get shelter from the heat ; and to be the means by which the distinctions of sex are regulated," you have told me the reason for a house. But now, when I ask you for what reason you make music, you say, " Music is for music's sake." It is as if you said, in answer to the same question about a house, that a house is for a house's sake.' " (*Kung Meng.*) The inference to be drawn from this is that the Mohists could say of the Confucianists that they talked about *jen* and *yi*, but they did not know the content of the ideas, nor did they know the function of *jen* and *yi*.

In these three passages we have criticisms which were possibly made by the Mohists against the Confucianists. When we say " possibly " here, we are not thinking of a theoretical possibility, but that as a matter of fact they did make such criticisms, although the historical evidence is inadequate.

Thus the Mohist criticism was not a statement to the effect that *jen* and *yi* were wrong, and that the Confucianists must not speak in this way, but to the effect that the Confucianists did not know how to put these principles into practice and did not know what their content was nor their function. Further, the Mohists did not come to doubt whether what the Confucianists called *jen* and *yi* were really *jen* and *yi*. The basic principle of *jen* and *yi* was what the Mohists approved. Thus, what they called " universal loving of each other " was to them the actual method of practising *jen*, indeed the whole content of *jen*. Then, what they called " the interchange of mutual profit " this was to them the actual method of practising righteousness (*yi*) : for them it was the whole content of righteousness.

The Confucianists for their part, although they openly stated that *jen* meant loving men (cf. *Lun Yü, Bk. XII*), yet directly criticized the Mohist conviction about universal love. As Mencius said, " universal love amounted to a man having no father." In this he was undoubtedly referring to the Mohist conviction that in loving, there should be no degrees of greater and less love. Thus, in the *Keng Chu Chapter*, we find one Wu Ma Tzu telling Master Mo that he was different from him, the Master. He explained himself as follows : " I am not able to love universally. I love the men of Tsou better than I love the men of Yueh. I love the men of Lu better than I love the men of Tsou. I love the men of my own district better than I love the men of Lu. I love the members of my own clan better than I love the men of my district. I love my parents better than I love the members of my clan. I love myself better than I love my parents." This Wu Ma Tzu was a Ju, and he could not love universally because he could not avoid making degrees in love. Thus, we see that the important thing about " universal love " was that it recognized no degrees in love. Mencius, in quoting a Mohist called Yi Chih, said that the Mohists recognized no degrees in love, whilst love really began with one's parents. (*Bk. III, A.*) Thus one great distinction between the two schools was that the Mohists affirmed that there were no degrees in love and the Confucianists were convinced that there were.

The representation of Wu Ma Tzŭ as saying " I love myself better than I love my parents ", comes from a Mohist source and for the most part is an exaggeration ; for the words do not agree with the Confucianist emphasis on filial piety. As to their conviction about degrees in love, Mencius said, " The man of honour in relation to the lower creatures, feels an affection (*ai*) for them, but he has no human-heartedness towards them ;

in relation to the common people, he has human-heartedness towards them, but no deep family love (*ch'ing*) for them. Have family love for the family, but human-heartedness (*jen*) for the people : have *jen* for the people, but an affection (*ai*) for the lower creatures. (*Bk. VII, A.*) He questioned whether the Mohist Yi Chih really believed that men loved their brothers' children in the same way as they loved their neighbours' children. The love for a brother's child is naturally much greater. So also with parents : a man loves his father and mother naturally more than he loves somebody else's father and mother. And the same applies to his own sons and daughters. This does not need to be corrected. What must be borne in mind is that while you love your parents, other men love their parents ; as also is the case with children. Thus, you must remember to arrange for other men, so that they are able to love their parents and children. At the very least, you must not hinder them doing so. As Mencius said, " Treat the aged men in your family as they should be treated, and extend this to the aged in other people's families. Extend the same treatment to other men's young folk as you give to your own young folk." As Mencius said of the men of old, " They were very able at extending the scope of their activity." Also he said, " Further, Heaven has in its bringing of life to all creatures made each come from one stock, whilst Yi Chih makes them come from two (i.e. from the man in the street as well as his father). To extend the care of the aged from one's own circle to the aged outside it, and the care of the young in the same fashion, this is the same principle as that in " *chung* and *shu* ", and this is " the method of *jen* ", the method by which *jen* is practised.

The practice of *chung* and *shu* [1] in full measure is equivalent to the practice of human-heartedness ; and there is nothing forced about the practice of *jen*, because men have in their original endowment " the mind of commiseration ", the mind which cannot bear to see the suffering of others. *Chung* and *shu* and *jen* are the development of this to the full. The Confucianists, in emphasizing that there were degrees in love, were not refraining from loving other men, but were loving their parents to a greater degree. Confucius himself said, " *Jen* is loving men," the very thing of which the Mohists approved. What they disapproved was men loving their parents to a greater degree. They insisted that the love of other men should be on a par with the love of

[1] Cf. Chapter I, p. 17.

parents, as, for that matter, that the love of parents should be on a par with the love of other men. Whether this meant loving one's parent less or loving others more, whatever the outcome, degrees of love should not exist. Should this happen, then it would not be enough to regard one's parents as one's parents only. That is why Mencius said that the Mohists' universal love meant " no more father ", and that was what he meant by his " double stock ". To recognize no degrees in love meant, in the strict sense, loving every individual equally. According to this, then, every individual is himself a stock. As Chu Hsi said, " With no degrees in love, why stop at two stocks ? You might as well have a thousand."

The Mohists might well have said that although they were convinced that there were no degrees in love, yet they also believed that parents were the beginning of this. To this the Confucianists might have replied by asking for what reason they thought parents were the beginning. If the reason for this is that according to basic principles you must first love your parents, this is equivalent to saying that you love your parents better than you do other men, and this entails that there are degrees of love. If because your parents, as a matter of fact, are by your side, therefore you must love them above all others, this " must " has a condition attached to it. Suppose your parents are not by your side, then it is not necessary that love " will begin with parents ". That being so, then " beginning with parents " does not help us to get over the difficulty in taking love as having no degrees.

The Mohist universal love and the Confucianist *jen* differ in this fashion. This was pointed out not only by Mencius, but also by others after him. Besides this there is in addition another even more important difference between the two schools, one to which Mencius and the others did not refer. We must now deal with it.

As we have noted, Confucius said " *Jen* is loving men ", and the Mohists agreed with him in this ; but if we ask for what reason the *jen* man loves others, the Mohist and Confucianist answers to this question are different. The Confucianist answer was that all men have a mind which cannot bear to see others suffer. " If the men of to-day see a child falling into a well, they are all alarmed and in a state of commiseration." (*Bk. II, A.*) Since this sense of commiseration is the bud of *jen*, when it is developed and brought to full measure, the result is the *jen* man.

The *jen* man working from this beginning in sympathy, cannot bear to see a man not in his right place, and therefore he loves him and does good to him.

The Mohist answer was that the principle of universal love is " hitting the target of profit for the state, for the hundred clans and every person in them ". They said, " The business of the *jen* man is the discharge of the necessary duty of benefiting the whole world and of removing the evils in the world ; but the question for to-day is which is the greatest of these evils ; and the answer is, the attacks made on small countries by great, the upsetting of the smaller clans by the larger, the oppression of the weak by the strong, the bullying of the minority by the majority, the deceiving of the simple by the cunning, the arrogant treatment of the lower classes by the upper. These are the great evils in the world. Now let us examine the source, as to whether there is evidence of social solidarity or of social discrimination. The answer cannot but be that there is evidence of social discrimination. But then this mutual social discrimination, of course, gives birth to the great evils in the world, does it not ? For this reason, I am opposed to social discrimination." Also, " the man who is opposed to anything, has a plan for remedying it " ; " therefore our Master Mo said that solidarity is the way to remedy discrimination." (*Chien Ai Shang.*) This, then, is the ground on which Mo Ti based his arguments for teaching people universal love. It is the utilitarian argument, the argument to which the Confucianists were violently opposed.

The ground of all the arguments which the Mohists used was utilitarian. For example, they were convinced that the expenditure on funerals should be cut down and the periods of mourning reduced. The theoretical basis they adduced for their position was as follows : " Elaborate funerals mean the waste of wealth, the long periods of mourning mean the holding up of ordinary business. To hide away and bury the wealth which has already been produced and to restrict, for a long period, the production of new wealth, all this with the aim of producing prosperity, is like forbidding the cultivation of the fields and expecting a harvest " ; " to do this with a view to getting a large population, is like making a man stab himself in order to obtain long life." (*Chieh Chuang Hsia.*)

The theoretical basis on which the Confucianists argued for elaborate funerals is in an entirely different category. Mencius accused the Mohist Yi Chih as follows : " The earlier generations had the custom of not burying their parents. When they died, they took them and left them in a dry gully. Passing that way later, there (they saw) foxes and wild cats eating them, the flies and gnats battening on them. The perspiration broke out on their foreheads, they turned their eyes away and could not look. And this sweat did not break out just to make a show for others to see. Their inmost heart was revealed on their faces, and so they came back and brought basketfuls of earth and covered them. If to cover them is really right, then there must be a right way for filial sons and *jen* men to do this." (*Mencius, Bk. III, A.*) Elaborate funerals are merely a way of bringing peace of mind to people, just as long periods of mourning have the same intention.[1] There is no nice calculation of the amount of profit and so of making the funeral elaborate and the period of mourning long.

The Mohists discussed the origin of the state and society on a utilitarian basis. What they said was, " In the very early days when man first began to live and there was no organization of government, in speaking with each other every man had his own ideas " ; " therefore, every man used his own ideas to contradict other men's ideas, with the result that there was mutual contradiction. Thus, in the family, fathers and sons and elder and younger brothers hated each other : they fell apart and could not live in harmony. Everywhere among the clans they used water and fire and poison to ill-treat each other to such a pitch that although a man had strength to spare he would not work for others, although he had materials in danger of rotting he would not share them out, whilst good ideas were hidden and not communicated. The confusion in the world was like that among the birds and beasts. The people understood that the reason why everywhere there was confusion clearly was because there was no one to take the head. The result was that they chose the worthiest among them to be a Son of Heaven." (*Shang T'ung Shang.*) The origin of the state and of society was like this, and therefore the basis of its continuance was also like this, namely, that if the state existed, it was beneficial, and if it did not exist, then there was harm. This kind of explanation is a utilitarian one.

The Confucianist explanation was a different one. Take Mencius' statement : " Hou Chi taught the people to sow and reap so that when the five kinds of grain were ripe, they might

---

[1] Cf. Confucius' remarks to Tsai Wo. (F. Y. L.)

be nourished. The human way is as follows : If men satisfy their hunger and have clothes to wear and live at ease but have no good teaching, then they are close to being like the birds and beasts. The sage [i.e. Yao] was distressed over this and appointed Hsieh as official instructor to teach men the basic relationships of life. Father and son should love each other ; king and subject should be just to each other ; husband and wife should distinguish their respective spheres ; elder and younger should have a sense of precedence ; between friends there should be good-faith." (*Bk. III, A.*) The existence of human relationships is the distinguishing mark between men and the birds and beasts. The state and society take their origin from the existence of these human relationships, and the reason why they must have them is because otherwise they would approach the level of the beasts.

There is a question which may be raised. The reason why the Mohists emphasized universal love was because thus " they hit the target of profit for state and people ". Now in Chapter I, the statement was made that the Confucianists also made public utility the content of righteousness. According to this the Mohist teaching of universal love may also truly be a teaching of men to act righteously. Is there any distinction here from the Confucianists ?

The question is a good one, and in spite of the Confucianist and Mohist conclusions given above, we may follow the question up and put another question which will throw fresh light on the difference between Mohism and Confucianism. As has been explained, for the Confucianists, the *jen* man loves men because he cannot bear to see others suffer, and in the development of this disposition to the full he becomes a *jen* man. Now let us go a step further. Why should a man develop this disposition ? The final Confucianist answer to this was that the possession of this disposition is the distinguishing mark between man and the beasts. Mencius said, " The difference between man and the beasts is a very slight one, and ordinary people lose it : the man of honour preserves it." (*Bk. IV, B.*) That which constitutes a man a man, i.e. that which distinguishes him from a beast, is that, being a man, he must manifest that which constitutes him a man. For men to develop their sympathetic disposition, this is to actualize that which constitutes a man a man. This is not because thereby there may be any benefit accruing.

The Mohist position was that men must have universal love because this was of benefit to the state and society. Here we follow up with a question : why should we aim at profiting the state and society ? The Mohist final answer was that to obtain the benefit of the whole was the best method for obtaining the benefit of the individual. They said, " Men are sure to follow on with loving those who love others, sure to follow on with serving the interests of those who serve the interests of others. Men are sure to follow on with hating those who hate others. Men are sure to follow on with injuring those who injure others." (*Chien Ai Chung.*) Not only so : according to the Mohist theory, Heaven will always reward the man who gives universal love, and so also will the spirits and the state. He can indeed get a great quantity of reward. As for the man without universal love, Heaven will punish him, and so will the spirits and the state. He will suffer a great quantity of punishment. Therefore, from the point of view of individual profit, to love universally will bring a hundred profits and not one injury, not to love universally will bring a hundred injuries and not one profit.

According to the Confucianist distinction between righteousness and profit, the man who for his own advantage practises universal love does deeds which, strictly speaking, are still profit-seeking and not righteous deeds at all. Man must practise universal love, because the very act in itself is of profit to him. To speak like the Mohists is to make the " obligation " in such acts one with conditions attached to it. Then acts of universal love are acts not done for their own sake. The basic difference between Confucianism and Mohism lies just here. We find in the *Mencius Book* the following statement : " Sung K'eng was on the way to Ch'u State. Mencius met him at Shih Chiu and asked him why he was going. Sung K'eng replied, ' I hear that Ch'in and Ch'u are getting their armed forces together. I want to get an audience of the king of Ch'u and stop this. If the king of Ch'u is unwilling, then I shall get an audience of the king of Ch'in and propose that he stop it. Among the two kings there will surely be one who will agree with me.' Mencius said, ' I will not ask in detail, I only want to hear the outline of how will you persuade them.' Sung K'eng said, ' I shall tell them of the unprofitableness.' Then Mencius said, ' Sir, your purpose is a great one, but the title you give to it is indefensible.' " (*Bk. VI, B.*) Mencius might have spoken to the Mohists in the same way.

According to the criterion which we proposed in the *Hsin Yüan Jen*, to do an act of universal love for one's own advantage is an action in accord with morality, but is not a moral action.

However much the action may be in accord with morality, the man who does it is not living in the moral sphere, but in the utilitarian sphere.

We may say that the Mohists only spoke of the utilitarian sphere. With regard to the criterion we set up, namely " attaining to the sublime but performing also the common task ", the Mohist theories were not in accord with the sublime side to the criterion.

This is not to say that the sphere in which Mo Ti and some of his followers lived was only that of the utilitarian one. With regard to Mo Ti himself, it was said of him that if he could benefit the world he would do it, in spite of suffering from head to heel. At the least, the sphere in which he lived was the moral sphere ; but those who listened to what he said and who sought their own advantage by means of universal love were living in the utilitarian sphere. This was the only sphere on which he spoke.

Neither do we mean that a man must not have universal love. If the universal love of the Mohist theories will not do, how much more will lack of universal love come short ? This is like the Taoists criticizing the Confucianists and saying, " away with *jen* and abolish *yi*." It was not that they taught men there was no need of *jen* and *yi*, but that the kind of *jen* and *yi*, if it was like that of the Confucianists, would not do. That being so, how much worse things would be without *jen* and *yi* !

CHAPTER III

THE DIALECTICIANS AND LOGICIANS

In Chapter I we said that the philosophy of the early Confucianists did not reach " the sphere of the abstract, nor ferry over into the beyond ". A philosophy which does reach the sphere of the abstract cannot avoid referring to what transcends shapes and features,[1] and the man who ferries himself over into the beyond is sure to be a wanderer in the world which transcends shapes and features. There must be a philosophy which deals with what transcends shapes and features, before there can be men who wander in this world. In other words, men must be able to reach the sphere of the abstract and be ferried over into the beyond before they can reach the highest sphere of living ; and philosophy must be a reaching of the sphere of the abstract and a ferrying over into the beyond, before it can be in accord with the criterion of attaining to the sublime.

The term " shapes and features " is characteristic of the actual. For instance, the big and the small, the square and the round, the long and the short, the black and the white, are each one class of shapes and features. Anything which is the object of experience of any sort, or can be the possible object of experience, has shape and feature and, we may rightly say, is within that world. We may also rightly say that everything which has shape and feature is an object or a possible object of an experience of some sort. We say " possible object of experience " because man's power of experiencing or any other creature's power of experiencing is limited. The term " objects of experience " is not adequate to exhaust all the shapes and features which exist. For example, what are called the atom and the electron in physics are what neither men can directly sense nor what any other creatures with the powers of sensation can directly sense. But this does not come from the atom or the electron being

---

[1] " Shapes and features " is a literal translation of Dr. Fung's Chinese, which, it should be noted, is a common term in Chinese philosophy. One's first impulse was to translate by " the phenomenal ". It may be thought that, as " phenomenal " is antithetical to noumenal this is correct. But there is no such antithesis in Chinese philosophy. Further " shapes and features " has a vivid quality of its own ; and who can tell whether some useful train of thought may not arise from the Western reader being reminded that the world of the phenomenal is a world of shapes *and* features ? (E. R. H.)

in principle impossible to be sensed. Supposing there were a more enhanced sensitivity in the senses, they could sense the atom and the electron, as we sense a table or a chair. Atoms and electrons are, then, examples of what we describe as possible objects of experience. All objects of experience are what we call things.[1]   Therefore what transcends shapes and features is equivalent to the term " outside the world of things ".

The expression " transcending shapes and features " does not mean the same as the common expression " supernatural ". Take religion. Amongst the religions, there are at least some in which God is supernatural. That is to say that God is above Nature or existed before Nature, and is not governed by Nature's laws. But, on the other hand, God has a personality, has a will, has knowledge, has power. Many qualifying expressions are used to qualify him so that God becomes an object or a possible object of experience of some sort. This, then, is to say that God has, at any rate, features, and that being so, God does not transcend shapes and features.

To transcend shapes and features does not necessarily refer to what in the *Hsin Li Hsüeh* [2] is called the " abstract ". " Abstract " is a term in Western philosophy, and represents the opposite to concrete. The abstract must necessarily transcend shapes and features, but not all that transcends shapes and features is necessarily abstract. For instance, the principle of " squareness " is abstract and of course transcends shapes and features. There are people who think squareness is square, and so (for them) squareness does not transcend shapes and features. This opinion is wrong. The principle of squareness is *that by which* square things are square. If a concrete thing is in accord with that by which square things are square, then it is a square thing. As to that by which square things are square, it is not a thing at all, and therefore it transcends shapes and features, nor can it be in that world. Thus a principle has no material property. We may legitimately say the principle of squareness is neither square nor not square. In precisely the same case is the principle of movement which itself does not move, or the principle of change which itself does not change. Of the one principle we may say that it may neither be called movable nor immovable,

---

[1] The Chinese " *wu* ", sometimes expressed more explicitly as " *shih wu* ", includes actual events as well as actual things. (E. R. H.)

[2] This is the title of the book published by Dr. Fung in 1938. *Li Hsüeh* is the term used to denote the Cheng-Chu school of philosophy in Sung and post-Sung times. *Hsin* means new. Cf. Author's Preface. (E. R. H.)

of the other that it may neither be called changeable nor unchangeable.

That which transcends shapes and features is not necessarily abstract. For example, in the *Hsin Li Hsüeh* what we called *ch'i* (matter in the Aristotelian sense) transcends shapes and features but is not abstract. *Ch'i* is so because we cannot employ any term to qualify it. We cannot say that it is a thing of any sort. And this is not because of defects in our knowledge or in our command of expression. It is because in principle *ch'i* is neither thinkable nor expressible. It transcends shapes and features. At the same time, it is not a principle. This is to say, it is not that by which any class of things becomes a class. For this reason it is not abstract.

In the *Hsin Li Hsüeh* we speak of " the universe " and " the evolution of the Tao " (*tao t'i*), and both of these transcend shapes and features, but they are not abstract. The universe is the whole of all that is ; the evolution of the Tao is the whole of all becoming. But both these wholes are unthinkable and inexpressible. If they were thought and expressed, then these thoughts and expressions would be themselves in the one case an existence, in the other case a becoming. This " existence " and this " becoming " would not be included in the wholes of which they are the thoughts. Therefore the wholes which are thought and expressed are not wholes : they are not the universe nor the evolution of the Tao. Since the universe and the evolution of the Tao are unthinkable and inexpressible—nor can they be objects of experience—therefore they transcend shapes and features. But " universe " also includes the concrete world, and " evolution of the Tao " includes all becoming. Therefore they are not abstract.

The universe and *ch'i* are not abstract ; neither are they concrete. *Ch'i* is not concrete, because a concrete thing must have *hsing* (quality) and *ch'i* has no quality. The universe is not concrete because in its wholeness it includes the abstract. The evolution of the Tao is concrete, but it transcends shapes and features.

The above is an exposition of what we mean by " transcending shapes and features ". In the history of Chinese philosophy, the first philosophy really of this kind of transcendence was the philosophy of the Logicians (*Ming Chia*, lit. Name School), the title given to the earliest specialists in logic in the fourth and third centuries B.C.

The Ming Chia logicians followed after the Dialecticians (Pien Chê), of whom the greatest teachers were Hui Shih and Kung-sun Lung. In the *Chiu Hsüeh Chapter* of the *Chuang Tzǔ Book* Kung-sun Lung is represented as saying, " I unified similarity and difference, and separated hardness and whiteness, proved the impossible as possible, and affirmed what others denied. I controverted the knowledge of all the philosophers. I refuted all the arguments brought against me." The *T'ien Hsia Chapter* says, " Huan T'uan and Kung-sun Lung belonged to the company of the Dialecticians. They threw a deceiving glamour over men's minds and altered their ideas. They could confute men's words, but they could not convince their minds. Herein lay the weakness of the Dialecticians. Yet Hui Shih regarded himself as the ablest of talkers. . . . In reality he simply contradicted people, yet wished to have the reputation of having confuted them. This is why he was at odds with everybody." Ssu-ma T'an said, " The Logicians made a minute examination of trifling points in complicated statements, so that it was impossible for others to get back to their own ideas. They considered terms only, and lost sight of common sense." (*Record of History, Discussion of Six Schools.*) These words, some of them purporting to be the Dialecticians' own words, are actual criticisms made of them in classical times and so represent the impression people got of them.

Regarding the ordinary Dialecticians, this criticism is on the whole right. These men argued for the sake of arguing. Whatever people regarded as so, they deliberately said it was not so ; and when everybody thought something was not so, they deliberately said that it was so. Thus, arguing as they did for the sake of arguing, their arguments had no other purpose except victory. As was said, " they regarded confuting people as highly reputable." This kind of arguing for the sake of arguing was indeed calculated to make those who argued with them often have no answer to make. It made those who argued with them constantly fall into confusion, so that they could not themselves know clearly what their ideas were, and so they themselves were not certain whether or not there were inconsistencies between their own words at different stages of the argument. This is what was said, " They threw a glamour over men's minds and altered their ideas," as also what was said about making minute examination of trifling points in complicated statements and making men unable to get back to their own ideas. But this kind of arguing only temporarily made people unable to find words to answer them with ; it did not necessarily make men pleased at being overcome by them. This is the weakness spoken of, namely that they overcame men's words, but not their minds.

The arguments, therefore, conducted by the Dialecticians were destructive. When others said East they said West, and when others said South they said North. " Their statements were at odds with everybody," but then that was precisely what they hoped would happen. They deliberately were different., It did not necessarily follow that they themselves could have systematic views regarding things, but only that they could argue for the sake of arguing, deliberately destroying other people's views and sometimes reducing them to silence. Their arguments were not necessarily such as to make men submit to them, nor were they necessarily true ; but none the less their arguments might make their opponents reflect on their own views. This did some real good to the opponents.

What everybody knows is for the most part confined to the world of shapes and features. A Dialectician's attitude to a common view was to regard it as not true. From the outset he made the not true true and the impossible possible. He, as a matter of course, criticized other people's views about things. The twenty-one examples cited in the Chuang Tzŭ, T'ien Hsia Chapter, of the Dialecticians' ways of thinking are all criticisms of people's views about things. According to the current idea, fire is hot, the shadow of a flying bird moves, a white puppy is white, a dog is a dog, a sheep is a sheep. The Dialecticians' rejoinder was, " fire is not hot, the shadow of a flying bird does not move, a white puppy is black, and a dog may be a sheep."

This kind of criticism may also be described as a criticism of the world of shapes and features. If a man caught hold of a Dialectician's hand and put it in the fire, telling him to test whether fire was hot or not, although he felt the fire was hot, he might still argue that fire was not hot. And the same would apply if somebody took him out to look at a white puppy : he might still argue that the puppy was black. His criticism of common views about things could be developed into a criticism of the world of shapes and features. He could not only deliberately set up a contrary view to other people's, he could also do the same for the world of shapes and features. All those examples cited in the T'ien Hsia Chapter are explainable in this fashion.

C

To go counter to the world of shapes and features and to criticize it, provided it is not merely argument for the sake of argument, implies that the critic has knowledge about the world which transcends shapes and features, and so has a criterion for purposes of criticism. It implies that the man knows there is such a world, from the angle of which he makes his criticism. If he has this knowledge, his statements are not merely destructive. The criticism which the ordinary Dialecticians made of everybody's views of things, as also their criticism generally of the world of shapes and features, was, in the main, argument for the sake of argument, and so merely destructive. But the two great masters among the Dialecticians, Hui Shih and Kung-sun Lung, whom we may call logicians, progressed to the point where they had a knowledge about the world which transcends shapes and features. Their arguments were not merely destructive. The Taoists were their opponents, but actually they established the Taoist philosophy on the foundation which it needed.

Hui Shih's theories are given in the *T'ien Hsia Chapter* under ten heads. The first is as follows : " the greatest has nothing beyond itself and is called the Great One ; the smallest has nothing within itself and is called the Little One." Using this criterion, from this angle of vision he might well criticize the world of shapes and features and the view that everybody had about things. The above two propositions are what are called formal propositions. With regard to what is actual, they make no assertion. Nor do they say what in the actual world is the largest thing, or what is the smallest. The assertion which they make is one about what transcends shapes and features. To get a full understanding of the significance of these two propositions, we must examine the *Chiu Hsüeh Chapter* in the *Chuang Tzŭ Book*.

In this chapter we find the following : " The River Spirit asked the Sea Spirit, ' Are we right in seeing our heaven and earth as supremely big and the tip of a hair as extremely small ? ' The Sea Spirit answered, ' What men know is less than what they do not know. The period of time in which they are alive is less than the period of time in which they are not alive. . . . How do we know that the tip of a hair is the *ne plus ultra* of the small, or that heaven and earth is the *ne plus ultra* of the big ? ' " What here is called " heaven and earth " is for the most part the physical heaven and earth. It is not the universe, nor the " Great One ". To say that heaven and earth is the biggest of things and the tip of a hair the smallest, is to make an assertion about what is actual. These two propositions are what we call positive propositions, and both may be untrue, because by experience only we have no means of drawing a sound conclusion that heaven and earth are the biggest of things and the tip of a hair the smallest. The big and the small things in the world of shapes and features are all relatively so. " If we call a thing big because it is bigger than something else, then among all the things in the world nothing is not big. If we call a thing small because it is smaller than something else, then among all the things in the world nothing is not small." (*Chiu Hsüeh.*) Everything in comparison with something smaller is bigger, and everything in comparison with something bigger is smaller. Because of this we cannot reach a certain conclusion that the tip of a hair is the *ne plus ultra* of smallness and that heaven and earth is the *ne plus ultra* of bigness.

We cannot, by experience, decide which thing is the biggest and which thing is the smallest in the world of shapes and features. But we can, apart from experience, say what supreme bigness is and what supreme smallness is. " Supreme bigness, with nothing beyond, is ' the great oneness ', and supreme smallness, with nothing within, is ' the small (indivisible) oneness ' ". These two propositions belong to the class of formal propositions. To be big with nothing bigger is to be absolutely big, and to be small, with nothing smaller, is to be absolutely small. Supreme bigness can only be supreme bigness, and supreme smallness can only be supreme smallness. Being absolute, these qualities are unchangeable. To assume the angle of vision of the absolute and the unchanging, to use the absolute and the unchanging as the criterion for looking at the world of shapes and features, is to see that the qualities of the things in that world and their differences are all relative and liable to change.

Now let us take the other nine of Hui Shih's heads. " The least possible thickness may in extent cover a thousand miles." This states that " big " and " small " are relative. For a thing to be the least possible thickness warrants us in calling it small ; but the area it covers warrants us in also calling it big.[1]

" The heavens are as low as the earth : the mountains are on the same level as the marshes." This states that " high " and " low " are relatively so. " The sun at noon is the sun declining :

[1] To the student of the Chinese text I must confess that Hui Shih's paradox here seems to me ambiguous in a way which Dr. Fung does not allow. (E. R. H.)

the creature born is the creature dying." This states that life and
death are relatively so. " A great similarity differs from a little
similarity." This is called small differentiation. " Things are
completely similar and completely different." This is called the
great differentiation. This is a statement that " similar and
' different ' are relative ". " The South has no limit but so has
a limit." This is a statement that " limited " and " unlimited "
are relatively so. " I go to the state of Yüeh to-day and arrived
there yesterday." This is a statement that " present " and
" past " are relatively so. " Connected rings can be separated."
This is a statement that " construction " and " destruction "
are relative. " I know the centre of the world : it is North of
Yen and South of Yüeh." [1] This is a statement that " to be at the
centre " and " to be at the side " are relative positions. " Love all
things equally : heaven-and-earth are one body." This is a
statement that the difference between things is not absolute.
" Things are completely similar and completely different." " If
we look at things from the point of view of their difference, the
liver and gall are distinguishable as are the states of Ch'u and
Yüeh. Looking at things from the point of view of their similarity,
all things are one." (Te Chung Fu.) This is the conclusion reached
in criticizing the world of shapes and features, and it is the
conclusion at which Hui Shih arrived.

When such a conclusion is reached there is a great step forward
made in relation to the knowledge of the world which transcends
shapes and features. At this point there is not only the knowledge
of how there is " great oneness ". There is also the knowledge
of what the great oneness is. " Love all things equally : heaven-
and-earth is one body." This one body is the great oneness.
Because this one body embraces heaven and earth and all creation,
it cannot have anything beyond itself. This then is the " nothing
beyond " in the words " supreme bigness, with nothing beyond
is the great oneness."

Kung-sun Lung also discovered a criterion and angle of vision
from which he could criticize the world of shapes and features or
the views held by everybody about things. He discovered what
in Western philosophy is called the " universal ". The actual
term he used was " chih " (literally " a finger " or " pointer ").
Two explanations may be given why he used " chih " to denote
universals. Chih is what a name indicates ; that is, to speak from

---

[1] Yen was the furthermost northern state and Yüeh the furthermost southern
state. (E. R. H.)

one aspect, what a name indicates is a particular. Thus Kung-sun Lung said, " A name is what designates an actuality." (*Ming Shih Lun.*) An actuality is a particular. But, from another aspect, what a name indicates is a universal. For example, the name " horse " can indicate this or that concrete horse, but it can also indicate the universal of horseness. Also the term " white " may indicate this or that white thing, but it can also indicate the universal of whiteness.[1] Thus Kung-sun Lung argued that " a white horse is not a horse ", and that " hardness and whiteness are unrelated " and in these " *pai ma* "'(white horse), " *ma* " (horse), " *chien* " (hard or hardness), " *pai* " (white or whiteness) indicate the universal. A universal is what a name (term) indicates. Thus he uses *chih* to denote a universal.

Perhaps we may also say that *chih* (a finger) and *chih* (an idea or concept) are interchangeable.[2] According to this explanation, when Kung-sun Lung mentions *chih* (finger) the meaning is really that of " concept " or " idea " in Western philosophy. This " idea " is not the subjective idea but the objective, the platonic idea.

The main proposition in Kung-sun Lung's *Discussion on a White Horse* is, " A white horse is not a horse." The argument with which he proves this proposition may be analysed as having three points, as follows.

The first point is, " The word horse denotes a shape, the word white denotes a colour. That which denotes colour does not denote shape. Therefore, I say that a white horse is not a horse." This, then, is to speak about the intention of the term " horse " and the term " white ". The intention of the one term is the shape of horses, whilst the intention of the other term is one kind of colour. The intention of the term " white horse " is a horse's shape, plus a colour. The intention of each of the three terms is different. Therefore a white horse is not a horse.

The second point is, " When a horse is required, a yellow horse or a black one may be brought forward. . . . Therefore the same yellow horse or black horse can respond to a call for a horse, but cannot respond to a call for a white horse. By this means it is demonstrated clearly that a white horse is not a horse." Also " the word horse neither excludes nor includes

---

[1] The Chinese for " white ", the adjective, and " whiteness " is the same character —*pai*. (E. R. H.)

[2] In Ssu-ma T'an's *Discussion of Six Schools* we find the expression " important *Chih* ". This *chih* is written like *chih* (finger), but what he discusses is important concepts or meanings. (E. R. H.)

colour. Therefore yellow ones and black ones may respond to it. But the term " white horse " both includes and excludes colour. Yellow and black horses are all excluded because of their colour. Therefore only a white horse can fit the requirements. That which does not exclude is not that which excludes. Therefore I say that a white horse is not a horse." Here then the reference is to the extension of the terms " horse " and " white horse ". The extension of " horse " includes all horses. The extension of the term " white horse " includes only white horses. Hence Kung-sun Lung's illustration of a man wanting just a horse and a yellow or black horse fitting the requirements and so forth. Since the extensions of the two terms " horse " and " white horse " are different, it follows that " a white horse is not a horse ".

The third point is, " Horses certainly have colour. Therefore there are white horses. Suppose there is a horse without colour, then we have a horse as such. How then can we get a white horse (at the same time) ? Therefore a white horse is not a horse. A white horse is ' horse ' plus ' white ' ; ' horse ' plus ' white ' is not ' horse '. Therefore I say that a white horse is not a horse." The reference here, then, is to the universal, " horseness ", the universal, " whiteness " and the universal, " white-horseness ". The universal horseness is the essential attribute of all horses, and this attribute contains no particular colour. It only equals the horse as such. The universal " white-horseness " then equals the attribute which all horses have in common, plus the attribute of whiteness. Hence the conclusion " a white horse is not a horse ".

Not only is it true that a white horse is not a horse, but also that it is not white. In the *Discussion on the White Horse* it is said, " The word ' white ' does not specify *what* is white : to forget that is permissible. But the words ' white horse ', in mentioning the white, specify what is white." What is there specified as white, is not the universal whiteness. The white colour which is seen in this or that white object is a specified, concrete white. The word " specified " (*ting*), has the meaning of determined. The white colour which is seen in this white thing is determined by this white thing. The universal " whiteness " may be stated to be " whiteness " as such, and it is not what is determined as that white thing or this white thing. It is whiteness unspecified. This meaning is what ordinary people do not take into account. The fact that they are not concerned with an unspecified whiteness has no visible consequence in their daily life ; as was said, " to forget is permissible." But the white colour which is specified in white objects is not unspecified whiteness. Since the white colour in a white horse is the white as specified, the specified concrete white is not whiteness. Therefore a white horse is not white.

Kung-sun Lung also had a *Discussion of Hardness and Whiteness*. The main proposition there is " Divorce hardness and whiteness ". The arguments which he used to prove his proposition have two points. We take them in the order of the text.

The first point is as follows in the dialogue. " Is it right to have three, viz. hard, white, and stone ? " The answer is that it is not right. " Is it right to have two ? " The answer is that it is right. " How is that ? " The answer is, " To have white colour without a hard surface gives a total of two. To have a hard surface without a white colour gives a total of two. Seeing does not give us what is hard but what is white, and there is no hardness about it. Touching does not give us what is white but what is hard, and there is no whiteness about it. . . . Our getting of this white (colour in the stone) and our getting of the hard (surface in the stone), depend on our perceiving or our not perceiving. To perceive [1] and not to perceive are entirely divorced from each other. The one does not infiltrate into the other, with the result that they are completely divorced from each other. To be divorced, equals to be concealed." This is the epistemological proof that the hard and the white are divorced from each other, i.e. are in separate categories. To illustrate : here we have a hard, white stone. If we use our eyes, we only get what is white ; we only get a white stone. If we use our hands, we only get what is hard ; we only get a hard stone. While we are sensing that the object is white, we cannot sense that it is hard ; and while we are sensing that the object is hard, we cannot sense that it is white. This is what is meant by " depending on our perceiving or our not perceiving ". Also, we see from this that " to perceive and not to perceive are entirely divorced ". So then, speaking epistemologically, there is only a hard stone here, there is only a white stone here : there is no hard, white stone here. Therefore, it is wrong to make a total of three from " hard ", " white " and " stone ". But it is right to make a total of two. " Hard " plus " stone " equals two, and " white " plus " stone " also equals two. And this fits in with the statement " the one does not infiltrate into the other, and there-fore they are completely divorced ". This " not infiltrating into

[1] Using Yü Yüeh's textual emendation, adding *chun* to perceive. (F. Y. L.)

the other " is equivalent to saying that there is no whiteness in hardness, and there is no hardness in whiteness.

The second point in the text is as follows. " Supposing a statement that some things are white, there is no *specifying* what things are white : supposing a statement that some things are hard, there is no specifying what things are hard. What is not specified is what is common to all white things and hard things respectively, so how can what is unspecified be in the stone ? [1] Hardness does not require to be incorporated in a stone for it to be hardness, but it is common to all hard things. It is not incorporation which makes hardness hardness. Hardness is of necessity hardness. Hardness is not the hardening of any stone or things, but is hardness itself. There is no such hardness in the world (of sense experience) ; and so hardness lies concealed (from the world, i.e. does not belong to that world). If whiteness cannot be whiteness in itself, how can it make other objects white ? Assuming that whiteness is necessarily white, then it is white, even though it does not make objects white. The same applies to yellowness and blackness. There may not be any stones at all. What need is there of a hard and white stone ? Therefore (these qualities) are divorced. This is the reason why they are so."

This is the metaphysical proof that hardness and whiteness are divorced from the stone. The universal " hardness " is unspecified, and the same is the case with the universal " whiteness ". The unspecified whiteness and the unspecified hardness are manifested respectively in all white things or all hard things. How can these be said to be in a stone ? The manifestation of hardness is not necessarily in a hard stone. It can be manifested in any hard object. Even if there is nothing which is hard, hardness is still hardness. If, in all the world, there were no hard stones or hard objects at all, then, in spite of hardness being of necessity hardness, it is not manifested. As was said, " it lies concealed." Unspecified whiteness must be whiteness in itself ; because, supposing a whiteness which could not be whiteness in itself, how could it make stones and other objects white ? If whiteness can be whiteness in itself, then it is not necessary for it to depend on anything else, but it is whiteness in itself. It is the same with yellow and black and all the colours. There might be no stone, and whiteness would still be whiteness. Why must it depend on a hard, white stone ? The conclusion,

[1] Emending *shen* to *ch'i* according to Ch'en Li's suggestion. (F. Y. L.)

obviously, is that hardness and whiteness are in a separate category from the stone.

Kung-sun Lung also wrote a *Discussion on Chih (Universals) and Things*. His main proposition there was, " There are no things which do not entail universals, but a universal is not universal." Thus things and universals are opposites. He also said, " Heaven-and-Earth and what it brings into existence are things. A thing is no more than a thing (i.e. a concrete actuality). It is also no less than a concrete actuality. It has a position." (*Ming Shih Lun.*) To use the terminology of Western philosophy, things are particulars, having position in space and time. A *chih* is a universal, a thing is a particular. A thing may be analysed into a number of universals. It is a number of universals put together. But a universal cannot be split up into a number of universals. Therefore, as was said, " There are no things which are not universals, but a universal is not universal." Examine a universal and it is but one universal. Each universal is separate from any other. This is what is said in Kung-sun Lung's " In the world each stands alone and is true." (*Chien Pai Lun.*)

Thus Kung-sun Lung discovers a world which transcends shapes and features. All universals indicated by names are in the transcendent world, though not all the universals in that world have names to indicate them. In that world hardness is hardness, whiteness is whiteness, horse-ness is horse-ness and white-horse-ness is white-horse-ness, in every case " each standing alone and being true ". The hardness in that world is not the specified hard, as also the whiteness is not the specified white : although if this hardness and whiteness are not actually thus specified they are not manifested. By this is meant that they are not in the world of shapes and features. As the *Chien Pai Lun* has it, " Hardness is not the hard-in-any-stone-or-thing but it is hardness in itself. There is no such hardness in the world (of sense experience) ; and so hardness lies concealed." The hardness which is not the hard-in-stones-and-things is the hardness which is not specified. Supposing, in the world of shapes and features, there are no concrete hard things, we nevertheless cannot say that there is no hardness. As was said, " hardness lies concealed." In this transcendent world there lie concealed the universals which subsist. This, then, is what the Sung Confucians described as " intangible, unmanifested, yet with a myriad symbols in due array ". Here, " intangible, unmanifested " refers to the world transcending shapes and features, and " a myriad symbols " refers to everything being there that must be there.

This is the contribution which the Logicians made to Chinese philosophy. From criticizing shapes and features they reached out to something beyond them. Hui Shih, starting with " Heaven-and-Earth as one body ", drew the moral that all things should be loved equally. Kung-sun Lung " wished to extend this argument to making right the correspondence between names and actualities, so as to transform the world." (*Kung-sun Lung Tzŭ, Chi Fu Chapter.*) They regarded themselves as also speaking about " sageness within and kingliness without ". None the less, we may say that they did not make full use of their knowledge in relation to what transcends shapes and features, with a view to obtaining a corresponding manner of life.

The Taoists were opposed to the Logicians. Their opposition was one of going beyond them, not an opposition on the same level. The authors of the *Mo Ching* [1] and *Hsün Tzŭ* opposed the Logicians, and their opposition was on the same level. The Taoists, having passed through the stage of criticism in relation to the world of shapes and features, went beyond the Logicians. In doing this, they attained to the sublime sphere of living. In this connection, the utility of the Logicians' criticism was like what was described as " *Ch'üan t'i* " (a trap for trapping fish and a trap for catching rabbits), the saying being that " after the fish and the rabbits are caught, the traps can be forgotten." (*Chuang Tzŭ Book.*) " When the rabbits are dead, the dogs can be cooked ; when the birds are shot, the bow can be stored away." " To destroy the bridge after crossing the river " may be highly immoral, but in philosophizing, if we do not apply this method, we fail to reach the sublime.

[1] This is a part of the *Mo Tzŭ Book* quite distinct from the other parts. In this part the author (? authors) takes issue with the Logicians. (E. R. H.)

CHAPTER IV

LAO TZŬ AND CHUANG TZŬ

Ssu-ma T'an (died 110 B.C.) said, " The Logicians only settled terms and so lost common sense." As for that, all philosophy involves the loss of common sense, because the ordinary people, in their knowledge, are limited by shapes and features and the highest aim of philosophy is to discover what transcends shapes and features. It has to deal with this before it can be in accord with a transcendental criterion. Most people cannot use abstract thinking, whilst philosophy is entirely concerned with the use of such. To use the term of the *Hsin Li Hsüeh*, abstract thinking is pure thought (*shih*), it is not pictorial thought (*hsiang*). Most men only manage to have pictorial thought, i.e. mental images ; they cannot rise to pure thought. And so, looking at philosophy from the viewpoint of pictorial thought, it is something which " loses common sense ". In the *Lao Tzŭ Book* there are the words, " The high type of gentleman hears the Tao and sets himself to practise it ; the middling type hears the Tao and is as if he had it and as if he had it not ; the low type hears the Tao and laughs loudly at it. If he did not laugh, the Tao would not suffice to be the Tao " (c. 41). We may say the same about philosophy.

Then with regard to settling terms, although we cannot agree with the prevalent opinion that the Logicians' business was to settle terms, yet their thoughts and their arguments did all start with terms. Kung-sun Lung was specially so. Most men's knowledge is restricted to shapes and features, and shapes and features are what Logicians call the actual. That is all that most men know, namely the actual ; that is all they pay attention to ; they do not pay attention to names. Logicians do pay attention to names. Although they do not necessarily know what Kung-sun Lung knew about the universals indicated by names, they still are interested in names. What they talk about is what is nameable. In the history of philosophy those philosophers called nominalists have held that only the actual is real and that names are but empty names. The thoughts of these nominalists, although nearer to common knowledge, are yet on a higher level than the thought of ordinary people. Most people, seeing the actual, have no difficulty in expressing it ; and, although they use names for it, they are not conscious that names are names. With regard to thoughts about names, they all come from thoughts about thoughts, or from reflection on thought as such. Hence it makes no difference whether they are according to the nominalist theory or according to Kung-sun Lung : all thoughts dealing with names are on a higher level than the plain man's thoughts.

In the last chapter, we said that the Taoists had the same experiences as the Logicians, but had risen above them. Their thoughts were on a higher level. Thus, with regard to criticism of shapes and features, whereas the Logicians talked only of the nameable, the Taoists went a step further and spoke of the unnameable. The unnameable stands in contrast to the nameable, and the fact that they had something in contrast to the nameable shows the extent to which they went further than the Logicians.

In the first chapter of the *Lao Tzŭ Book* we find " The Tao that can be comprised in words is not the abiding Tao ; the names that can be named are not unchangeable names. The unnameable is the beginning of heaven and earth ; the nameable is the ' mother of all things '." Again, in Chapter 32, " The Tao abides unchanging, nameless, the Uncarved Block.[1] . . . Once the block is carved, there are names." And again, in Chapter 41, " The Tao lying hid, nameless." In the *Chuang Tzŭ Book* there is " In the very beginning there was non-being, and non-being had no name." (*T'ien Ti Chapter*.) In the Taoist system, being and non-being are opposites, the nameable and the unnameable are opposites. These two, in reality, are one opposite ; and what is spoken of as non-being and being is really a short name for the unnameable and the nameable.[2] The unnameable is the beginning of heaven and earth ; the nameable is the " mother of all things ". There is an alternative reading of this passage, namely " non-being is the name for the beginning of heaven and earth ; being is the name for the mother of all things." These two ways of reading the passage do not make any real difference. In the Taoist system, the Tao was designated as *wu*, non-being ; heaven and earth and all creation as *yu*, being. To say that the Tao was called " non-being " is to say " the Tao is the uncarved block of the unnameable ", that it " lies hid, nameless ". To speak of heaven and earth and all things as things which are designated

[1] " Uncarved Block " is Mr. Arthur Waley's admirable translation of '*p'o* in his *The Way and its Power*. (E. R. H.)
[2] In the Chinese nameable is *yu ming* and unnameable *wu ming*, being is *yu* and non-being *wu*. (E. R. H.)

as being, is to say that they have names ; heaven the name " heaven ", earth the name " earth ", and this kind or the other kind, the name of " this kind " and " the other kind ". There is heaven, there is the name " heaven ", and so also with earth and this and that kind of thing. As was said, " once the block is carved, there are names." The Tao is unnameable, but it is that by which the nameable comes to be. This is why it is said, " The unnameable was the beginning of heaven and earth ; the nameable was the mother of all things."

" The Tao is abiding, unnameable, the Uncarved ,Block." Since it is unnameable, therefore it cannot be comprised in words, but having to designate it, we say " the Tao ", that is, we give it a name which is not a name. " From the past to the present, its name has not ceased to be, having its visualization of all beginnings " (c. 21). The Tao is that by which anything and everything comes to be ; therefore its name does not cease to be. A name that does not cease to be is an abiding name. An abiding name is in reality a name which is not a name, one which it is impossible to make a name. This is why it is said " if a name can be named, it is not an abiding name ".

" The unnameable was the beginning of heaven and earth." This proposition is only a formal one, not a positive one. It does not give any information about facts : with regard to the actual it makes no assertion. The Taoists thought that since there were all things, there must be something whereby all things came to be. This something cannot be named, and for that reason it is called the Tao. The idea of Tao is a formal idea, not a positive one. It only asserts that there is something whereby all things come to be. What that something is, it does not assert. Nevertheless, it does assert that this something, whereby all things come to be, is not in the same category as all things. For " all things " means the sum total of things, and if the Tao is in the same category as these things, then it is not that whereby the sum total of things comes to be, because then the words " sum total " would include the Tao itself. In the *Chuang Tzǔ Book* there is the statement " That which makes things to be things is not a thing." (Chapter 11.) The Tao is that which makes things to be things ; therefore it is of necessity not a thing.[1] Every kind of thing has a

---

[1] Of course in Lao Tzǔ we find the statement *Tao chih wei wu*, of which the natural translation is " The Tao as a thing ". But it is inconceivable that the author meant " thing " here in the same category as all things in creation, or indeed any sort of thing in the ordinary sense of the term. Such things all belong to the nameable. The passage, therefore, is to be taken as " In the case of the Tao ". (F. Y. L.)

name. The Tao is not anything of that sort. Therefore it is " the Uncarved Block without a name ". " If an uncarved block is split up into fragments, then it becomes utensils." (*Lao Tzǔ Book*, c. 28.) Utensils are nameable, have being : the Tao is unnameable, is non-being.

The fact that all things have being involves something having being first of all. By the words " first of all " is not meant first in point of time, but first in the logical sense. For instance, we speak of a certain species of animal coming first, for example apes, and afterwards there being men. Here " first " means in point of time. If, however, we say that first there must be animals before there are men, the word "first" is in the logical sense. The existence of men implies the existence of animals. The heavens and the earth and all creatures all have being ; therefore the existence of the heavens and the earth and all creatures implies the being of being. Since that is so, therefore being is something which stands first of all. " All the creatures under heaven come into being from being ; and being comes into being from non-being." (*Lao Tzǔ Book*, c. 40.) This does not necessarily mean that there was a time when there was only non-being and nothing, and that then there came a time when being came into being from non-being. It only means that if we analyse the existence of the heavens and the earth and all creatures, then we see that there must first be being before there can be beings such as the heavens and the earth and all creatures. Therefore, speaking logically, being is something which stands first of all. The meaning of "first" here is not first in point of time, and the meaning of " being " is not being in point of actuality. From the point of view of actual existences, there cannot be being but only beings.

Speaking of " being " as distinct from beings, there can only be one " being ". In the *Lao Tzǔ Book* there is also the statement, " The Tao produces one, one produces two, two produces three, three produces creation " (c. 42). The " one " referred to here is " being ". Then there is the Tao plus " being " ; the total is two. There is one, plus this total of two ; the total is three. These " one " and " two " and " three " are all formal ideas. There is no assertion as to what " one " is, or what " two " is or what " three " is.

These Taoist ideas with which we have been dealing may well be described as " the settling of terms and so losing common sense." Indeed, in this respect the effect which the Logicians had on the Taoists is very clear.

" The Tao," " non-being," " being," " one," these are not any sort of thing, therefore they transcend shapes and features. The *Chuang Tzŭ Book, T'ien Hsia Chapter,* says of Kuan Yin and Lao Tan that " for building up (their system of thought) they used invariability, non-being and being. For the leading idea they used supreme oneness ". " Supreme oneness," this is the Tao. As also is said in the *Chuang Tzŭ Book,* " In the great beginning, there was non-being, and this non-being had no name : it is that from which oneness originated. There was oneness, but it had not yet form." The Tao is that from which oneness came to be, i.e. " the Tao brought oneness into being ". Since it did that, it is the supreme oneness (*T'ai Yi*).[1]

" *Chang*," which has been translated " abiding " or " invariable ", is the opposite to changing. Things are changing things : the Tao does not change. That is why it may be spoken of as " the invariable or abiding Tao ". The law, according to which things change, is an unchanging law. Therefore, in the *Lao Tzŭ Book,* this law is constantly referred to in that way. For instance, " the conquest of the world comes invariably from doing nothing " (c. 48). " The way the people do their business is invariably to spoil it just at the point of completing it " (c. 64). " The Tao of Heaven has no favourites : it is invariably given to good men " (c. 79). The invariability of law is like that : as we say, " a law of nature."

In a law of nature, the fundamental principle is what we find expressed in Chapter XL : " A complete reversing is the movement of the Tao." If the quality of a thing has developed to its highest pitch, then that quality inevitably changes and becomes its opposite. That is what *fan* (complete reversing) signifies. In the *Lao Tzŭ Book,* we find " To be supreme means to go away from, to go away from means to get further and further, to get further and further means to revert back " (c. 25).

This is one of the basic meanings in the philosophy of the *Lao Tzŭ Book.* There are many statements in this book which are not easy to comprehend, but once we have comprehended this basic idea, then the other difficulties are more easily overcome.

Since " reversing " is the characteristic movement of the Tao, therefore " it is upon calamity that happiness leans, upon happiness that calamity rests. . . . The normal turns round and

---

[1] This " *t'ai* " (supreme) is the *t'ai* found in the titles " *T'ai shang Huang* " (emperor above the emperor, i.e. the emperor's father, " *Huang t'ai Hau* " (the emperor's mother), " *lao t'ai yeh* " (master above master), so that *T'ai Yi* means something higher than just " one ". (F. Y. L.)

becomes the abnormal ; goodness turns round and becomes wickedness " (c. 58). Because this is so, " the twisted will become whole, the crooked will grow straight, the low ground will be filled with water, the ruined will start afresh, those with little will acquire, those with much will be led astray " (c. 22). And because that is so, " a hurricane never lasts the whole morning, nor a rainstorm the whole day " (c. 23). And because that is so, " He who by the Tao helps a ruler of men, does not war down the world by force of arms, for such things invite reprisals " (c. 30). Because that is so, " Is not the Tao of Heaven like the stretching of a bow ? [1] What is high becomes low, and what is low becomes high. From those who have too much, the Tao takes away, and for those who are inadequately supplied, it increases their store " (c. 77). And because this is so, " The most yielding thing in the world (i.e. water) masters the most unyielding " (c. 43), and " Nothing in the world is more yielding than water, but when it attacks things which are hard and resistant, there is nothing more overpowering " (c. 78). And just because this is so, " Diminish a thing, and it will increase ; increase a thing, and it will diminish " (c. 42). Now, the general law which governs all these changes is what the *Lao Tzŭ Book* sets forth in detail. In doing this, it is not deliberately making fantastic and paradoxical theories, although among the mass of men there are a number who regard them as such. This is why it is said in the *Lao Tzŭ Book* " true words appear to be the direct reverse (of what they are) " (c. 78), and why it is said, " the low type of gentleman, on hearing the Tao, laughs loudly at it ; if he did not laugh, it would not suffice to be the Tao " (c. 41).

This is what is referred to under the term " invariable ". " To know the invariable means having illumination : not to know the invariable and to do blindly is to come to disaster " (c. 16). The *Chuang Tzŭ Book, T'ien Hsia Chapter*, says of Kuan Yin and Lao Tzŭ, " they made weakness and humility their outward expression . . . they were aware of the masculine, but they maintained the feminine . . . they were conscious of good repute, but also maintained no repute." The reason why they were so is because, according to " the invariable " described above, to maintain the feminine is the true means for finding

[1] The Chinese bow when at rest is in one position. When it is stretched it is in the reverse position. Hence the connection of this sentence with the succeeding one. (E. R. H.)

the masculine, to maintain no repute is the true means for avoiding real disgrace. This is the method the author of the *Lao Tzŭ Book* discovered for making life whole and shunning injury.

The influence which the Logicians had on Chuang Chou is very clear. On many points, Chuang Chou was the continuation of Hui Shih. In Chapter 3, we gave a short explanation of Hui Shih's Ten Points. Because the *T'ien Hsia Chapter* account is too much in outline, we cannot be entirely certain that Hui Shih's original meaning was really as described. On the other hand, we are able to say with more confidence about the first stages of reasoning in the *Ch'i Wu Lun Chapter* (*Chuang Tzŭ Book*) that it belongs to the class of reasoning which Hui Shih practised.

At this stage the distinctions which ordinary people make between things in the world of shapes and features are pointed out as relative distinctions. From these distinctions are built up men's views of the world of shapes and features ; and these views are shown to disagree in ten thousand ways : what the *Ch'i Wu Lun Chapter* describes as " a myriad hollow roarings from the blowing of the wind ".

Amongst the views which most attracted people's attention at the time were the Confucianist and the Mohist. So also the controversy which most attracted attention was that between these two schools. The *Ch'i Wu Lun Chapter* says, " How is it that the Tao is so obscured that we have truth and error ? How is it that speech is so obscured that we have (a statement) both affirmed and denied ? How can the Tao leave (us) and cease to exist (for us) ? How can statements continue to be made and be utterly fallacious ? The Tao is obscured by narrow conclusions (about it). Statements are obscured by the embroideries (added to them). The result is the affirmations and denials of the Confucianists and Mohists, the one school regarding as right what the other regards as wrong, and as wrong what the other regards as right." And again, " The Tao has no limit : words are not unchanging." The Tao is not confined to being one thing : therefore it has no limit. The whole of the truth requires stating from many aspects ; therefore statements are made from many points of view, and therefore are continually subject to change. This is how there is the question, " How can the Tao leave (us) and cease to be (with us) and how can statements continue to be made and be utterly fallacious ? "

If we realize this, then we know that statements from every

point of view are all capable of being statements of one or other aspect of the truth. From this point of view, the statements made are not in the last resort affirmable or deniable in relation to each other. The origin of " right " and " wrong " lies in the limited range of vision which each man has in viewing things. Because of this every man has his one-sided view, his " narrow conclusion ". Not being aware that his view is so, he regards it as inclusive. That being so, " the Tao is obscured." And not only is every man unaware that he is one-sided, he also embroiders the statement of his view in the hope that it may be regarded as having good ground for it. Thus, truth-demonstrating speech is nowhere to be found : and " speech is obscured by ornamentation ". To Chuang Chou, the arguments of the Confucianists and the Mohists were of this kind.

This kind of arguing, with the one side saying No to the other side's Yes, and Yes to their No, is like a circle turning without end, for there is no stopping place. There is no way in which a final conclusion can be reached, no way to determine that what is right is really right and what is wrong is really wrong. A dialectician thinks that it is possible to decide by argument what is true and what is not. But how can argument decide this question ? As the *Ch'i Wu Lun Chapter* says, " Suppose you and I are engaged in an argument. If you defeat me, I have not defeated you. But does it necessarily follow that you are right and I am wrong ? If I defeat you, you have not defeated me. But does it necessarily follow that you are right and I am wrong ? Is either of us right or wrong, or are both of us right or both wrong ? Since neither you nor I can know, others also are all in the dark. Whom shall we ask to produce the right decision ? If we ask someone who agrees with you, the decision will go in your favour. If we ask someone who agrees with me, the decision will go in my favour. How can we get a right decision ? If we ask someone who disagrees with both you and me, then his decision will be different from both of us. If we ask someone who agrees with both of us, how can he make the right decision ? " This passage in the *Ch'i Wu Lun Chapter* is considerably in the manner of the Dialecticians. It may appear to say " something is so when it is not so, is possible when it is not possible ". But, whereas the Dialecticians spoke in this way in contradiction of common knowledge, the *Ch'i Wu Lun Chapter* speaks in this way in contradiction of the Dialecticians.

If we know that the notions of right and wrong originate in

the views which men have of things, each from his own limited angle of vision, and if we assume a higher standpoint, we see that the things in the world of shapes and features are as the *Ch'i Wu Lun Chapter* says. Thus, " When there is life there is death, and when there is death there is life ; when there is possibility there is impossibility, and when there is impossibility there is possibility. Because there is the right, there is the wrong, and because there is the wrong, there is the right." Things are subject to change and have many aspects, so that every sort of theory may be proposed about these aspects. If we look at the matter in this way, then there is no need to make a decision about the argument on the right and the wrong : the argument explains itself. This is the meaning of the words in the *Ch'i Wu Lun Chapter*. " This is why a sage does not follow : he sees things in the light of Heaven." " Does not follow " means that he does not follow the ordinary point of view in looking at things. " Sees things in the light of Heaven," means that he looks at things from the viewpoint of the transcendent. That viewpoint is a higher view-point, as also is the viewpoint of the Tao. From a finite viewpoint, a " that " is a system of right and wrong, and a " this " is also a system of right and wrong. A " that " and a " this " exist in contrast to each other and make what is called " a pair ". If we take our stand at the higher viewpoint, then our position is not relative to a " that " or a " this ". This is described in the *Ch'i Wu Lun Chapter* as follows : ' If a ' that ' and a ' this ' be not contrasted, it (i.e. the resultant point of view) can be described as the Tao Axis. An axis is the centre of a revolving system, in which it responds to changes endlessly. The right is wholly endless, the wrong wholly endless in their changes." Thus, a " that " and a " this ", in their mutual contrast of right and wrong, are like a circle revolving without start or finish. Thus, a man who has reached the central position of the Tao and looks at things from that viewpoint, does not see things as " that " or " this ", which are in contrast to each other. His position is like that described in Ssu Kung T'i's *Critique of Poetry*, in which he says, " Transcend shapes and features : attain to the axis." Only if we transcend the world of shapes and features, can we attain to the axis of the Tao.

This viewing of things from the viewpoint of the Tao is mentioned in the *Ch'iu Hsüeh Chapter* directly, as that of " using the Tao to view things ". If we do that, then every thing has what it can do and what it cannot do. As the *Ch'i Wu Lun Chapter* says, " The possible is possible and the impossible is the impossible. The Tao acts and makes them so. We speak of things as ' being so ', but how about this ' being so ' ? It is just as it is. But how about its being not so ? It is just as it is not. A thing must be something and have what it can do. There is nothing which is not something nor has nothing which it can do. Thus it is that there are roof slates alongside of solid pillars, ugliness alongside of beauty, the peculiar and the extraordinary : all these by means of the Tao interpenetrate and become one." Although things differ from each other, they are alike in this that they all are good for something and are something. They all alike come from the Tao. Therefore, from the viewpoint of the Tao, things which are different " interpenetrate and become one ".

The distinctions which people make between things are also relative. The *Ch'i Wu Lun Chapter* says, " To make a distinction is to construct something. Construction is destruction. For all things there is no construction and destruction, but they turn back and interpenetrate the Tao and become one." Clouds change and become rain. With regard to the rain, then, it may be said to have been constructed ; with regard to the clouds, they may be said to be destroyed. Each of these expressions, construction and destruction, are made from one angle of vision. From a limited viewpoint this is so : but from the viewpoint of the Tao, there is neither construction nor destruction, but interpenetration and oneness.

From the viewpoint of the Tao not only are the distinctions which men make relative. It may also be said that the natures respectively of all things are relative. So also is the difference between the " I " of me and other things. We all equally come from the Tao, and therefore the Tao interpenetrates and makes us one. The *Ch'i Wu Lun Chapter* says, " There is nothing larger in the world than the point of a hair, nothing smaller than Mount T'ai, nothing older than a dead child, whilst Grandfather Peng had an untimely death. The heavens and the earth and I have come into existence together, and all creation and I are one." This conclusion is the same as the one in Hui Shih's dictum, " Love all things equally, for heaven-and-earth is one body."

In the above paragraphs, the subject for consideration has been the first stage of reasoning in the *Ch'i Wu Lun Chapter* : one which we also find in Hui Shih's philosophy, since it also taught men to view the world of things from a higher viewpoint and thus be able to criticize men's approach to the world of things. This is not to say that the *Ch'i Wu Lun Chapter* on this point and Hui Shih have entirely the same meaning, for Hui Shih was criticizing common knowledge, whilst the *Ch'i Wu Lun Chapter* also criticized the criticism of the Logicians, and its criticism of them was from the viewpoint of the Tao. For this reason, its criticism was on a higher level than the criticism of the Logicians.

For instance, the *Ch'i Wu Lun Chapter* criticizes Kung-sun Lung as follows : " To take *chih* [1] to illustrate that *chih* are not *chih*, is not so good as to take non-*chih* to illustrate that *chih* are not *chih*. To take a horse to illustrate that horses are not horses is not so good as to take non-horses to illustrate that horses are not horses. The universe is one *chih* : all things are one horse." Kung-sun Lung's position was, " there are no things which are not *chih*, but these *chih* are not *chih*." This was to take *chih* to illustrate that *chih* are not *chih*. Kung-sun Lung had also said that a white horse is not a horse, and in saying this he was taking a horse to prove that horses are not horses. But from the viewpoint of the Tao, " the Tao interpenetrates and makes oneness," so that a *chih* and a non-*chih* make a unit and horses with non-horses make a unit. Therefore it is said, " the universe is one *chih* : all things are one horse."

The Logicians used dialectic to criticize people's ordinary approach to the world of things, whilst the *Ch'i Wu Lun Chapter* uses the Tao to criticize the Logicians' dialectic. In doing this the *Ch'i Wu Lun Chapter* says, " In arguing, there are aspects of things which do not emerge to view. The supreme form of argument is not in words." This arguing without words is arguing on a higher level. This is why we said that the Taoists had gone through criticism of the Dialecticians to reach a higher level on which to criticize.

In the *Ch'i Wu Lun Chapter*, in the passage where it said " all creation and I are one ", it goes on to say, " Since all things are one, what room is there for speech ? But since I have already spoken of the one, is this not already speech ? One, plus speech, makes two : two plus one makes three. Going on from this, even the most skilful reckoner will not be able to reach the end, so how much less able to do so are ordinary people ! If proceeding from nothing to something, we can reach three, how much further shall we reach, if we proceed from something to something ! Let

---

[1] Cf. Chapter 3, p. 53, on *chih* as universals.

us not proceed. Let us stop here." It is in this rejoinder that Chuang Chou advanced a step ahead of Hui Shih : and this is the second stage in the reasoning of the *Ch'i Wu Lun Chapter*. The " one " in " all creation and I are one " is a one which transcends shapes and features. It is impossible to conceive it or put it into words. The reason is that once there is thought and speech about the one, this one dealt with in that thought and speech immediately becomes an object of thought and speech, is in contrast to that thought and speech, and at the same time, is in contrast to this " I " of me. The " one " like this is not the " one " in the statement " all creation and I are one." Chuang Chou says that the one is inexpressible, and in so doing, he shows true understanding of " the one ". Hui Shih said, " The greatest has nothing beyond itself, and is called the Great One ". He only knew that there was a " Great One " ; he did not know that the Great One is inexpressible. The Taoists knew that it is inexpressible, and knowing this they advanced one step beyond the Logicians in their knowledge of the world transcending shapes and features. The Logicians regarded ordinary people as wrong in what they took to be knowledge. In doing this, the Logicians themselves were also wrong. " The Tao has no limit. Words are not unchanging. How can the Tao leave (us) and cease to exist (for us) ? How can statements continue to be made and be utterly fallacious ? " The common approach to things is also one aspect of the truth. The only point where this approach is open to criticism, is that people are not conscious that their respective approaches are only partial aspects of the truth. They are not conscious, and therefore their approach is a one-sided one. If they knew that their approach was one-sided, that approach would at once cease to be one-sided. To go a step further, the arguing as to " right " and " wrong " is part of " the ever-changing voice of Nature ". Every creature cannot but regard himself as right, and those things which are different from him as wrong. This also is natural in every case ; and from the viewpoint of the Tao this is inevitable, and the creature is to be let alone to do this. The result is that the man who has reached " the axis of the wheel " does not need to discard the ordinary man's interpretation or argue over right and wrong. The only thing is that he " does not follow them, but views things in the light of Heaven ". This, then, is not destroying but transcending. As the *Ch'i Wu Lun Chapter* puts it, " This is why a sage harmonizes the different systems of right and wrong, and rests in the revolving of Nature " (*T'ien chun*), this feature being described as " following two courses at one and the same time ". This " revolving of Nature " represents the spontaneous revolving change going on in all things. Since there is " right " and " wrong ", let them be as " right " and " wrong ", let them follow this spontaneous, revolving process. They are relative. The truth of the interpretation which people make of things is also relative. The natures which things respectively have, are also relative. Yet " all creation and I are one ", and this one is absolute. Not to discard the relative and to achieve the absolute, this is " to follow two courses at one and the same time ".

This is the point where Chuang Chou advanced a step further than Hui Shih. The latter only knew how to argue : he did not know the arguing of non-arguing. He knew words but not the words which go beyond words. Knowing that the common interpretation was open to criticism as wrong, he did not know that it also can be said that there is nothing wrong. Therefore the Logicians " were not in harmony with the mass of the people " (*T'ien Hsia Chapter*), whilst the Taoists " went back and forth with the spirit of the Universe, and had not a proud attitude towards the world of things " (*ibid.*). " They did not discard the right and the wrong, but lived in the ordinary world " (*ibid.*). This is why we say that the Taoists went beyond the Dialecticians.

On the other hand, the Taoists only knew that the unnameable transcends shapes and features. They did not know that the nameable also can transcend shapes and features. Thus, if what a name denotes is an object or thing, then the nameable is in the world of shapes and features. If, on the other hand, a name denotes a universal, then it also transcends the world of shapes and features. Hardness, whiteness, horseness, white-horseness, in Kung Sun-lung are not unnameable, but they transcend shapes and features. From this point of view, although the Taoists, in contrast with the Logicians, spoke of the unnameable, yet with regard to what the Logicians called the nameable, they still did not have a complete understanding. In their system they had arrived at transcending shapes and features, but not at the abstract.

We find in the *Ch'i Wu Lun Chapter* the following terms : " to be " and " not to be ", " to be thus " and " not to be thus ". If to be is necessarily to be, then it is different from not to be. About this there is no need of argument. Also, if to be thus is necessarily to be thus, then it is different from not being thus.

About this also there is no need of argument. " The ever-changing voices of Nature, whether relative to each other or not : let us amalgamate these in accord with the apportioning of Heaven. Let them follow their own courses indefinitely ; and in this way we can complete our term of years. Forget the passage of time ; forget the distinctions of right and wrong. Leap into the boundless, and so dwell in the boundless." This is the realm in which the man who has attained to the axis of the Tao lives. As was said above, " The Tao interpenetrates and makes one," and also, " The heavens and the earth have come into existence together : all creation and I make one." These words refer to the knowledge of the man at the axis of the Tao. Such a man not only has this kind of knowledge. What is more, he also has this kind of experience, and his experience is an experience of living in " the sphere of identification with Heaven ". Given a man of this sphere, he has forgotten all distinctions. In his experience there is only the undifferentiable " one ". He has forgotten the passage of time and distinctions of right and wrong ; that is, he has forgotten all distinctions. He dwells in the boundless ; that is, he dwells in the undifferentiable one.

Because he needs to forget distinctions, therefore he needs to discard knowledge ; and this is the method which the Taoists employed in aiming at the highest sphere. What is called " knowledge " here is the common meaning of the term. The prime task of this kind of knowledge is to make distinctions between things. To know a thing is to know the difference between it and some other thing. Given that that thing is distinguishable, then it is not undifferentiable. To discard knowledge, then, is to forget all these distinctions. Once all distinctions are forgotten, there remains only undifferentiable oneness. As we found in the *Lao Tzŭ Book*, " In learning, we daily get more and more ; in cultivating the Tao, we daily get less and less." To learn is to increase our knowledge, and therefore we " daily get more and more ". In cultivating the Tao, we do the reverse with our knowledge, and therefore we " daily get less and less ".

The term " Tao " has two meanings. One denotes that by which all things come into being. The other denotes the knowledge of that by which all things come into being. Now, according to the first meaning, Tao is unthinkable and inexpressible ; for, if we do think of it and put it into words, it acquires a definite quality, and we give it a name. But it is unnameable ; it is impossible to take any name for naming it. Because it is so, therefore it cannot be the object of knowledge. From this it follows, in regard to knowledge of the Tao, that it is knowledge which is not knowledge. " Who knows the dialectic which is not in words ? Who knows the Tao which is inexpressible ? " The knowledge which is not knowledge is then the height of knowledge. As the *T'ien Ti Chapter* puts it, " The Yellow Emperor travelled to the north of the Red Water and climbed the K'un Lun peaks ; but, on his return home to the south, he lost his mystic pearl [i.e. the Tao]. He set Chih to find it, but he failed to find it. He set Li Chu, and he failed. He set Ch'ieh Kou, and he failed. Then he set Hsiang Wang, and he found it." " Chih " represents knowledge in the ordinary sense, " Li Chu " represents perception, " Ch'ieh Kou " dialectic. All these could not find the Tao. Only Hsiang Wang could find it, and " Hsiang Wang " is equivalent to " *wu hsiang* " (without features), and that means " transcending shapes and features ". As has been said above, " rise above shapes and features," and afterwards you can " reach the centre of the circle ". This kind of knowledge is then a knowledge which is not knowledge, that is to say, it is the highest kind of knowledge.

To seek the highest sphere entails discarding knowledge. First discard knowledge, and then you can attain to undifferentiable oneness. To seek the highest kind of knowledge also entails discarding knowledge. First discard knowledge, and then you will obtain the knowledge which is not knowledge. To sum up, the method of " cultivating the Tao " is to discard knowledge. There are many passages in the *Chuang Tzŭ Book* where mention is made of the procedure by which one " cultivates the Tao " ; and these are the steps by which one advances in this cultivating. The *Ta Tsung Shih Chapter* says, " Nan Po Tzu K'uei said to Nü Nü, ' Sir, you are a great age, but your complexion is like a babe's. How is this ? ' The answer was, ' I have learnt the Tao from a teacher.' " " Nan Po Tzu then asked whether it was possible for him to be taught the Tao. The answer was, ' It is quite impossible, you are not the right kind of man. There was Pu Liang Yi, who had the gifts of a sage, but not the Tao of a sage. I have the Tao of a sage, but not the gifts. Had I wanted to teach him the Tao, is it likely that he would have become a sage man ? No, it is not likely. But by means of the Tao of a sage to impart to one with the gifts of a sage, that was an easy matter. I was reserved with him, and so imparted to him. In three days' time, the world of men was outside his purview. I was again reserved with him for nine days, and after that life itself was outside his purview. That being so, there then came the dawn of illumination. Being illumined, he could then see the One ; seeing the One, then past and present ceased to exist (for him) ; past and present having ceased to exist (for him) he was then able to enter into eternity [lit. non-dying and non-living]. In regard to things, there is nothing he does not accompany, nothing he does not welcome, nothing which is not to him destruction, nothing to him which is not construction. This is called tranquillity in the midst of activity, the significance of which is that the tranquillity found in activity is the perfect tranquillity.' "

In the expressions *wai t'ien hsia* (the world of men is outside his purview) and *wai wu* (the world of things is outside his purview), the *wai* (outside) means that he ceased to know, he forgot all about them. Pu Liang Yi ceased to know that there was a world of men : he forgot all about it. Now, the world of men is a particular thing, and that is relatively easy to forget. Things in general are more difficult to forget ; so that it was seven days after he had forgotten the world of men before he could forget the world of things, i.e. not know that they existed. The most difficult thing to forget is one's life. It took, therefore, another nine days before he could not know, or had forgotten that he was alive. When things in general and life itself are outside our purview, then the distinction between what is called " I " and things, the gulf between the " I " and the " not-I ", from the point of view of knowledge, ceases to exist. In this fashion one comes into an undifferentiated condition in relation to oneself and to things and is identified with " the undifferentiable One ". This undifferentiated state is what was called " the dawn of illumination " and this seems to be equivalent to *huo jan kuan t'ung*, " mystic enlightenment." At such a time, what a man sees is only the undifferentiable One, hence the words " he sees the One ". The One includes everything, it is the Great Whole. For the Great Whole there is no past and present, for past and present are measurements of time, and since the Great Whole includes time, we cannot have any time with its measurement of past and present outside this whole. In this Great Whole there is neither death nor life. Because the Great Whole cannot cease to be, therefore there is no real death. Because the Great Whole did not begin at any particular time, therefore there is no mortal life. This being so, the man who is one with the Great Whole also has no past or present : death and life have no meaning to him. The man who dwells in this sphere, regarding the material world from the point of view of the Great Whole, sees all things as neither being constructed nor being destroyed. At the same time he can also say that there is nothing which is not being constructed and not being destroyed. So we have the words " *ying ning* ", *ying* to be in a state of activity, *ning* to be in a state of tranquillity. Hence *ying ning* means a condition of tranquillity which is not incompatible with the confused activity of things.

The *Ta Tsung Shih Chapter* also has the following. " Yen Hui [1] said, ' I am getting on.' When Confucius asked him what he meant, he replied, ' I have forgotten human-heartedness and righteousness.' ' Good,' said Confucius, ' but that is not enough.' Another day, Yen Hui again saw Confucius and said, ' I am getting on ' ; and in reply to the question of what he meant, he said, ' I have forgotten rituals and music.' Confucius said, ' Good, but this is not enough.' When, on another day, Yen Hui saw Confucius and told him he was getting on and Confucius asked him what he meant, he replied, ' I sit in forgetfulness.' At this Confucius changed countenance and said, ' What do you mean by " sitting in forgetfulness " ? ' Yen Hui replied, ' With my limbs nerveless and my intelligence dimmed, I part from my body and abandon knowledge. I am one with the Great Interpenetration. This is what I mean by sitting in forget-fulness.' Confucius said, ' If you have become one with the Great Interpenetration, you have no personal likes and dislikes. If you become one with the Great Revolving, then nothing remains the same in you. If you really have this virtue, I should like to follow in your steps.' "

Here the forgetting of human-heartedness and righteousness corresponds with what in the previous quotation was described as things coming to be outside a man's purview. Human-heartedness and righteousness are abstractions and are, therefore, relatively easy to forget. Rituals and music are concrete and therefore more difficult to forget. " To sit in forgetfulness," means " one's limbs being nerveless and intelligence dimmed, being parted from one's body and abandoning knowledge " ; and all this agrees with what in the previous quotation was called " life coming to be outside one's purview ", whilst " being one with the Great Interpenetration " is equivalent to the " dawn of illumination and seeing the One ". So also having no

---

[1] Confucius' most intimate disciple, the man who understood him best. (E. R. H.)

personal likings, corresponds to " accompanying everything and welcoming everything." " Nothing remains the same " corresponds in consequence to " everything is construction and everything is destruction ". " To be one with the Great Inter-penetration," " the dawn of illumination," and " to see the One ", these phrases denote the sphere in which the man who sits in forgetfulness lives. " To be one with the Great Inter-penetration and so have no private likings, to be one with the Great Revolving and so for nothing to remain the same in you ", this is the activity which the man who sits in forgetfulness may have.

Some people may well ask about the statement above, about the Taoists not destroying the right and the wrong, but transcending the right and the wrong by taking two courses at one and the same time. Also we say that the cultivation of the Tao entails the discarding of knowledge and the forgetting of distinctions. This discarding and this forgetting surely mean destroying knowledge and distinctions. To this question we answer that to speak of discarding knowledge and forgetting distinctions is to speak of the sphere of the sage. This belongs to the aspect of " sageness within ". Not to destroy the right and the wrong and not to forget distinctions, this, then, is to speak of the sage's handling of business in the world. It belongs to the aspect of " kingliness without ". The sage handles the business of the world and yet can have his special sphere. This is what has been described as *ying ning*, tranquillity-in-activity, which is equivalent to " going two ways at one and the same time ". The sage has the highest of spheres, and at the same time has absolute " *sao yao* ". By " *sao yao* " Chuang Chou meant the joy of freedom. In his *Sao Yao Yü Chapter*, at the beginning, he speaks of the great roc [1] and the small birds, of small knowledge and great knowledge, of short life and long life. The difference between the large birds and the small ones is great, but if birds follow each their own nature, they all have joy in freedom. Nevertheless, their joy in freedom is conditioned. As the *Sao Yao Yü Chapter* says, " Master Lieh could drive the wind as a team and go, borne aloft. . . . Yet in this, although he had no need to walk, there was still something which conditioned him [viz. the wind]. Supposing, however, one who is borne on the normality of the universe, driving a team of the six elements in their changes,

---

[1] A fabulous bird of prodigious size. Chuang Chou in this passage speaks of its back as measuring several thousand miles across. (E. R. H.)

and thus wandering freely in infinity, would there be anything then which conditioned him ? " Without the wind, Master Lieh could not have gone as he did, so that his joy in freedom was conditioned by the wind. The great roc made a flight of ninety thousand miles, and his joy in freedom was conditioned by making this long flight. For the great *chuang* tree, eight thousand years was one spring, eight thousand years one autumn.[1] Its joy in freedom was conditioned by having a very long life. All these represent conditions, joy in freedom existing under conditions. The sage roams in infinity, and, doing this, he is what the *Ch'i Wu Lun Chapter* described as " leaping into the boundless and dwelling in the boundless ". He will accompany everything and welcome everything, everything being in the course of being constructed and in the course of being destroyed. Hence he cannot but obtain joy in freedom, and his joy is unconditioned.

The early Taoists originally sought only to keep life whole and so to avoid injury to life. But one must get to the highest sphere of living : only then is it possible to make injury not injurious. In the *T'ien Tzu Fang Chapter* we find, " All that is below the sky is that by which the myriad creatures are one. If a man attain to be one with that which makes oneness, then his body and limbs will be but the dust of the earth, and life and death, a beginning and an end, become but as a day and a night, and they can in no way trouble him. How much less trifles such as gaining and losing, bad or good fortune ! " Men must reach this highest sphere of all before they can keep life whole. In the *Ta Tsung Shih Chapter* we find, " A boat may be hidden in a creek, and a net may be hidden in a lake. These may be said to be safe enough. But at midnight a strong man may come and carry them away on his back. The ignorant do not see that, however well you may conceal things [i.e., smaller ones in larger ones], there will always be a chance for them to get lost. But if you conceal the world in the world, there will be no room left for it to get lost. This is the great fact about things. Hence, the sage roams amidst that which cannot get lost and exists along with it." This is the true way of keeping life whole and avoiding injury. And this is the solution which the *Chuang Tzŭ Book* made when faced with the problems of the early Taoists. From the world's point of view, in the book there is no solution much to any problem. What it said did not help men in any real way to live long and defy death ; nor in

[1] This illustration is also taken from the *Sao Yao Yü Chapter*. (E. R. H.)

fact did it enable men to avoid injury to life. Nevertheless, it was able to abolish these problems. According to what it said, the problem of how to achieve wholeness in life and avoid injury is no longer a problem. In fact, we may be paradoxical and say that it made a solution which was no solution.

The Taoists' method of seeking the highest kind of knowledge and the highest sphere, was that of discarding knowledge. The fruit of discarding knowledge is no knowledge, but this kind of no-knowledge comes from having passed through a stage of knowledge. It is not the no-knowledge of original ignorance. To make the distinction clear, we shall call this " post-gained no-knowledge ". The man with the no-knowledge of ignorance lives in the unselfconsciously natural sphere, the man with the post-gained no-knowledge lives in the transcendent sphere.

These two kinds of no-knowledge appear to be like each other, as also do the two corresponding spheres. The sphere of the unselfconsciously natural is an undifferentiable sphere, and the sphere of the transcendent also appears to be undifferentiable. The man in the unselfconsciously natural sphere does not know how to make a lot of distinctions between things. The man in the sphere of the transcendent has forgotten the distinctions which he used to make between things. The reason why the Taoists spoke of forgetting was that the man in the sphere of the trans- cendent is not without knowledge, nor has he never made distinctions between things. He is one who, having made distinctions, has forgotten them. The other man, who has not made distinctions, has not reached this level. The act of forgetting these distinctions is the act of rising above the lower level. As Wang Jung (late third century A.D.) said, " The highest position of all, is to forget feeling, the lowest stage is to have feeling." (*Shih Shuo Hsin Yü* ; *Shang Shih Chapter*.) From the point of view of knowledge the situation is like that. Original ignorance has not arrived at knowledge, and the man in that state may well be described in respect to knowledge as undifferentiably one with all creation. But he is unconscious of it. It is because he has not this kind of self-consciousness that he belongs to the sphere of the unselfconsciously natural. Post-gained no-knowledge transcends knowledge, and the man who belongs to this sphere is conscious that he has done so. It is because he has this kind of self-consciousness that he belongs to the sphere of the transcendent.

This point the Taoists often failed to recognize clearly. In their discussions of society, they constantly praised the primitive state of society, and in discussing the individual they constantly praised a babe and the ignorant man. Because the babes and ignorant fools of a primitive society in their undifferentiable fashion have no knowledge, therefore they may appear to be sages. Actually this appearance is entirely misleading. The difference between the two spheres is that of being poles asunder. The sphere to which the sage of the Taoists really belongs is that of the transcendent, but there were times when what they praised merely belonged to the unselfconsciously natural sphere.

The Taoists were opposed to the Confucianists' treatment of *jen* and *yi*. This is not to say that they insisted on men being not-*jen* and not-*yi*. Their position was that *jen* and *yi* alone are not enough. Because the man who practises *jen* and *yi* belongs to the moral sphere, then from the standpoint of the transcendent sphere we see the moral sphere and the man of the moral sphere to be bound up in society. The Taoists distinguished being in the world and being out of the world. The man who is bound up in society is one who " roams in the world ", whilst the man who gets outside society is one who " roams outside the world ". This latter " is a man alongside of the Creator (*tsao wu chieh*) and roams in the single *ch'i* [i.e., undifferentiated matter, ὕλη] of the universe. To him life is a huge tumour from which death sets him free. He considers his body as borrowed from various kinds of materials and temporarily entrusted to him for the purpose of making a body. He forgets his liver and gall and dispenses with his ears and eyes. Back and forth he goes between the end and the beginning, with nothing to take hold of as he goes, forgetting everything, wandering beyond the dust of the world, free within the sphere of inaction." The men who roam in the world " are troubled about the customary rituals, in order that they may be seen of men ". (*Ta Tsung Shih Chapter.*) The Taoists regarded Confucius and Mencius as men like this, namely in the world.[1] If this view of them is true, then the sphere to which Confucius and Mencius belonged was a low one.

Confucius and Mencius, however, were not in the world in this way. They sought the highest sphere, but the method which they used was different from that used by the Taoists. The Taoist method was to discard knowledge, and so to forget the self, and by this means to enter the sphere of undifferentiable oneness

---

[1] Cf. p. 75 on Yen Hui, where we see the other Taoist method of depreciating the Confucianists, viz. claiming that Confucius had an esoteric Taoist side to him of which his ordinary followers were ignorant. (E. R. H.)

with all creation. Confucius' and Mencius' method was the accumulation of righteousness, by this to overcome the self and so be able to enter the sphere of undifferentiable oneness with all creation. Using this method, the oneness which they attained was an emotional oneness. The oneness which the Taoists attained by their method was an intellectual one. Therefore the Confucianist sage always had what is called a heart of loving people as one's brother, of loving all creatures as one's friends, whilst the Taoist sages " abandoned the world and lived independently of it ". The Confucianist sages were enthusiastic souls, the Taoist sages men of imperturbable calm.

If the method of accumulation of righteousness be used, then there must be no distinction between being in the world and being out of the world. The discarding of knowledge may entail having such a distinction, and the Taoists called the men who were out of the world " squatters ", that is to say " men who squatted alongside of men but who were companions of Heaven ". With this we may compare, " Heaven's little men are men's gentlemen : men's gentlemen are Heaven's little men." (*Ta Tsung Shih Chapter.*) The Taoist philosophy thus had this antithesis in it, and although it exalted the sublime, yet it still was not in accord with our criterion of attaining to the sublime and performing the common task.

There can be no doubt the Taoists were devoted to what they called " taking two courses at one and the same time ". " In their oneness they belonged to the divine, in their not-oneness they belonged to the human, and for them there was no striving for victory between the two sides. This is what I call a true man." (*Ta Tsung Shih Chapter.*) Here is a " taking of two courses at one and the same time, one the divine, the other the human " ; and also, " not discarding the right and the wrong, but living in the world of custom." (*T'ien Hsïa Chapter.*) This, then, is the two courses of being in the world and being out of the world. None the less, taking our criterion of attaining to the sublime and performing the common task, to speak of two courses is open to criticism, because, according to this standard, attention to the sublime and to the daily round of common affairs are not two courses but one and the same course.

CHAPTER V

THE YI SCRIPTURE AMPLIFICATIONS AND THE CHUNG YUNG [1]

We said in Chapter I that although the Confucianists were famous for their principles of *jen* and *yi*, yet the scope of their teaching was not restricted to *jen* and *yi* : the sphere of living with which they dealt, was not merely the moral sphere. Nevertheless, if we apply the test of our criterion of attaining to the sublime and yet performing the common task, their teaching may be said to have been sublime but not to the highest degree.

After Mencius' time at the end of the era of the Warring States amongst the Confucianists of that time was Hsün Tzŭ (Hsün Ch'ing), a very great teacher. He was influenced by the naturalistic tendency of Taoist thought. Among the earlier Confucianists, when they spoke of " Heaven " they were thinking of it as Ruler. Mencius' " Heaven " in the main was one which was the source of moral principle and our human lot. Hsün Tzŭ's " Heaven " was a Heaven of " Nature " in the sense of the natural order. Here we see the influence of Taoism on him, though this influence was not sufficient to raise his philosophy to the completely sublime. Thus, in the Confucianist philosophy, he represents more the specialists in ritual conduct and music. That is to say, the sphere he dealt with was restricted to the moral.

With regard to other systems of thought in his day, and in respect to a certain restricted field, Hsün Ch'ing had an extremely clear apprehension and made most apposite criticism. Thus he said, " Lao Tzŭ had a vision of how to be abased, but not of how to abound. Mo Tzŭ had a vision of social uniformity, but not of individuality." (*Book of Hsün Tzŭ, T'ien Lün Chapter.*) And again, " Mo Tzŭ's vision was obscured by utility and he did not understand culture. Hui Tzŭ's vision was obscured by terms, and he did not understand the actual. Chuang Tzŭ's vision was obscured by Nature, and he did not understand man. . . . Hence from the standpoint of utility, the Tao is nothing more than

---

[1] The *Yi Scripture Amplifications* are what are commonly known in China as the *Ten Wings*, but which are called appendixes in Legge's translation (*vide Sacred Books of the East*, vol. xvi). The *Chung Yung* is what is commonly known as *The Doctrine of the Mean* (*vide* Legge's translation). In my translation (Dent, 1942) it is entitled *The Mean-in-Action*. (E. R. H.)

profit ; from the standpoint of dialectic, the Tao is nothing more than cogency of argument ; from the standpoint of Nature, the Tao is nothing more than *laissez faire*. Each of these items refers to one aspect of the Tao. As to the Tao itself, it is the essence of unchangeability and yet exhausts the possibilities of change. One aspect cannot express it adequately. A man with lop-sided knowledge, observing only one corner of the Tao, cannot understand it. The result is that if he thinks he has an adequate understanding of it, his mind is thrown into confusion on the one hand, and on the other hand he misleads others. For those above to obscure the vision of those below, and for those below to obscure the vision of those above, this is the calamity of benightedness." (*Chieh Pi Pien Chapter*.) In these criticisms which Hsün Ch'ing made of the other schools, his main attitude has certain resemblances with that of the *T'ien Hsia Chapter* in the *Chuang Tzŭ Book*. As has been said, his criticism is extremely apposite, but, since he was only concerned with the moral sphere, he was neither able to appreciate nor to criticize the Taoists' tenets with regard to the transcendent sphere. In the statements about Lao Tzŭ and Chuang Tzŭ just quoted he is in one respect very much to the point ; but the highest principle of their philosophy is not in this connection. That is why we said, " within a certain restricted field."

Those Confucianists who were influenced by the Taoists and so were able to advance in their philosophical thinking, were the authors of the *Amplifications of the Yi Scripture* and the *Chung Yung*. According to traditional scholarship, Confucius was the author of these amplifications, but modern historical criticism has proved that this view is not true. So also with the *Chung Yung*, the traditional view has been that Confucius' grandson, Tzŭ Ssŭ, was the author. On the whole, one section of it probably was by him, but the rest came from a later group of Confucianists who maintained a Tzŭ-Ssŭ tradition. Neither the *Yi Amplifications* nor the *Chung Yung* were the work of one man. Speaking generally, these late writers had come under the influence of the Taoists. In the *Lao Tzŭ Book* it is said, " the Tao unchanging, without name, the Uncarved Block " (c. 32), and also, " when the block is separated into pieces, we get utensils " (c. 28). The Tao and utensils are opposites. The *Hsi Tz'ŭ* [1] also says, " That which is above shapes and features is the· Tao : that which is of shapes

---

[1] This is one chapter of the Amplifications and the significance of the title *Hsi Tz'ŭ* is " Judgments attached to the *Yi* ". (E. R. H.)

and features is the utensil." In the same way the Tao and utensils are opposites.

The *Hsi Tz'ǔ* has the following, " These operations (i.e. the functional operations symbolized by the sages' hexagrams) are indeed numinous, supernal, with the result that without hurrying they move quickly, without travelling they arrive." The *Chung Yung* has the following, " Anything like this (i.e. the Reality in the Universe) is invisible and yet clearly visible, does not stir things and yet changes them, takes no action and yet completes them." To speak like this is very like what is described in the *Lao Tzǔ Book* as the Tao which raises loud laughter in the low kind of scholar. When the *Hsi Tz'ǔ* speaks of the Tao as transcending shapes and features and the *Chung Yung* speaks of it in the words of the *Odes* as " spiritual power (*tê*), weightless as a hair, although a hair has a weight for comparison, whilst the deeds of High Heaven have neither sound nor smell, that is to say are perfect ", what these two books are speaking of is what transcends shapes and features.

Mencius, as we have shown, spoke of the " great morale which pervades all between Heaven and Earth ", so that " the sage flows together with Heaven and Earth ". The Heaven and Earth to which he refers is a Heaven-and-Earth which may be described as transcending shapes and features, although it would seem that Mencius himself was not fully conscious of this implication. The authors of the *Hsi Tz'ǔ* and *Chung Yung* were referring to what transcended shapes and features, and they were fully conscious of doing so. In this respect, therefore, they rose into the sphere of the sublime.

Although the authors of the *Yi Amplifications* and the *Chung Yung* were under the influence of the Taoists, yet they differed from them. They accepted the Confucianist tradition and emphasized a concern for the common task. This is one difference. There is another one. In Chapter IV we stated that the Taoists only knew that the nameless transcended shapes and features : they did not know that the nameable might also transcend shapes and features. When the Taoists spoke of what transcended shapes and features they were thinking of non-being, whilst the authors of the *Yi Amplifications* and the *Chung Yung* had a different approach. When the latter speaks of Heaven's deeds as without sound or smell, the meaning is that they are not the object of sense-experience ; and when the former speaks of " the numinous as neither ' here ' nor ' there ', and the contents of the *Yi* not (limited to) ' this ' or ' that ' ", he is thinking of the numinous, as something essentially fraught with mystery, so that the contents of the *Yi* are not to be subjected to a rigid interpretation. Although these words contain " *wu* ", it does not denote the negative in the term *wu ming*, i.e. the nameless.[1] For them, what transcends shapes and features was not nameless. Here lies a fundamental difference between these thinkers and the Taoist thinkers. Because they also took into account the transcendent, therefore in the era of the Wei and Chin Dynasties (roughly third and fourth centuries A.D.) the Mystical School of philosophy classed the *Yi Scripture* along with the *Lao Tzŭ Book* and the *Chuang Tzŭ Book*, and named them " The Three Mystical Scriptures ". At that time also there were those who wrote commentaries on the *Chung Yung* in the same spirit. It was, however, difficult for them to distinguish the *Yi* from the *Lao Tzŭ Book* and the *Chuang Tzŭ Book*. This defect in understanding on the part of these mystical or transcendental philosophers was not cleared up until the Sung and Ming Neo-Confucianists proved that they were wrong.

With regard to the question of the transcendent being restricted or not to what is nameless, as we have said, if the object denoted by a name is a concrete object, then it is of course within the sphere of shapes and features ; but when the object denoted is a universal, then it transcends shapes and features. For instance, Kung-sun Lung's hardness, white-ness, horse-ness and white-horse-ness, these transcend shapes and features. These universals are not merely nameable, but, what is more, are really entitled to have names. The statement from the *Lao Tzŭ Book* about " The name continuing the same from the past to the present " thus may be applied to them. Hardness from everlasting to everlasting must be called hardness ; and the same applies to whiteness and horseness.

The universal " hardness " is that by which hard things are hard. That may be described as the tao or principle of hardness : the same applies to the universal " whiteness ", or the principle of whiteness. This use of the word *tao* is the same as that in " the tao of kingliness ", " the tao of ministership," " the tao of fatherhood," " the tao of sonship." [2]

According to statements coming in the *Amplifications to the Yi*

---

[1] Cf. Chapter IV, pp. 72–3.

[2] Tao in this sense is what the Neo-Confucianists in Sung times called " *li* ". By so doing the Neo-Confucianists took into use this term *li* which the amplifiers of the *Yi Scripture* apparently were the first to use in the more philosophical sense. (E. R. H.)

Scripture, the book is concerned with *li* (principles). Thus, in the *Hsi Tz'ŭ* we find, " The Ch'ien hexagram, by its easiness, is knowable, the K'un by its simplicity is do-able : if easy, then easy to know ; if simple, then simple in application. . . . With ease and simplicity, then all principles in the world are successfully obtained." The *Shuo Kua Amplification* says, " In bygone days the sages made the *Yi*. In it they dealt exhaustively with the principle and nature of every kind of thing with a view to arriving at understanding of (Heaven's) decrees," and again, " in bygone days when the sages made the *Yi*, their aim was conformity with the principles of the natures which things possess and of the different lots which Heaven decrees. Therefore they established the Tao of Heaven described as the action of Yin and Yang, and the Tao of Earth described as the soft and the hard, and the Tao of man described as human-heartedness and righteousness." Thus, although these two works speak of *li*, yet they do not specify clearly what a *li* is. In this connection we cannot, just on the appearance of the character *li*, decide that it has the same meaning as *li* in the vocabulary of the *Hsin Li Hsüeh*. The quotation from the *Shuo Kua* shows that for its author *li* and *tao* are synonyms. The use of *tao* is " such as we find in the *tao* of wifeliness and the *tao* of ministership " (vid., *Wen Yen Amplification* on the K'un Hexagram), and this is the same as the *Hsin Li Hsüeh's li*. In the passage, " First a round of Yin, then a round of Yang, this equals the Tao," there is something like what the *Hsin Li Hsüeh* calls *li*.[1]

On the other hand, the Tao of the Taoists is something like what the *Hsin Li Hsüeh* calls *ch'i*.[2] Thus the Tao of the Taoists and the Tao of the *Amplifications* are completely different. Unfortunately, the mystical philosophers of the Wei and Chin periods, in their preoccupation with the Three Mystical Scriptures, constantly used the Laotzian and Chuangtzian " Tao " to explain the " Tao " of the *Amplifications*. For example, the passage, " First a round of Yin and then a round of Yang, equals the Tao," is explained by Han K'ang-Po in the following way : " What is the Tao here ? It is the designation of non-being. There is nothing which is not interpenetrated by it, nothing which does not come from it. Being known as the Tao, the meaning is that it is without content and activity, is neither this nor that, has neither shape nor feature. When the function of being is at its height, the achievement of non-being is revealed. The result is

---

[1] The full explanation will appear in Chapter X.
[2] Cf. " matter " in the Aristotelian sense. (E. R. H.)

that the numinous is neither here nor there, the contents of the *Yi Scripture* are not limited to this or that, and hereby the Tao is revealed." This kind of explanation is, from a historical view-point, entirely wrong.

I have said above that what the Taoists called Tao is " something like " what the *Hsin Li Hsüeh* calls *ch'i* : no more than something like, because things cannot come into existence in sole dependence on *ch'i* in the *Hsin Li Hsüeh* sense, whilst the Taoists' Tao can produce things. The words " something like " also apply to the likeness between the *Yi Amplifications'* Tao and the *Hsin Li Hsüeh's li*, because things cannot come into existence in sole dependence on this *li*, whilst that Tao could produce things. We may say that the Taoists' *tao* is an unclear version of the concept which figures in the *Hsin Li Hsüeh* as *ch'i* ; and the Tao of the *Yi Amplifications* is an unclear version of the concept which figures in the *Hsin Li Hsüeh* as *li*.

The *Yi Scripture* was originally a book of divination, its nature being of the same character as books like the *Ya Pei Shen Shu*. The sentences in those books cannot be rigidly interpreted. E.g., in the use of the *Ya Pei Shen Shu*, the dealing of the cards may give, for example, the combination of *hsia-hsia*, *hsia-hsia*, *shang-shang* (down-down, down-down, up-up = two very bads to one very good). The oracle-key book gives for this combination, " Three campaigns : three times defeated : no cause for you to be ashamed. You will save the empire and rule over the feudatories." On the face of it, this oracle is concerned with an army being first defeated and then obtaining a victory, but actually it means first suffering bad luck, and afterwards being blessed with good luck. It is as if there was a bag containing all forms of bad luck changing to good. The wording of the *Yi* originally had the same significance. Later the amplifiers of the *Yi*, following the lead contained in these rough figures, woke up to the idea of a formula. According to their theory, what the *Yi* contained was a number of formulae, every one of them representing one or a number of *tao* (principles), the total of formulae being a perfect representation of as many principles as there are. That is what is maintained in the *Yi Amplifications*.

According to the *Hsi Tz'ŭ*, " The *Yi* consists of symbols ; the sixty-four hexagrams and the three hundred and eighty-four *yao* (the single lines which comprise the hexagrams) are all symbols." Symbols are like what, in symbolic logic, are called variables, and a variable can be substituted for a class or a number of classes of objects. An object or a class of objects only needs to satisfy certain conditions, and they can have a variable as their substitute. As the *Hsi Tz'ŭ* expresses it, " Objects come to be aggregated through being classified : things come to be distinguished through being grouped." Every object must belong to one class or another. The objects in this or that class only need to satisfy certain conditions for them to be substituted by a certain hexagram or by a certain *yao*. The judgment attached to a hexagram or a *yao* is a formula representing the *tao* which the objects in this class, being subject to these conditions, either obey or ought to obey. If they do obey this *tao*, that is good fortune : if they do not obey it, that is bad fortune.

We must examine this. The *Hsi Tz'ŭ* says, " The *Yi* illuminates what has gone by and what is yet to come, and thus what is obscure becomes clear." That is to say, the hexagrams and the *yao* are formulae which are applicable to every event in the past and every event in the future. Now, although the formula may be clear, it is not necessarily the case that the *tao* which it sets forth is obvious. In these so-called " judgments " which the author of the *Hsi Tz'ŭ* regarded as " judgments made through the rectification of names ", a particular hexagram or a particular *yao* may be the substitute for more than one class of object. Of these classes one, as was realized at the time, may be of no particular importance, whilst another may be very important. Also, one class may be near at hand and easily recognized, another class remote and hard to recognize : as was said, " the idea contained in it (i.e., a certain hexagram under discussion) is far-reaching ". Also, sometimes in a judgment there may be no direct reference to a certain class of object and it may be ascertainable only through its connection with another class. It was said of these judgments that they " have the quality of art : the words, although indirect, yet hit the mark." Thus, whilst a judgment may appear to be dealing with material things, what it really represents is the principles underlying those things, and thus, " the thing (under observation) is both obvious and not obvious." And further, these principles are guides for men in matters of conduct. There is a passage in the *Hsi Tz'ŭ* which, in spite of the obvious corruption of the text in two of its words, has quite clearly the meaning that if men follow this guidance they are successful in action, and if they do not follow it they fail. There is direct reference to a recompense, either one of success or one of failure. As is stated in another passage, " The terms ' good fortune ' and ' bad fortune ' refer to success and failure in action."

We go on to the actual hexagrams and *yao*, each one of them the substitute for one or more classes of objects. The *Hsi Tz'ŭ* says, " With expansion of the use of the hexagrams, new classes can be included and everything that man can do in the world is there." Wang Pi (A.D. 226–249) in his *Treatise on the Yi* says, " Postulating the definite meaning of ' virility in the ascendant ', what is the necessity about the horse (with its virile nature) ? Postulating the class of ' docility in the ascendant ', what is the necessity about the cow (with its docile temper) ? Postulating this *yao* here as conforming with docility, what is the necessity which makes the K'un hexagram apply to the cow ? Postulating the particular meaning of ' virility in the ascendant ', what is the necessity which makes the Ch'ien hexagram apply to the horse ? " The *Shuo Kua* says, " The Ch'ien includes the horse, the K'un includes the cow." The horse and the cow may come under the categories represented by these two hexagrams, but the Ch'ien and the K'un are not the substitutes for the horse and the cow alone. Any thing which has the virile nature can have the Ch'ien hexagram as its substitute ; and so also with any thing with the docile nature and the K'un hexagram. In the *Wen Yen*, in the section dealing with the K'un, there are the words, " With regard to the Yin qualities, admirable though they are, the use of them in the carrying out of the king's business entails that they dare not aim at their own completion. This is the tao of earth, the tao of wifeliness, the tao of ministership." The earth, the wife, the minister, have docility as the right course for them : hence, they all come under the K'un. It is the symbol of each one of them. The judgments which come under this hexagram and its *yao* give the principles of earth-ness, wifeliness, ministership. The opposite to the K'un hexagram is the Ch'ien hexagram, the symbol of Heaven, of being a true husband, of being a true monarch. The judgments under this hexagram and its *yao* give the principles of Heaven-ness, of husband-ness, of monarch-ness. Every one of the hexagrams in the *Yi* represents more than one class of object, and the judgments attached to the hexagrams and their *yao* deal with the principles of more than one class of object. Hence, as the *Hsi Tz'ŭ* puts it, " The *Yi*, as a book, must not be out of your mind. It is based on unceasing change." Also, " The *Yi* is not subject to rigid interpretation : the interpretation varies with the circumstances."

The whole *Yi* book is then a system of symbols. As the *Hsi Tz'ŭ* says, " The result is that (the contents of) the *Yi* are symbols. By symbol, is meant something resembling." Also it says, " The sages made observations of all the complex phenomena under the sky, and then considered their characteristic forms and symbolized their types. That is why they are called symbols. The sages made observations of all the movements under the sky, directing their attention to the interpenetrations which take place in them, this with a view to putting into effect right rituals. They made appended judgments, so that decisions might be made as to what brings good fortune and what brings bad fortune. This is why they are called *yao*. They dealt with the most complex phenomena under the sky in this way, in order that there might be no revulsion of feeling against them [i.e., the phenomena]. They dealt with the most mutable things under the sky in this way, in order that there might be no confusion." In other words, all the things in the universe are complex, for ever changing. If there are symbols and judgments attached to them, representing principles, then among the complexities simplicity can be found, among the changes something unchanging. With such simplicities there can be no revulsion of feeling against (the universe), with such an unchanging quality introduced there can be no confusion in the world.

In the *Chien Tsu T'u*, among the Wei books of the *Yi*,[1] and in Cheng K'ang-chen's *Praise of the Yi* and his *Discussion of the Yi* we find the following statement : " What is included in the one word ' *Yi* ' is three meanings, (1) ease and simplicity, (2) variability, (3) invariability." [2] The *Yi* in the midst of complexities reveals simplicity. As the *Hsi Tz'ŭ* puts it, " the Ch'ien by its easiness is knowable, the K'un by its simplicity is do-able. If easy, then easy to know ; if simple, then simple in application. With ease and simplicity, then all the principles in the world of man are successfully obtained." This is the idea of ease and simplicity attached to the *Yi*. It also reveals an element of invariability in the midst of variability. As the *Hsi Tz'ŭ* says, " Movement and quiescence are invariably what they are. There is the definite distinction between the virile [i.e. movement]

[1] From the middle of the First Han, a certain type of scholar exercised great ingenuity in building up a pseudo-science of omens in relation to the *Six Classics* (Ching). These were quite popular for some 300 years. The term *wei* means the weft complementary to *ching* (the warp). (E. R. H.)

[2] These works are lost. The above is K'ung Ying-ta's quotation from them (in the T'ang era) in his commentary on Wang Pi's exegesis of the *Yi*. (E. R. H.)

and the docile [i.e. quiescence]." It also says, "All the movements in the world are true to their invariability." This is the idea of invariability in the *Yi*. Thus the symbols and formulae in the *Yi* are simple and invariable, but since they are the substitutes for any and every class of object, the *Yi* is not subject to rigid interpretation. The interpretation varies according to the circumstances. This is the idea of variability in the *Yi*.

According to the *Hsi Tz'ü's* interpretation, although the *Yi* has only sixty-four hexagrams and three hundred and eighty-four *yao*, yet with these as a framework, one can continuously expand their scope to include new classes. The conclusion drawn is that its symbols and the judgments attached to them include every principle there is. Thus it is said, " The *Yi* dovetails (chün) with Heaven and Earth, with the result that it completely interweaves the governing principles of Heaven and Earth." Dovetailing (*chün*) means corresponding (*teng*) at every point, whilst the interweaving emphasizes the inclusion of all the governing principles in Heaven and Earth. As is said, " What does the *Yi* accomplish ? The *Yi* opens the door to the myriad things in Nature and brings man's task to completion : it embraces all the governing principles in the world. This and no more and no less is what the *Yi* accomplishes." The reference here is to " the principles in man's world ". The " governing principles of Heaven and Earth " refers to those laws which everything obeys. For instance, the principle of kingliness, and the principle of ministership, that of being a good husband and that of being a good wife, these illustrate the first class, whilst the principle known as " one round of Yin and one round of Yang ", refers to the second class.

Whatever exists as an event or a thing cannot divorce itself from the Tao, nor can it disobey it. Concrete things may be defective : in the Tao, there can be no defect. The symbols of the *Yi* include every kind of tao there is, and these symbols and their formulae are, therefore, what events and things cannot be divorced from and what they cannot disobey. That is to say, there can be no defect about them. That is the *Hsi Tz'ü's* position, as it shows : " There is a similarity here with Heaven-and-Earth, with the result that the *Yi* is necessarily not disobeyable. The knowledge (in the *Yi*) embraces all things, and the principles here are of assistance to all beneath the sky, with the result that there are no defects in the *Yi*." Also, " The *Yi* includes within its scope all the transformations in Heaven and Earth without any defect. In multifarious ways it completes all things, leaving out none." Also, " How wide its scope, how great ! To speak of its furthest (implication), there is no limit to it ; to speak of its nearest (meaning), it rests in its proper place : to speak of it in relation to all that lies between Heaven and Earth, it is completely furnished (with explanations)." Also, " So great are its principles that with every kind of thing it does not fail." These statements show that the symbols with their formulae represent whatever kind of tao there is.

In the *Hsi Tz'ŭ*, there are two sets of statement, one with regard to the Tao, the other with regard to *hsiang* (symbols), along with which go a number of formulae with which the Tao is dovetailed. With regard to the symbols, there is the statement, " The *Yi* contains the Supreme Ultimate from which came into being the Two Modes [i.e. the Yin and Yang], from which came into being the Four Hsiang [i.e. the Yin and Yang each under two phases], from which came into existence the Eight Trigrams, by which the good and bad issues of events are determined, from which comes great achievement." With regard to the Tao, there is the statement already quoted, " one round of the Yin and then one round of the Yang," which " equals the Tao ". " That which ensues from this is goodness, that which is completed thereby is the natures (of men and things). As seen by the human-hearted man it [i.e. the Tao] is called humanheartedness : as seen by the wise man it is called wisdom. The common people have it in daily use, but are not aware of it, with the result that the tao of the man of moral intelligence is seldom found. Whilst it is revealed in humanheartedness, its functioning is in secret, stimulating the myriad creatures but without creating the anxieties which the sages endured. How prolific is the virtue of this and how great the achievement ! The abundance of it is what is indicated by the term ' great achievement ' and the daily renewal of it by the term ' prolific virtue '."

In both these statements there is reference to " great achievement ', but the meaning is not the same. " Great achievement," in relation to the Supreme Ultimate, consists in the symbols and formulae connected with the sixty-four hexagrams and three hundred and eighty-four yao. " Great achievement," in relation to the Tao, consists in all the concrete events and things in the universe. Thus, the two meanings are different. But, although they differ, yet they are made completely to dovetail into each other. As the *Hsi Tz'ŭ* says, " In its breadth and greatness (the *Yi*) corresponds (p'ei) [1] to Heaven and Earth, its transformations to the four seasons, the idea of Yin and Yang to the sun and the moon, its ease and simplicity to the highest spiritual power."

The Tao achieves "the great achievement", it being abundant and daily renewed. Indeed, its achievement is achieved in daily renewal. As the *Hsi Tz'ŭ* says, " When the sun goes, the moon comes ; and when the moon goes, the sun comes. Thus, the sun and the moon give place to each other, and light continues in existence. When the winter goes, the summer comes ; and when the summer goes, the winter comes. Thus, winter and summer give way to each other, and the year is completed. That which goes wanes ; that which comes waxes. Waxing and waning have a mutual influence, so that results accrue." This is what is described as being " the great achievement revealed in transformation ". As the *Hsi Tz'ŭ* says, " The supreme virtue of Heaven is to produce." Production, then, is the prolific virtue which is " daily renewed ". Also all the transformations which come in it are mysterious (*shen*). As the *Hsi Tz'ŭ* says, " The inexplorable nature of the Yin and the Yang is what is called mysterious." It also says, " The man who comprehends the tao of transformation, comprehends what the mysterious does."

The things in the universe are not static. They are all part of " the unceasing movement going on in the world ". The symbols in the *Yi* and their formulae are for the most part concerned with movement and change. As the *Hsi Tz'ŭ* says, " The supreme virtue of Heaven is to produce," and " production and reproduction are what the *Yi* represents ". Now, this of course does not mean that the *Yi* itself can produce, but that in the *Yi* there are many symbols which are concerned with producing, and many formulae in accordance with which producing and reproducing go on. As is said, " The lines are imitations of all the movements and changes in the world," the meaning of which of course is not that the lines can make things move or that they themselves move. It only means that a line is the symbol of a certain type of movement, and this being so, the judgment attached to that line is the formula of that type of movement.

" A round of Yin and then a round of Yang equals the Tao," this is the formula for the production of all creatures. In the

---

[1] Here the term "*p'ei*" (corresponds) is synonymous with the term "chün" (dovetail) above. (E. R. H.)

third-line judgment of the eleventh hexagram, we find, " There is no level place without a bank, no going away without a coming back." This denotes the tao of transformation, by which is meant that this is the formula according to which things undergo change. Now, when a thing is produced it must have had something which was able to produce it, and there must have been the materials out of which the producer made it, the former being the active element in the situation, the latter the passive. Using the terminology of the *Yi Amplifications*, one element is the strong and virile, the other element is the soft and yielding ; one is *yang* and the other is *yin*. Using the *Amplifications'* symbols, the *yang* symbol is *ch'ien*, the *yin* symbol is *k'un*. As the *Hsi Tz'ŭ* says, " *Ch'ien* symbolizes *yang* subjects, *K'un* symbolizes *yin* subjects " ; and again, " *Ch'ien* symbolizes the mastery (*chih*) in a great origination, *K'un* symbolizes the process of completion." As we have said, the *Ch'ien* is the active element in the process, is the symbol of that which directs, the *K'un* is the passive element, the symbol of that which completes. Thus there is the statement, " Take the *Ch'ien* : when it is quiescent it is self-contained ; when it is active, it goes straight ahead. This is why it produces on the grand scale. Take the *K'un* : when it is quiescent, it is shut in ; when it is active, it opens out. This is why it produces on a wide scale." Thus the *Ch'ien* and *K'un* complement each other, the *Ch'ien* being the active, initiatory element, the *K'un* being the passive, compliant element. And then, take the *Ch'ien* in itself and the *K'un* in itself, each has its quiescent side and its active side. The *Ch'ien* being (by its nature) originatory, is in a state of quiescence when it is not actually originating. When it is actually originating, then it is in a state of action. The *K'un* being (by its nature) responsive to originative power, is quiescent when it is not actually in a state of responding (or being acted upon) ; when it is actually responding, then it is in a state of action. " Self-contained," and " straight ahead ", qualify the *Ch'ien* as the originating element ; " shut in " and " opening out " qualify the *K'un* as the responsive element. *Hsi* (shut in) means a state of preparation to be acted upon. *P'i* (opening out) means being open to be acted upon. All things in their times of origination come under the category of Yang ; all things in their times of responding come under the category of Yin. All the things in the Yang category can be represented by the *Ch'ien* hexagram, and the six *yao* of that hexagram represent the formulae according to which there is the originative activity. And the same applies to the *K'un* hexagram and its six *yao* and their formulae in relation to responsive activity.

Everything can be a *yang* thing and everything can be a *yin* thing at one stage or another. But the Yang from which every thing is produced can only be *yang*, and the Yin from which every thing is produced can only be *yin*. Although the two hexagrams *Ch'ien* and *K'un* can be substitutes for the things with predominantly virile and docile natures respectively, yet the line of argument in the *Amplifications* is predominantly to take them as the symbols of the Yang and the Yin from which all things are produced. As is said, " *Ch'ien* represents the highest pitch of virility in the world ; *K'un* represents the highest pitch of docility in the world." This refers to the Yin and the Yang, from which all things are produced. According to this, the Yin element can only be the Yin element, representing in consequence the highest pitch of docility, whilst the Yang element can only be the Yang element, representing in consequence the highest pitch of virility. The " one round of Yin and then one round of Yang " is then that which produces every thing in the world. With regard to this reciprocating process which " equals the Tao ", taken in a general sense this is a reference to the *yin* and *yang* elements in any particular situation. Taken in a special sense, this refers to the Yin and Yang, by which all things are produced.

If a thing reaches the point of completion, then it follows necessarily that it has attained to its right position, has attained to the right way [i.e. the mean], has attained to the proper time for it. By this is meant that it is in the place where it ought to be, that its development is within its proper limits, that it has its proper environment. Let us explore this according to the *Yi Amplifications'* line of explanation, where the second and fourth lines in a hexagram (counting from the bottom up) are *yin* positions, the third and the fifth are *yang* positions.[1] The *Hsi Tz'ŭ* says, " The second and fourth lines, although their positions are different, have a like value. But the good (issues which they symbolize) are different. Line 2 is the subject of much praise, Line 4 of many fears, the latter because it is too near to the highest position [i.e. the fifth-line position]. According to the tao for a *jou* (yielding, i.e. broken line), it is not advantageous to be far from Line 1. But in essence, no harm accrues, because the yielding *yao* is in a central position. (Further,) Line 3 and Line 5

---

[1] According to Wang Pi's *Treatise on the Yi*, the First and Sixth Lines were not counted as " positions ". (F. Y. L.)

have a like value, although their positions are different. Line 3 represents many misfortunes, Line 5 many achievements, their two positions being different by one being higher than the other. In this case, the *jou* represents being subject to danger, whilst the *kang* (the strong, i.e. unbroken line) represents being triumphantly successful." Now, " for a *yin* element to take the lead entails going astray, losing its way. To follow is its right course." (Vide *Tuan Judgments* [1] *in re the K'un Hexagram.*) Thus (according to this line of explanation), Line 4, being near to Line 5, represents a liability to take the lead and so the loss of its proper rôle. This is the reason for " many fears ". Line 2 being not far from Line 1 and being in the centre of the lower trigram, there is much praise. The Yang element's rôle is to take the lead. Since Line 5 is a high position in the hexagram and is also a *yang* position, the result is many achievements. Since Line 3 is a lowly position in the hexagram, the result is many misfortunes.

Among the hexagrams, a *yang* unbroken line may be in a *yin* position, or a *yin* broken line may be in a *yang* position. Those are said to be improper positions. Unless there are special circumstances, the rule is that improper positions give a bad issue. A *yang* line in a *yang* position and a *yin* line in a *yin* position, these are said to be in their proper positions, and apart from special circumstances the rule is that a proper position gives a good issue. For a line to attain to a proper position is often described as achieving the right for it. In the *Tuan Judgments* on the *Chia Jen* (the Members of a Family) Hexagram, there is a discussion of proper position, and the statement is made, " Take the members of a family : the wife has her right position in her relation to internal affairs, the husband has his right position in relation to external affairs. For men and women to be in right relationship is a basic part of the justice in the world. Among the members of a family there is sovereign headship. Let the father be a father, the son be a son, the husband a husband, the wife a wife ; then the tao of the family is rectified. With the family rectified, the great society of man is stable." For the parents and the children and for the husband and the wife to be truly rectified is for each to be in its right position.

Again, according to the explanations of the *Amplifications*, the second and the fifth lines in a hexagram are in central positions, the second being in the centre of the lower trigram and the fifth

---

[1] This is another section in the *Amplifications*.

in the centre of the upper. Thus they do not err either by excess or by defect. In this sense they attain the mean. This, speaking generally, entails what the *Yi* calls " *chi* " (a good and happy issue to any transaction or affair of any sort). Even if a *yin* broken line or a *yang* unbroken line is not in a proper position, it can still have a good issue provided it be in a central position [i.e. in a second or fifth position]. Thus in the second-line Hsiang judgment of the Wei Ch'i hexagram we find " Line 2 represents an oracle of happy issue. The right action is achieved by it being done according to the mean ". This line is a *yang* line in a *yin* position, in other words in an improper position. But since it has attained to its centrality (i.e. being in the centre of the lower trigram), it still symbolizes a happy issue. Wang Pi's comment is that, " although its position is improper, centrality makes the action right." Supposing a *yang* line is in the fifth position or a *yin* line in the second, then this has to be called both central and right ; and if there are no special circumstances, the rule is that it symbolizes a happy issue.

The development of a thing cannot go counter to its *shih* (time, i.e. circumstance, time plus environment). That is, for a development to succeed it must be at the proper time in the proper environment. The *Tuan Judgments* on the Feng Hexagram say, " When the sun has reached its meridian height, then it begins to go down. When the moon is full, it begins to wane. The heavens and the earth may be in a brimming state or in an empty state, growing or diminishing, according to the seasons. How much more then with man ! How much more with the manes and the gods ! The heavens and the earth cannot go counter to the *shih* factor. How much more is this in regard to the other things ! " According to the explanations in the *Hsi Tz'ŭ*, with regard to the single lines in a hexagram, if a development is at the right *shih*, then there is a happy issue, if a line symbolizes the missing of the right *shih*, then there is an unhappy issue. In the Judgment for Line 2 of the Tse Hexagram, we find, " Not to go beyond the threshold brings about a bad issue," and the Hsiang Judgment says, " Not to go beyond the threshold brings a bad issue because it symbolizes the complete missing of the right *shih*." Now, in the judgment for Line 5 of the Chi Chi Hexagram we find, " For your neighbour in the east to slay an ox (for a major sacrifice), is not so good as your neighbour in the west observing a minor sacrifice for which he actually receives a blessing." The Hsiang Judgment here says, " The action for the sacrifice is not so good in point of *shih* as the action for the minor sacrifice."

The slaying of an ox is symbolic of a major sacrifice, but the blessing coming with the major sacrifice is paradoxically not so good as that coming from the minor sacrifice. This is because the circumstances visualized for the former sacrifice are not right, whilst those of the latter are.[1] The *Amplifications* constantly refer to " an action as going arm-in-arm with a *shih* ", and this entails " desisting at the right time to desist, acting at the right time to act : in movement and quiescence not to miss the right time, the tao of this is brilliantly clear [i.e. self-evident] ". (*Tuan Judgment, in re the Keng Hexagram.*) As the *Hsi Tz'ŭ* puts it, " The virile and the docile make the basis on which the calculation is made. A transformation and its successful accomplishment is in accordance with the factors of time and environment."

There are many places in the *Amplifications* where the subject of consideration is the *shih* factor. A hexagram, as also a *yao*, can represent a particular condition of time-plus-environment. The only hexagram in which the six lines all have their right positions is the Chi Chi Hexagram (☲☵), which has the meaning of having made an achievement. There the *yin* and *yang* elements which produce a thing are all in the positions which it is proper for them to occupy. That means that each of the elements completely fulfils its tao. If that takes place, then the completion of the producing process is without question a success. But the *Hsiang Judgment* of the Chi Chi Hexagram says, " The morally intelligent man accordingly takes thought for possible dangers and takes precautions against these." For what reason at the time when success is coming should there be thought of dangers and the taking of precautions ? This question brings us to the point where we need to speak about the tao of transformation.

As we have said above, " there is no level place without a bank, no going away without a coming back." This denotes " the tao of transformation ". The complement to going is coming. As the *Hsi Tz'ŭ* says, " The shutting of a door comes in the category of *K'un*, the opening of a door in the category of *Ch'ien*. A whole act of shutting plus a whole act of opening is the meaning of transformation. The unceasing process, first of moving one way and then moving the other, is designated

---

[1] Why this is so would need a detailed explanation for which the only relative importance of the point here hardly warrants us using the reader's time. It is a situation with which anthropologists are familiar. (E. R. H.)

as effective evolving." It is also stated, " That which goes away wanes, that which comes waxes. Waxing and waning have a mutual influence, so that results accrue." The content of the course of transformation in the universe is a process of construction and destruction in things. And this process of construction-plus-destruction in things is the opening and shutting referred to in the explanations of the *Ch'ien* and the *K'un*. The constructive part of the process is equivalent to the " coming forward ", the destructive part is equivalent to the " going away ". A whole act of coming forward, plus a whole act of going away, that is transformation. This going and coming has no end to it, and just because this is so, therefore the universe is without limit of time. Therefore it is said, " the unceasing moving one way and the other is designated as effective evolving." The process is without limit, because what comes must go and what goes must come back again : the advancing thing also retires and the retiring thing comes back again (*fu*). The words, " there is no level place without a bank," indicate the same idea, that there is no coming without going and no going without coming back.

The *Hsi Tz'ŭ* says, " Whenever a climax is reached, there is transformation. Whenever there is transformation, there is effective evolving. Whenever there is effective evolving, there is continuous survival." Because the *Yi* emphasizes effective evolving, therefore it also lays emphasis on returning (*fu*). There is a Fu Hexagram, and in the *Tuan Judgments* we find : " Does not the Fu Hexagram reveal the mind of Heaven and Earth ? " In regard to the great flux of transformation in the universe, wherever we cut athwart it, what we see is a returning. This is because there has been no original coming. As the *Lao Tzŭ Book* says (c. 16), " All things arise side by side ; so I watch for their returning." The meaning of *fu* here is that indicated in the words "back to their root,[1] back to their destined condition". The *Lao Tzŭ Book* also says, " All things sprout luxuriantly, and each of them turns back home again to its root. To be back in its root is to be what is called quiescent, and that means back again to a destined state." In other words, all things emerge from the Tao and return to it. Wang Pi's comment here is, " All things come from emptiness [? infinity], all movements begin in quiescence. The result is that all things, although they in every case move and act, yet in the end go back to emptiness and quiescence." So also with, " Does not the Fu Hexagram reveal the mind of Heaven and Earth ? "

---

[1] Root: " groundstock " ; cf. the German " Grundlage ". (E. R. H.)

Wang Pi's comment is, " The meaning of *fu* is a reverse movement back to the origin, and the reference to the mind of Heaven and Earth is to the original root. If there is desistance from movement, this is quiescence. Quiescence is not the opposite to movement. To desist from speaking is to be silent, but silence is not the opposite to speaking. That being so, although Heaven-and-Earth is so vast and is filled with myriads of things, with such transformations as thunder moving and the wind travelling, yet the silence of non-being is the original root of it all."

This interpretation amounts to the use of the Laotzian ideas in explanation of the *Yi*; it is not true to the original idea of the *Yi*. The Laotzian returning is one of return to the root, to the destined condition, and the emphasis here is on Non-being, whilst in the *Yi Amplifications* the emphasis is on going and coming without end, i.e. on Being. Here, as we have shown, lay the fundamental difference between the Confucianists and the Taoists. None the less, here is where the *Yi Amplifications* and the *Lao Tzŭ Book* come nearest to each other. In the old days there was the saying, based on the point we have been considering, that " the *Yi* and *Lao Tzŭ* are mutually explanatory ". Both books agree that for a thing to reach the highest point of its development is for it to start going in the reverse direction. This is the general law to which transformations conform. What that section of the *Amplifications* called *The Order of the Hexagrams* has to say about the order of the sixty-four Hexagrams represents this general law. The mutually opposed hexagrams always go together in pairs. Thus in this amplification we find the " T'ai ䷊ (Prosperity) Hexagram symbolizes having free course. Things cannot have that for ever, with the result that P'i ䷋ (Lack of Prosperity) succeeds T'ai ". " P'o ䷖ (Disintegration) symbolizes things disintegrating. It is impossible that a thing should be entirely obliterated. When the process of disintegration is ended, the reverse process begins. The result is that the succeeding hexagram is the Fu ䷗ (Return)." Further, " Chen ䷲ (Startling Movement) symbolizes movement. But things cannot keep moving for ever, with the result that the next hexagram is the Ken ䷳ (Arrested Movement)." Also, next to the Chi Chi ䷾ (Having Accomplished) Hexagram comes the Wei Chi ䷿ (Not Yet Accomplished) Hexagram, about which the *Order of the Hexagrams* says, " It is impossible that events and things come to a final end. The result is that the *Yi Scripture* concludes with the Hexagram Wei Chi (Not Yet Accomplished)."

The *Yi Amplifications* and the *Lao Tzŭ Book* agree in thinking that if it be desirable that a thing should be preserved, it is highly necessary that its development should be prevented from reaching its climax, as also that preparations should be made to include some elements of its opposites : that if this be done, it is possible to avoid the opposite coming into effect. Hence, in the *Hsiang Judgments*, the following is found on the Chi Chi Hexagram : " The morally intelligent man accordingly takes thought for possible dangers and takes precautions against them." If the morally intelligent man do this, he can protect and consolidate what he has achieved. As the *Hsi Tzŭ* says, " The man who keeps danger in mind is the one who retains his position ; the man who keeps ruin in mind is the one who survives ; the man who keeps disorder in mind is the one who has control over society. The result is that the man of moral intelligence, when all is peaceful, does not forget danger ; when he is carrying on does not forget about ruin ; when he has society well under control, does not forget disorder. Hence it is possible, with his own person secure, for him to protect the state. As the *Yi* says, ' Am I to perish ? Am I to perish ? (No, the situation) is bound to a clump of mulberry trees [i.e. in a very stable condition].' " (Cf. the Second Line Judgment to the Twelfth Hexagram.) Not to forget danger in times of peace, to think of mischances and to take precautions against them, this is an attitude of mind also denoted as " knowing the hidden springs (of the future) ". Thus, in the *Hsi Tzŭ*, we find, " To know the hidden springs, is not this to have numinous wisdom ? The man of moral intelligence in his intercourse with those of higher rank does not flatter, in his intercourse with those of lower rank is not vulgarly free. Surely he is aware of the hidden springs. A hidden spring is the first slight indication of a movement (in any direction), the initial appearance of good fortune (or bad)." This is what the *Yi* sets out to teach, namely to know, to be aware of, the hidden spring or pivot of what is likely to happen. As the *Hsi Tzŭ* puts it, " With the *Yi* the sages went deep (into the future) and so studied the hidden springs." If the man who knows the hidden springs does not forget dangers in times of peace, he can protect his peace ; if he does not forget ruin in times of security, he can preserve that security ; if he does not forget disorder in times of successful control, he can guard that control.

Those who have this capacity, display the quality of modesty. In the *Tuan Judgments*, on the Ch'ien (Modesty) Hexagram, we find, " It is the tao of Heaven to diminish the puffed up and to augment the modest. It is the tao of Earth to subvert the puffed up and to give free course to the modest. The gods and the manes bring calamity on the puffed up and blessing on the modest. It is the tao of man to hate the puffed up and to delight in the modest. Modesty in a high position sheds a lustre on it ; in a low position cannot be passed by unobserved. This is the final goal of the man of moral intelligence." The *Amplifications* pay attention to this quality, as also does the *Lao Tzŭ Book*.

On the other hand, the sphere in which this type of man lives is not the highest sphere of all. In the *Amplifications*, the man who lives in the highest sphere of all is what is called " the sage man ", also what is called " the great man ". Thus, in the *Wen Yen's* remarks on the Ch'ien Hexagram, we find, " The Great Man has a spiritual power which is in accord with Heaven and Earth, sheds a light like that of the sun and moon, proceeds in such orderly fashion as the four seasons ; in his (mastery of) the good and bad issues he is like the manes and the gods. When he acts before Heaven, Heaven does not go counter to him ; when he acts after Heaven, he serves the timeliness of Heaven's acts. Since Heaven does not go counter to him, how much less do his fellow men ! How much less do the manes and the gods ! "

In other words, the sphere in which the sage man lives is what the *Hsin Yüan Jen* describes as the sphere of identification with Heaven. The mind of the sage man is completely identified with the Tao. Since the Tao existed before shapes and features, and shapes and features cannot go counter to the Tao, it follows that the sage man can " act before Heaven does and Heaven not go counter to him ". But the sage man's body is in the world of shapes and features, and being so it has to obey what shapes and features obey. Thus also, " acting after Heaven acts he serves the timeliness of Heaven's acts." In this highest of all spheres he, of course, has the capacity of the man of moral intelligence. As the *Wen Yen* remarks on the oracle attached to the Ch'ien Hexagram, " An overbearing dragon entailing remorse. . . . The force of this ' overbearing ' is seen in an awareness to advance, coupled with an unawareness to retreat, an awareness to things holding together, coupled with an unawareness to them going to ruin, an awareness to success, coupled with an unawareness to failure. It is the sage and no other who is aware of both progressing and retrogressing, of holding together and going to ruin, and throughout maintaining rectitude of conduct. It is indeed the sage and no other." The sage does this as a matter of course, not deliberately seeking any profit or avoiding any injury. He does not think in terms of profit and loss, but solely of maintaining rectitude in his conduct.

The sage attains to the highest sphere because he has the highest form of knowledge. According to the *Amplifications*, the *Yi* contains that by which man can attain to this kind of knowledge. As the *Hsi Tz'ŭ* says, " How sublime is the *Yi* ! It was by the *Yi* that the sages were able to exalt their spiritual power and extend the scope of their transactions. Their knowledge was exalted, their code of manners yielding : being exalted, after the pattern of Heaven ; being yielding, after the pattern of Earth." Thus the scope of the knowledge contained in the *Yi* is supposed to be the widest possible. As the *Hsi Tz'ŭ* says, " The *Yi* fits perfectly with Heaven and Earth, with the result that it can knit together the ways of Heaven and Earth. Thus, in looking above, the *Yi* observes the artistry of the heavens, in looking below, it examines the order of the earth. And the result is that there is knowledge of the causes of darkness and light. The *Yi* traces the beginning and the end of things, with the result, a knowledge which explains life and death. . . . Knowledge embraces all things. . . . Knowledge through comprehension of the tao of day and night." Also it says, " To understand the spiritual fully and to know transformation, this is the peak of spiritual power." Now, in both the *Hsin Li Hsüeh* and the *Hsin Yüan Jen*, we have urged that the knowledge which embraces all things can only be a formal knowledge. To enable man to reach a higher sphere, this kind of knowledge is all that is needed. The *Amplifications*, however, on this point seem to regard the *Yi* as enabling man to have a positive knowledge : as if, by the method of observing and examining, man is enabled positively to have an all-embracing knowledge of all phenomena. This is impossible. This is one reason why the *Yi Amplifications* are not in entire accord with our criterion of attaining to the sublime.

The sage man has the highest kind of knowledge. He knows that " one round of Yin, plus one round of Yang, equals the Tao ". And this is the Tao which the common people use day by day, only they are not aware that what they daily use is the Tao. In spite of the sage man being aware of this, this Tao remains unaffected. Although he may act in advance of Heaven and Heaven not go counter to him, he still may act after Heaven and serve the timeliness of Heaven. Hence, although his knowledge embraces all phenomena, he yet in regard to action is " one who is trustworthy in ordinary speech and is careful about ordinary action. . . . He occupies a high position and is not arrogant ; is low in the social scale and is not distressed." (Vide *Wen Yen* on the Ch'ien Hexagram.) The transactions he engages in are still those in which all men engage in the corresponding station in life. None the less, the sphere in which he lives is the transcendent sphere.

There are many respects in which the main thesis of the *Chung Yung* corresponds with the main thesis of the *Yi Amplifications*. The language in the *Chung Yung* also, to a certain extent, resembles the phraseology of the *Amplifications*. Thus, in the *Wen Yen's* statements about the Ch'ien Hexagram we find, " He does not change with the world, neither is he completed by the addition of fame. To be in obscure retirement does not distress him. To be opposed by all does not distress him." The *Chung Yung* also says, " The man of moral intelligence acts in accordance with the mean in common action. That he should be in obscure retirement and not known to the world does not hurt him." Compare also what the *Wen Yen* says, " Trustworthy in ordinary speech, careful in ordinary acts," with what the *Chung Yung* says, " acts of ordinary virtue, the carefulness exercised in ordinary speech." Again, the *Wen Yen* says, " The great man has a spiritual power which is in accord with Heaven and Earth ; the light which he sheds is like that of the sun and the moon ; he proceeds in such orderly fashion as the four seasons ; in his mastery of good and bad issues he is like the manes and the gods." Also we find in the *Chung Yung* the following remark about Confucius : " He is to be compared with the heavens and the earth, in that there is nothing which they do not uphold and maintain, nothing which they do not cover and envelop ; to be compared with the four seasons in their interaction, with the light of the sun and the moon giving place to each other." The above statements have a considerable resemblance. Both the *Yi Amplifications* and the *Chung Yung* came from more than one hand. Owing to the resemblances between them, it is open to conjecture that one or more of the authors of the one had a hand in the other. Whether this was the case or not, there is a close affinity between the two works.

In the opening section of the *Chung Yung* there is this : " That which Heaven entrusts to man is to be called his nature. The following out of this nature is to be called the Way (Tao). The building up of the Way is to be called spiritual culture." The word " Tao " here means the Way of man [i.e. the Highway for man], a different meaning from that in the *Hsi Tz'ü's* " one round of Yin, plus one round of Yang, equals the Tao ". There, Tao means the Tao of Heaven. Then in regard to those initial words of the *Chung Yung* about Heaven entrusting man with his nature, in the *Hsi Tz'ü* the statement about one round of Yin and one round of Yang is followed by, " that which passes it (i.e. the Tao) on is goodness, that which completes it is the nature (of man and things)."

All this is an attempt to state clearly the origin of man's nature and the connection of it with Heaven. In this connection compare what the *Mencius Book* says, " The function of the mind is thought. With thought, the mind accomplishes something, whilst without thought, it fails to do so. It is what Heaven gives to me." (*Bk. VI, B.*) Assuming that since the mind is given by Heaven, the nature also is given by Heaven, and that the mind and the nature of man are in relationship with Heaven, the *Mencius Book* says, " The man who develops his mind to its highest capacity knows his nature ; and if he knows his nature, it follows that he knows Heaven." (*Bk. VII, A.*) A similar meaning is to be found in the *Yi Amplifications* and the *Chung Yung*.

To follow the dictates of his nature in action is the Tao (Highway) for man. Since man's nature is what Heaven has given into his charge, and since following the dictates of this nature is the Tao for man, it follows that the Tao of man is also the Tao of Heaven, that the virtue (*te*) of man is also the virtue of Heaven. Adding to this the *Chung Yung* affirmation, " Reaching to the height of the virtue of Heaven," we may say of the man who only knows the virtue of man as the virtue of man, that his sphere of living can only be the moral sphere. But the sphere in which the man lives who knows that the virtue of man is also the virtue of Heaven, that is the transcendent sphere.

We come to, " the building (*hsiu*) of the Way is to be called spiritual culture (*chiao*) ". The word *hsiu* here has the meaning of constructing a house or constructing a road. Thus, " *chiao* " is equivalent to taking in hand the construction of the Highway for man. Now the *Chung Yung* says, " It is impossible for the Tao to be separated from any man for a moment. If it could be separated, it would not be the Tao." Now, since the Tao is such, the question arises as to what necessity there can be for it to be constructed. To answer this question two points need to be considered.

The first point is that it is impossible for ordinary people to be separated from the Tao for a moment. All men at all times have their feet on the Way, but the point is that they do not know that this is so. Compare what we were considering, " they are using it daily without knowing that it is the Way." The *Chung Yung* maintains that, " Amongst men, there are none who do not eat and drink, but there are few who appreciate flavours." The function of spiritual culture is to enable men to appreciate that the Way is one which it is impossible for them to leave for a moment, to appreciate that their feet are at all times in the Way ; or, to use a metaphor, to enable men to be aware of the flavour (to this fact). The Way, by its intrinsic nature, is one which cannot be left for a moment : man, by his intrinsic nature, at all times has his feet in the Way. Speaking from this angle, there is no necessity for the Way to be constructed ; but speaking from the angle of man's conscious knowledge, the Way does need construction.

The second point is that although all men at all times have their feet in the Way, it does not necessarily follow that they actually fulfil all the requirements of the Way. Following out one's nature is to be called the Way. Hence, to fulfil all the requirements of the Way is to fulfil all the requirements of man's nature. In the *Chung Yung* we find, " It is only the man who is entirely real in this world (of experience), who has the capacity to fulfil all the requirements of his human nature." This does not mean that it can be done without application to learning. Thus, the function of spiritual culture is to enable men to fulfil all the requirements of their human nature, and thereby to fulfil all the requirements of the Way. The *Chung Yung* states, " Unless there be spiritual personality (*te*) at its highest, the highest (results of) the Way cannot be consolidated." The man who fulfils all the requirements of his human nature, he possesses spiritual personality at its highest, that is the Tao at its highest. Thus, although " from the angle of ordinary following of the Tao there is no need of construction, from the angle of the Tao at its highest there is need ".

The Way which the sage man knows, is the same way as that which it is impossible for men to leave for a moment, but which they follow without knowing that they follow it. The Way at its highest is also that which it is impossible for men to leave for a moment, the only difference being that the sage fulfils its highest requirements. As the *Chung Yung* puts it, " the Way of the morally intelligent man is obvious and yet obscure. The ordinary man and ordinary woman, in all their ignorance, can yet have (some) knowledge of it. And yet at its highest even a sage man finds that there is something there which he does not know. The ordinary man and ordinary woman, with all their stupidity, can yet practise it, and yet at its height, the sage finds there is something there which he cannot practise. . . . Thus the Way of the man of moral intelligence : its first shoots coming into existence through the relationship of husband and wife, but in its ultimate extent to be examined in relation to Heaven-and-Earth." These first shoots are the acts which all men are already performing. This does not require any construction of the Way. But if there be examination in relation to Heaven-and-Earth, then there is need for construction.

Since a sage man's " Way at its highest " is the same " Way which all men at all times are walking ", it follows that it may be called *yung* (common to all).[1] Because this Way is what all men are already practising, it is ordinary. It is also what they cannot leave for a moment, and therefore it is invariable. Sage men also walk this road and also fulfil its highest requirements. Now this means reaching the point of being exactly good, by which is meant achieving the Mean. As Chu Hsi said, " Achieving the Mean is the name for not erring to one side or the other, for being neither too much nor too little." That is what is meant by being exactly good. This is the highest form of goodness, and it is something which is the hardest of all to achieve. As the *Chung Yung* says, " How perfect is the Mean in ordinary action ! " and again, " The states and families in the Great Society might have equal divisions of wealth. Men might refuse noble station and the wealth that goes with it. They might trample the naked sword under foot. But to achieve the Mean in ordinary action, it is impossible for them to do that." [2]   To make an equality

---

[1] Chu Hsi's comment on *yung* was " What is ordinarily found ", and he also quoted Cheng Tzŭ as saying, " What is invariable is to be called *yung* ".   (F. Y. L.)

[2] One can only surmise that the author used the term *pu k'o* (impossible) with the connotation that it is extremely hard, so hard that if a man does achieve it, he is a sage.   (E. R. H.)

among states and families, to refuse noble station and its wealth, to trample the sword under foot, these are very difficult to do. But in the matter of equal division of wealth it is necessary that the moral imperative should be just so. So also with the refusal of high station. So also with trampling the naked sword under foot. Only so will these actions be in accord with the Mean. This is much more difficult to do.

In the *Chung Yung* we find, " To have no emotions of pleasure and anger and sorrow and joy welling up, this is to be described as being in a state of equilibrium. To have these emotions welling up but in due proportion, this is to be described as being in a state of harmony. This state of equilibrium is the chief foundation of the Great Society, this state of harmony the great highway for the Great Society. Once equilibrium and harmony are established, the heavens and the earth maintain their proper positions and all creatures are nourished." When the emotions described here do not well up, the mind in no way errs in one direction or another, it neither goes too far nor comes too short. This state of equilibrium is included in the idea of the Mean. This is to indicate one particular state of affairs and to regard it as an illustration of the Mean. It does not mean that only this is a state of the Mean. To have the emotions welling up and yet in due proportion is also a state of the Mean. The force of this emphasis on harmony lies in the fact that to harmonize is the function of the Mean and a state of harmony its result. Harmony and sameness are not to be confused. In the Cheng State section of the *Kuo Yü*, Shih Po is quoted as saying, " It is harmony which brings things into existence. Sameness has no offspring. To ameliorate one thing with another is the meaning of harmony. The result is flourishing and growth, and thereby creatures coming into existence. But supposing uniformity is supplemented by uniformity, nothing new can be produced." So also in the *Tso Chuan* (Duke Chao, 20th year) we find, " Harmony is different from sameness," and Yen Tzŭ is quoted as saying, " Harmony is like soup. There being water and heat, sour flavouring and pickles, salt and peaches, with a bright fire of wood, the cook harmonizing all the ingredients in the cooking of the fish and flesh. . . . If water be used to help out water, who could eat it ? If the harp and the lute were the same, who would delight in them ? In this way sameness is of no practical use." To ameliorate one thing with another is the meaning of harmony, as in adding a salty taste to a bitter, with a new taste resulting.

The salt flavouring is the other to the bitter, and the bitter is the other to the salt. With these two " others " combining in due proportions and a new flavour emerging, this is what is expressed in " harmony " and what brings things into existence. Where water helps out water, the result is just the flavour of water, and that is what is expressed in " sameness supplementing sameness ", and " sameness having no offspring ". Sameness and difference are opposite concepts. A harmony includes differences, with all the differences harmonized to produce a state of harmony. None the less, if differences are to produce a state of harmony, then it is necessary that all the differences should have each its own due proportion and be " exactly good " to that extent, neither exceeding nor coming short. What is described as " achieving the Mean ", and also as " in due proportion " amounts to all the differences each being neither too much nor too little, if a state of harmony is to be achieved. That is why it is said, " (when the emotions) well up, they are all in due proportion, and this is called harmony."

This also is setting up a particular state of affairs as an illustration of harmony, and it does not mean that only this constitutes a state of harmony. On the scale of the universe for " all things alike to be nourished and not to injure each other, for all the tao (plural) to be practised and there to be no mutual contradictions ", this also is a state of harmony. Hence the affirmation, " when harmony is carried to the highest, the heavens and the earth maintain their right positions, and all creatures are nourished." This state of harmony is not merely that of man with man in the world. Hence, in the *Yi Amplifications* there is what is called " the Supreme Harmony ", and in the *Tuan Judgments* on the Ch'ien Hexagram there is the ejaculation, " How vast is the originating (power) symbolized by the Ch'ien . . . protecting the Supreme Harmony in unison. This indeed is profitable and auspicious."

The *Chung Yung* says, " Reality is the Way of Heaven ; making oneself real is the Way of man." Also, it says that the " quality of realness is the Way of combining the inward and the outward ". " Heaven " already includes everything with no distinction between inward and outward. Men make the distinction between the " I " and the " not-I ", i.e. the distinction between the inward and the outward. The cause of their making this distinction is that they do not know that each and every man's human nature, together with the natures of all the species of

" things " are equally a charge entrusted by Heaven. All these natures alike come from one source. This state of not knowing can be called unenlightenment. In the *Chung Yung* there is the statement, " (To be able) to proceed from realness to a state of enlightenment is to be ascribed to the nature of man. To proceed from enlightenment to a state of realness is to be ascribed to spiritual culture." This proceeding from realness to enlightenment has the same significance as the statement in the beginning of the *Chung Yung* : " That which Heaven entrusts to man is to be called his human nature and the following out of this nature is to be called the Way." The proceeding from enlightenment to realness has the same significance as " the building of the Way ", namely " spiritual culture ". It means making one's self real.

This matter of enlightenment leading on to realness has been discussed in the *Hsin Yüan Jen*, where the argument is that by proceeding from understanding and self-conciousness the highest sphere of living can be attained. It is this step from understanding and self-conciousness which the *Chung Yung* calls *ming* (becoming enlightened). Without this step being taken there is unenlightenment. With regard to " realness being the Way by which the inward and the outward are combined ", this is what the *Hsin Yüan Jen* described as the sphere of identification with Heaven. This sphere the *Chung Yung* describes as " the height of realness ".

The *Chung Yung* says : " It is only the man who is entirely real in this world who has the capacity to give full development to his human nature. If he has that capacity, it follows that he has the capacity to give full development to other men's human nature. If he has that capacity, it follows that he has the capacity to give full development to the natures of all species of things. Thus it is possible for him to be assisting the transforming and nourishing work of Heaven-and-Earth. That being so, it is possible for him to be part of a trinity of Heaven, Earth and himself." Now, the first half of this passage can be explained along a certain logical line. We may say that the entirely real being is a man and also a thing, that he has the nature of a man and also has the nature of a thing, and for this reason by implication he who is capable of developing his own human nature also is capable of developing the human nature of man and the natures of things in general. But this is not the logic of the *Chung Yung*. The position maintained by the *Chung Yung* is that the nature of each and every man, together with the natures

of all species of things, all equally come from one source, and it is
for this reason that the man who is entirely real is capable of
extending the scope of his high activities from himself to other
men and to the whole world of creation.

In what sense is complete realness able to assist in the
transforming and nourishing work of Heaven-and-Earth ? The
Chung Yung says, " It is only the man who is completely real in
the world, who can weave the fabric of the great basic strands in
human society, who can establish the great foundations of this
world, and who can understand the transforming and nourishing
work of Heaven-and-Earth." Compare this with the statement,
" There are nine basic strands which constitute the society of
man and its constituent states and families," and " this quality
of the Mean, is the main foundation of human society ". The
main strands and the main foundation referred to are the same,
and to understand the transforming and nourishing work of
Heaven-and-Earth, this is on all fours with assisting those
processes. " The hawk beats its way to the height of the heavens,
the fish dives down in the abyss." These are part of the
transforming and nourishing processes of the universe. In man's
life, every phase of activity is also part of the transforming and
nourishing processes of the universe. If men have a full understanding that this is so, then every phase of their activity is of
assistance to these transforming and nourishing processes. Given
the man who can do that, the result is that he is part of a trinity
of Heaven and Earth and man. If men have not a full understanding that every phase of their activity is so, then they are only
transformed and nourished by Heaven : in other words, they
are just things, creatures, and cannot be part of this trinity. The
Taoists constantly said, " To thing things, but not to be thinged
by things." The things which assist the transforming and
nourishing processes, these are not merely in the category of
things (i.e. not to be thinged by things). The distinction between
those two classes consists in whether they have enlightenment
or not.

The conclusion to be drawn is that the man who is entirely
real is not necessarily compelled to engage in acts which are
different from the main bulk of mankind. He may quite well,
in point of action, be engaged " in the deeds of ordinary virtue
and devote himself to ordinary speech ". But in regard to his
sphere of living, it is one with the universe. It is of the same order
as the quality of realness which the *Chung Yung* describes in the

following terms : " In its substantiality, it pairs with Earth, in its sublimity it pairs with Heaven, in its permanence it is infinite time."

The sage men referred to in the *Yi Amplifications* and the *Chung Yung* are all engaged in the deeds of ordinary virtue, and careful about ordinary speech. The method they employ in aspiring to the highest sphere of all is that described by Mencius as, " the marriage of righteousness and the Tao." The moral sphere is attained by means of the accumulation of righteousness. The transcendent sphere can also be attained by the method of accumulating righteousness, but the difference in the sphere attained to lies in the kind of Tao to which righteousness is " married ". There are higher and lower kinds of tao. The fruit of accumulating righteousness is the quality of unselfishness, and unselfishness entails self-sacrifice. The man who lives in the moral sphere is without selfishness, as also is the man who lives in the transcendent sphere. If a man can be like this, it follows that then the sphere in which he lives depends on the loftiness of the tao to which he is devoted. By using this method we avoid the Taoists' distinction between the inward and the outward. In the last resort these two lines of activity make one course, not two.

There is, however, this to be considered.

The authors of the *Yi Amplifications* and the *Chung Yung* knew that the nameable can also transcend shapes and features. But they did not know that for a perfect discussion of what transcends shapes and features it is necessary that the unnameable should also be considered. It is not necessary that what transcends shapes and features should be unnameable, but it is necessary that what transcends shapes and features should not be restricted to the nameable. Arguing from this, we are in a position to maintain that the philosophical system in the two books with which this chapter has dealt is entirely in accord with the criterion of performing the common task, but is still not entirely in accord with the criterion of attaining to the sublime. Thus, the kind of life attained through this philosophy is still inadequate for " absorption in the Abstract and ferrying over into the Beyond ".

CHAPTER VI

THE HAN SCHOLARS

There are a number of ancient philosophical works the date of which we cannot fix in relation to whether they were written in the pre-Ch'in era or in the Han era. On the other hand, with regard to those works which we can date as Han productions, those reveal one special feature. This feature is that the thought expressed in them is unable to " transcend shapes and features ". As we have seen, the early Taoists were the ones to lay the strongest emphasis on transcending shapes and features. Yet the Han Taoists, in their theorizing, were restricted to the world of shapes and features.

The Han scholars believed that the book the *Huai Nan Hung Lieh*, produced by the King of the Huai Nan area, Liu An, and his guests was, " in principle close to the *Lao Tzŭ Book*, with its emphasis on fewness of desires and inaction, with its planting of its feet in emptiness and its maintenance of quiescence." (Cf. Kao Yu's *Commentary*, the Preface.) In the last chapter of this book the authors speak of their intention in writing the book. One statement is, " If I speak of the Tao and not of mundane things, then I am not immersed in swimming with the world. If I speak of mundane things and not of the Tao, then I am not at rest in the freedom of transformation." One part at least of this book comes from the hands of Han era Taoists. These Taoists continued to use the Lao-Chuang terminology as also the actual sentences in the Lao-Chuang books. In that Lao-Chuang philosophy, however, there are terms which originally represented only formal concepts, sentences which represented formal propositions. The authors of the *Huai Nan Hung Lieh* gave positive interpretations, and although they were the inheritors of the Lao-Chuang philosophy, their outlook was nevertheless restricted to shapes and features.

In the Lao-Chuang philosophy, the terms " the Supreme One ", " being," " non-being," and the like represent concepts which are only formal concepts. But the Taoist authors of the *Huai Nang Hung Lieh* gave a positive interpretation to them. Thus, in the *T'ien Wen Hsün Chapter* we find, " Before the heavens and the earth took shape, there was an abyss without form and void : hence the expression Supreme Light. The Tao began with emptiness, and this emptiness produced the universe. The universe produced *ch'i* (vital gas), and this was a winding stream with a bank to it. The pure *ch'i*, being tenuous and loosely dispersed made the heavens, the heavy, muddy *ch'i* being coagulated and hard to move made the earth. The pure and delicate *ch'i* coming together and making a whole, was an easy matter, the heavy and muddied solidification was difficult. The result was that the heavens were finished first and the earth became solid later. The combined essence of heaven-and-earth became the Yin and the Yang, and four special forms of the Yin and the Yang made the four seasons, whilst the dispersed essence of the four seasons made all creatures." This was what the Han age imagined to be the process by which the world came into existence. " The Tao " would appear thus to exist before the heavens and the earth, to be the primordial raw material. In that case, the Tao is a thing, and the concept of the Tao is a positive one, and " the Tao is " is a positive proposition. To speak of abyss without form is to ascribe a form to it, is to make it a possible object of experience. That being so, it does not transcend shapes and features.

In the *Ch'i Wu Lun Chapter* of the *Chuang Tzŭ Book*, there is the statement : " If there was the beginning (of creation), then there was the non-beginning before the beginning and a non-non-beginning to that non-beginning of the beginning. If there is being (*yu*), then there is non-being (*wu*) and a non-beginning to non-being and a non-non-beginning to that non-beginning of non-being. When suddenly there was non-being, there was no telling whether it existed (*yu*) or did not exist(*wu*)." These are formal propositions. They do not assert that there is something which had a beginning or a non-beginning, something which has being or non-being. Still less do they assert what that is which had beginning or non-beginning, or what that is which has being or non-being. That is to say, in these propositions there is no affirmation about the actual.

This statement is also found in the *Shu Ching Hsün* (i.e. teaching on the real) *Chapter* in the *Huai Nan Book* ; but the author of that chapter gave a positive interpretation. Having quoted the statement,[1] he explained the different sections in the following way. About " the beginning " he said : " Before proliferation

[1] There are one or two slight alterations in the quotation, slight but very important, as the reader will see. Further, whereas the original statement requires " non-beginning " as the correct translation, the viewpoint of the *Huai Nan Book* would make pre-beginning more representative of what it had in mind. (E. R. H.)

took place, there was a fore-shadowing, a groundstock ready for the burgeoning, and this was before there was any hard and fast shape to anything." About the non-beginning to the beginning, he said, " With the *ch'i* (vital gas) of the heavens beginning to descend and the *ch'i* of the earth beginning to ascend and the Yin and the Yang in reciprocal agreement, these (forces) were intermixing with things, but no foreshadowing of individuality had emerged." About " a non-non-beginning to the beginning ", he said : " With the heavenly harmonizing influence not yet descending and the earthly *ch'i* not yet spreading abroad, there was emptiness and silence . . . the great indiscriminate mass entirely dark." About " being ", he said that there was a time when " all things became mixed together, so that they could be separated and handled and numbered and measured ". About " non-being ", he said that this was like " looking for but seeing no form, listening for but hearing no sound, a vast desert to which no features attach, over which no measurement can be made but through which light penetrates ". About " the non-beginning to being and non-being ", he said, " it enveloped the heavens and the earth and had a moulding control over all things, with this great indiscriminate mass entirely dark, (namely) a depth and width of space outside which it were impossible there should be anything, and inside which it were impossible there should be anything smaller than the split section of a hair tip, so that with no supporting base the root of being and non-being is produced." About " a non-non-beginning to the non-beginning of being and non-being ", he said : " With the heavens and the earth not yet split asunder, the Yin and the Yang not yet separated, the four seasons not yet distinguishable and the myriad things not yet born, it was like a vast lake, level and still, colourless and transparent, without form and void."

It was with this kind of theorizing that most of the Han thinkers imagined the process by which the universe came into existence. Even the idea in the expression " without form and void ", does not transcend shapes and features. Thus the formal concepts of the *Chuang Tzŭ Book* were changed into positive concepts and its formal propositions into positive propositions.

In the *Ch'üan Yen Hsün* (i.e. teaching in explanation of terms) *Chapter* of the *Huai Nan Book* there is the following : " When the heavens and the earth were still an abyss, still a chaotic mass, this was before the creation of the myriad things. To this condition is given the name of ' the Supreme Oneness '. All things emerged from this oneness, each after its kind, birds, beasts and fishes. To this is given the name 'the differentiation of things'. Creatures became grouped according to their genus, classified according to their species. The natures allotted to each are different, but all have form in the category of being. They are divided into quite distinct classes and so become the myriad things with none able to return to the essence (i.e. the original oneness). The result is that as active beings they are spoken of as being alive, and when they die they are spoken of as having come to an end. All these are things : none of them is able to thing things (*wu wu*). That which things things is not in the midst of the myriad things." The gist of this passage is akin to the Lao-Chuang position. But if the words " abyss ", " chaos," " mass," used as describing the heavens and the earth at a pre-beginning stage, have the same meaning as the terms in the *T'ien Wen Hsün* quotation, then the Supreme Oneness is in the category of shapes and features. It is, after all, no more than a thing.

According to these quotations from the *Huai Nan Book*, the treatment of the concepts of " Tao " and " being " and " non-being " is such that what we are given is knowledge of a certain kind of history, that is to say, the history of the way in which the universe came to be. It comes in the category of natural science, just as astronomy and geology do.

Natural science can increase man's knowledge, but it cannot elevate man's sphere of living. Philosophy can elevate man's sphere of living, but cannot increase his knowledge. Take the statement in the *Lao Tzŭ Book* : " Heaven and earth and the myriad things are produced from being, and being is produced from non-being." Now these words cannot afford us any knowledge of heaven and earth and the myriad things, as to how they came into existence ; but what the *Huai Nan Book* sets out to do is to tell us how all things actually came into existence—the only trouble being that, as far as we can see, what it says is simply not true. The difference in the two outlooks marks the difference between philosophy and science.

Strictly speaking, the Han era possessed religion and science but had no pure philosophy. The main concepts and propositions in pure philosophy are all formal concepts and propositions ; they make no assertion about actuality. The concepts and propositions in religion and science, on the other hand, are all positive and do make assertions about actuality. In recent years, religion and science constantly have taken up opposing positions, but in ancient society the early forms of religion and the early forms of science were inextricably mixed. Amongst the pre-Ch'in philosophers, there was the Yin-Yang school, which carried on the ancient Chinese tradition in its religious and scientific aspects. Ssu-ma T'an has the statement in his *Discussion of Six Schools of Thought*, " With regard to the techniques in connection with the Yin-Yang school, they went too much into detail [1] and were full of taboos, putting people in a quandary and so making many of them afraid. And yet this school makes order out of the great procession of the seasons, and for this reason it is indispensable." In the first half of this passage we can see how this school took over the old religious tradition, the second half, how this school took over the old scientific tradition. This meant utilizing the old scientific knowledge and the old religion, developing and systematizing them, so that this school gave a positive systematic explanation of the world as it is. This is the viewpoint of the Yin-Yang school, this is its essential spirit.

The Han era laid special emphasis on the actual. Its thinkers were either unable or unwilling to indulge in abstract thinking, and they were unable to understand that element in the earlier philosophers which is illustrated by the words " the mystery of mysteries ". In the field of politics they succeeded in unifying the government of the whole country, and the corollary of this was to them the unification of the whole world. In the intellectual realm similarly they were attempting to find the unity of the universe. Hence the Yin-Yang school's theories, theories which were as the *Shih Chi* stated " of so vast a scope that they became untrustworthy ", yet did fulfil the requirements of the Han era. It makes no difference whether the thinkers of that era regarded themselves as Taoists or as Confucianists ; all their viewpoints embodied the viewpoint of the Yin-Yang school and its essential spirit.

The actual process of the development according to which, as the *Huai Nan Book* depicted, the world came into existence, this is what the pre-Ch'in Taoists did not speak of, indeed could not speak of. The reason for this is that the problem of the actual is not soluble through the use of formal concepts and propositions. That the Han Taoists did discuss this problem, is due to the influence of the Yin-Yang school, and the theories which they used for the most part came from the same quarter.

---

[1] Using the Han Shu version of this passage as against the ordinary printed version of the *Shih Chi* (F. Y. L.)

With regard to this influence, it comes for the most part under two heads, one the scientific influence, the other the religious influence. The scientific influence went very far with the Taoists, the religious influence with the Confucianists. With regard to the former, there is no central figure to be taken as representative, for their ideas were not at all systematized. Apart from an early stage in the Han era, their thoughts did not belong to the main stream of Han thought. It was the Confucianists who represent the main stream, and in this they had a representative, namely Tung Chung-shu.

Turning to the Confucianists, Tung Chung-shu inherited the tradition of Tzŭ Ssŭ and Mencius, and their branch of Confucianism. Mencius had spoken of men's nature as good, regarding men from the beginning as all having " shoots of goodness ". Tung Chung-shu had the same conviction with regard to these " shoots ", but he was unable to subscribe to the idea that the nature of man is good. He said, " Mencius levelled down the natural disposition (of man) to that of the birds and beasts and their doings, and this is how he came to say that man's nature is good. For myself, I elevate the natural disposition to that of the sages and their doings, with the result that I say that man's nature is not yet good." (*Ch'un Ch'iu Fan Lu, Sheng Ch'a Ming Hao Chapter*, i.e. the examination of terms and titles.) From this we can see clearly that his viewpoint in this question followed on from that of Mencius. Mencius said, " Confucius made the *Spring and Autumn* (Classic), and this book deals with the affairs of the Son of Heaven." Tung Chung-shu expanded the idea, saying that Confucius received a charge from Heaven to succeed the Chou house in its sovereign position, and in the *Ch'un Ch'iu* he created the institutions for a new dynasty. The *Chung Yung* affirmed that it was possible for man to make a trinity with Heaven and Earth. Tung Chung-shu also maintained this position. Thus we can see that he inherited this branch of the Confucian tradition.

Apparently Confucius, Tzŭ Ssŭ, and Mencius did not entirely abandon the ancient religious point of view. Hence, what they had to say sometimes has the colour of the Yin-Yang school. Confucius said, " The phœnix does not come, the River does not produce the Chart : I am finished." (*Lun Yü*, Bk. IX) ; and the *Chung Yung* says, " When a country is flourishing, there are bound to be omens of happy augury : when it is about to fall into ruin, there are bound to be omens of calamity." These words have the same religious colouring as the Yin-Yang school's ideas about bad and good fortune. Mencius said, " Heaven's gift of life to the people has continued for a great period now, (and with it) there is one round of peaceful control and one round of anarchy." (*Bk. III, B.*) He also said, " Within the space of five hundred years there is bound to be a king of real kingly quality." (*Bk. II, B.*) This theory is like that of the Yin-Yang school in its philosophy of history built round the excellences of the Five *Hsing* (Physical Forces) [1] coming each in turn. Tzŭ Ssŭ and Mencius " stood by the old but created a new thing and called it the Five Forces." (*Hsün Tzŭ, Fei Ju Chapter.*) This criticism from Hsün Tzŭ shows that their thought had been coloured by the Yin-Yang school.

Tung Chung-shu maintained this feature in the Confucianist tradition, and gave yet more pronounced expression to the Yin-Yang school's religious and scientific attitude. The broad success of this in Han thought lay in the establishment of a new order for the universe. He also extended the Confucianist social and ethical philosophy, and so made a theoretical justification for the new order in the society of his day. These were his contributions to the Han era. The Han scholars applauded him as " the head of all the Ju " (vide *Han History, Tung Chung-shu Biography*), and this was not just an idle statement.

According to Tung Chung-shu's theories the universe is composed of ten parts ; as he says, " the heavens, the earth, the Yin, the Yang, wood, fire, soil, metal, water [= the Five Hsing], nine component parts making with man ten parts, Heaven's fixed total thus being complete." (*Ch'un Ch'iu Fan Lu, Heaven and Earth and Yin and Yang Chapter.*) This " heaven " (*t'ien*) at the head of the list is the sky which complements the earth. But the " Heaven " (*t'ien*) at the end of the passage, this denotes the universe, the universe of science, though not the universe of philosophy. This universe of science is a structure, and the concept here is a positive one, whilst the universe of philosophy is only the sum total of all that is and the concept there is only a formal one. Now Tung Chung-shu's " Heaven " actually denotes a structure with ten component parts. Hence, his concept of the universe is a positive one.

To Tung Chung-shu the Yin and Yang were two kinds of *ch'i*. As he says, " Within the area of heaven and earth there is the Yin *ch'i* and the Yang *ch'i*, permanently imbuing men, as water imbues the fish in it, that which constitutes the difference

[1] See infra for the meaning of " the Five Hsing".

between water and *ch'i* being that the one is visible and the other is invisible." " In the area of heaven and earth, although it appears to be nothing, yet it is something. Man is permanently imbued with this stream (of the two *ch'i*), and the two *ch'i* are mixed with the two *ch'i* of order and disorder."

In the Chinese language the term *ch'i* is one with an exceptional variety of meanings. Thus a man may have a *ch'i* of pleasure or a *ch'i* of anger, referring to the appearance of the man. There is the " proper *ch'i* ", or the " basic *ch'i* ", i.e. the healthy element in any thing or state of affairs, and even for the heavens and the earth there is this *ch'i*. Turning to the four seasons they can be spoken of as having " improper *ch'i* ", denoting an unseasonable season which produces sickness in man or plant, etc., whilst yet more to-day in common speech we talk of *k'ung ch'i* (the air) and *tien ch'i* (electricity).

In Chinese philosophy also the term has an exceptionally varied number of meanings. There is Yin *ch'i* and Yang *ch'i*, and the *ch'i* of social order. Tung Chung-shu also speaks of " the *ch'i* of heaven and earth making a unity, which divides into Yin and Yang, splits up into the four seasons, makes a series of Five Hsing (Forces). The term ' *hsing* ', means in a state of activity, and here each of the activities is different from the other, so that all these forces are called *hsing*." (*Wu Hsing Hsiang Sheng Chapter*.) According to this statement, there is also the *ch'i* of heaven and of earth, which is the source of the Yin *ch'i* and the Yang *ch'i*.

The tendency in ancient times with regard to any thing or any force which was invisible and intangible was to describe it as *ch'i*, whilst in recent times the use of *k'ung* (empty) *ch'i* for air and *tien* (lightning) *ch'i* for electricity has arisen in the same way. To use modern terminology, what is called " the *ch'i* of heaven and earth ", may be paraphrased as the basic force of the physical universe.

The Five Forces were sometimes called five kinds of *ch'i*. In the Ming Lüeh section of the *Yui Shih Lan Chapter* of the *Lü Shih Ch'un Ch'iu* this is done, as also in the *Pai Hu T'ung Yi* in which we find, " What is meant by the Five Forces? The term refers to metal, wood, water, fire and soil, and the idea conveyed is that they activate the *ch'i* on behalf of Heaven." This corresponds quite closely with Tung Chung-shu's meaning as quoted above. According to the *Pai Hu T'ung Yi's* interpretation, the earth (*ti*) is represented by the soil (*t'u*) in the series, and it says, " With regard to the earth assisting the heavens, it is like a wife serving her husband, a minister serving his sovereign. Their position is lowly. Because that is so, they personally undertake these duties, with the result that it (i.e. the earth), is equivalent to one of the Five Forces. In this way the position of Heaven is exalted.

According to this way of thinking, the universe is an organic structure, and the controlling power in this structure is Heaven. Heaven and earth are the boundary wall, whilst the Yin and Yang and the Five Forces are the framework of the structure. In terms of space, wood belongs to the east, fire to the south, metal to the west and water to the north, whilst soil occupies the central position. These five forces are very like pillars supporting the universe. In terms of time, four of the five forces control the four seasons, and each is the *ch'i* of one season, wood being that of spring, fire that of summer, metal that of autumn, and water that of winter. Soil has nothing particular which it controls, but it is the central authority of the four seasons. As Tung Chung-shu put it, " The soil is the main agent of Heaven, and since its intrinsic power is on a bountiful scale, its controlling influence cannot be concerned with merely one season ; so that with the Five Forces and the Four Seasons, soil is in them all alike. Although metal, wood, water and fire, each has its own office, yet these are not effectual unless they are based on soil. Unless the sour, acid, peppery and bitter tastes be based on the richly sweet, none of them can be one of the standard flavours. The sweet is the basis of the five flavours. The soil is the controller of the Five Forces, and without the *ch'i* of soil nothing can be accomplished." (*Ch'un Ch'iu Fan Lu, Wu Hsing Chih Yi Chapter.*)

The changes of the seasons, spring, summer, autumn and winter, make a cycle, and this cycle is completed every year with a subsequent return to the beginning. That which is the cause of these transformations is the *ch'i* of the Yin and the Yang, with an alternation of flourishing and declining. In the Chapter on " The unitary nature of the Tao of Heaven " (*Ch'un Ch'iu Fan Lu*), there is the statement : " The unchanging Tao of Heaven is that things of opposing nature are not permitted to start at the same time. The result is that this Tao is unitary, that is, it is one and not two, this being the process of Heaven in action." " The Yin and the Yang are of opposing nature." Hence, if the Yin flourishes, the Yang declines ; and if the Yang flourishes, the Yin declines. When the Yang flourishes, it helps wood, enabling the *ch'i* of wood to be dominant. When this happens, it is spring. It helps fire, enabling the *ch'i* of fire to be dominant. When this happens, it is summer. When the Yin flourishes, it helps metal, enabling its *ch'i* to be dominant. When this happens, it is autumn. It helps water, enabling its *ch'i* to be dominant. When this happens, it is winter.

Taking the four seasons, when spring comes, all things give birth : when summer comes, all things make their growth : when autumn comes, all things bear fruit ; when winter comes, all things go into seclusion. The changes in the seasons are caused by the flourishing and the decline of the Yin and the Yang. The Yang is advantageous in regard to birth and growth. The Yin is disadvantageous in regard to birth and growth. Hence the Yang is " the blessing of Heaven ", the Yin is " the punishment of Heaven ". " Heaven also has a *ch'i* of pleasure and a *ch'i* of anger, a heart of sorrow and a heart of joy, just as happens in men, so that men and Heaven belong to the same class (both having feeling)." (*Yin Yang Yi Chapter.*) These *ch'i* of pleasure and of anger and these hearts of sorrow and joy in normal conditions are revealed in the transformations of the seasons. On the other hand, Heaven gives free rein to the Yang but not to the Yin, it delights in blessing and dislikes punishing. Hence among the four seasons, " spring is full of flower, autumn is full of fruit," that is, autumn (although a Yin season) is not disadvantageous to creation. Only one season does not bring positive advantage, and that is winter. Hence Tung Chung-shu's statement : " The *ch'i* of Heaven throughout three seasons produces life, in one season (only) is loss and death." (*Yin Yang Yi Chapter.*)

In this structure of the universe there are the myriad things, and among them the most imbued with spiritual quality and the highest in the scale of value is man. Man and Heaven complement each other. Man is Heaven's second edition, Heaven's shadow in brief. As Tung Chung-shu said : " There is nothing more subtle than *ch'i*, there is nothing more endowed with wealth than Earth, nothing more numinous than Heaven, and of the essence of Heaven and Earth whereby things are brought to life, there is nothing of higher estate than man." Hence, with his head erect, man faces Heaven, whilst the plants with their heads [i.e. their roots] face Earth, and the animals with their heads bent down are different from men and plants. " The heads of those which receive less from Heaven and Earth bend down : the heads of those which receive more from Heaven and Earth are erect and face

Heaven. This shows man in his superiority to ordinary things and in his intimate association with Heaven and Earth." Not only so : man's bodily structure also is a second edition of Heaven. "There is a tallying of Heaven and Earth and a reproduction of the Yin and the Yang permanently established in the human body." "In the body there are three hundred and sixty-six small component parts, making the sum total of the days in the year, and twelve major parts, making the sum total of the months in the year. Within, there are five viscera, making the sum total of the Five Forces. Without, there are four limbs, making the sum total of the four seasons." "At one time man's senses work [i.e. he is awake], at another time they are dormant [i.e. he sleeps], thus putting him in the category of day and night. At one time man is assertive and at another time yielding, putting him thus in the category of summer and winter. At one time he feels sorrows and at another he feels joy, putting him thus in the category of the Yin and the Yang. With those (features) which can be numbered, there is correspondence in number, with those (qualities) which cannot be numbered, there is correspondence in category. In every respect man is a second edition of Heaven, nothing less." (vid. the chapter on "Man an Edition of Heaven.") Thus, according to Tung Chung-shu's system, man is a shadow in brief of the universe : he is a microcosm to the macrocosm, and the universe may be described as man on a vast scale, in short as the "great man".

Man being thus, it follows that he stands along with Heaven and Earth, and they make together a total of three, or to use a previous expression, "a trinity." In the chapter on the theory of a Primordial Spirit we find, "Heaven, Earth and Man are the basis of all creation. Heaven produces them, Earth nourishes them, and man completes them." Man's task is to make a perfect completion of what Heaven and Earth have left uncompleted. This is the prime contribution which man has to make in relation to the universe. As we have shown above in the quotations from the *Chung Yung*, especially in "making a trinity with Heaven and Earth", the statements there were formal ones. Here they are positive ones.

Speaking from the psychological point of view, in man there is the mind with its special nature (*hsing*) and there is the affectional element, and these are on all fours with Heaven with its Yin and Yang. The chapter on the examination of terms and titles has the statement : "The individual person has his nature and his affectional side, just as Heaven has the Yin and the Yang. To speak of a man's constitution and leave out the affectional side would be like speaking of Heaven's Yang and leaving out its Yin. Man's nature is revealed without in human-heartedness, his affectional side is revealed without in greed." The same chapter also says, " The reality of the individual person has both greed and humanheartedness, the *ch'i* of both these qualities being in the individual. In speaking of *shen* (body or person or individual), this is derived from Heaven ; for Heaven employs both the Yin and the Yang and the individual has a constitution which includes both greed and humanheartedness."

Heaven gives rein to the Yang and not to the Yin. So men also ought " to use their nature to restrict the affectional element ". This is the function of the mind. " The mind is that which prevents all evils from within, so that they cannot manifest themselves without, with the result that as Heaven has the Yang restricting the Yin, so the individual has his nature restricting the affectional. The principle is identical with that of Heaven. Hence the activities of the Yin do not succeed in having a bad effect in spring and summer, and the dark [lit. : ghost] of the moon has an aversion to the light of the sun, and there are times when the moon is waxing full and times when it is on the wane. Heaven's restriction of the Yin is like this. Surely man must lessen his desires and restrict the affectional, and thereby correspond to Heaven. This is restricting what Heaven restricts. To restrict what Heaven restricts is not restricting Heaven." (Examination of Terms and Titles.) Men are morally bound to restrict what Heaven restricts, and if they do, they can in time become perfectly good men. " For morality consists in men making up what Heaven leaves undone, accomplishing something extra, something outside not inside the compass of what Heaven itself performs. What Heaven performs has a limit, and Heaven stops at that point. That which is within this limit is ascribed to Heaven, that which is outside this limit is ascribed to kingly culture." (*Ibid.*)

The king is the one established by Heaven for the purpose of educating men in spiritual culture. As the chapter on examination of terms and titles says, " Heaven brought into existence the nature of ordinary people with its groundstock of goodness and its inability (of itself) to carry goodness to perfection. Thus on their behalf Heaven established the king in order to make them good. This is Heaven's aim. Ordinary people, having received from Heaven this nature with its inability to be (entirely) good, fall back on getting nature-fulfilling culture from the king. The king has this as his special office, namely to fulfil this human nature's requirements." The law and institutions by means of which the king instructs are called the Kingly Way and these are patterned after the Way of Heaven. For instance, part of this Kingly Way is what is called " The Three Basic Ties ", about which Tung Chung-shu says, " they can be found in Heaven." These ties are that of " sovereign and subject, father and son, husband and wife ". These are patterned on " the *tao* of Yin and Yang ". The chapter on basic principles says, " (The essence of) the Yin is to supplement the Yang, just as the wife supplements the husband, the son the father, the subject the sovereign. There is no creature which is without something to supplement it, there being a Yin and a Yang in each case." And again, " The principles underlying the relationships of sovereign and subject, of father and son and husband and wife are all derived from the *tao* of the Yin and the Yang."

Man being a second edition of Heaven, a shadow in brief of the universe, and his position in relation to the universe being so exalted, and the king being the one charged to educate men, it follows that if his actions are improper and go counter to the eternal verities, Heaven is aroused and reveals this in very visible and remarkable fashion, in other words in untoward and portentous occurrences. Whichever way the king acts, his actions call forth a response from Heaven. Tung Chung-shu had two theories. One is, " Where among the creatures of Heaven and Earth there are abnormal changes, these are what are known as portentous occurrences, the smaller variety being known as untoward occurrences. These latter invariably come first and the former follow later, they being reprimands from Heaven, the others being Heaven overawing the wicked. Where reprimands are not recognized, the use of terrors abounds." (Chapter on " There must be Humanheartedness as well as Wisdom.") According to this theory, untoward and portentous occurrences are caused by the displeasure of Heaven. The other theory is, " Good calls forth goodness, evil calls forth evil, this arising from like fulfilling like. If a horse whinnies, it is a horse that responds, whilst if a cow lows, it is a cow that answers . . . It is most sure that things invoke each other, like to like . . . Heaven has Yin and Yang : men also have Yin and Yang. When the Yin *ch'i* of Heaven and Earth is in the ascendancy, man's Yin *ch'i* responds by being in the ascendancy; and when man's Yin *ch'i* is in the ascendancy, the Yin *ch'i* of Heaven and Earth rightly responds by being in the ascendancy." (Chapter on " Mutual Effect of Things of the Same Class.") According to this theory, these evils eventuate through a kind of mechanical reaction. These two theories are very different from each other, and appear to be mutually incompatible. The first is a teleological theory and is close to religion, whilst the second is a mechanistic theory and is close to science, though neither the Yin-Yang school nor Tung Chung-shu were conscious of this modern distinction. This was because in their systems, religion and science were inextricably mixed.

In Tung Chung-shu's system, man has the most exalted position in the universe. Not only is it open for him to be a trinity with Heaven and Earth, but in very fact he is a trinity with Heaven and Earth. Nevertheless, although this theory puts man in so exalted a position, yet it cannot enable him to live in the highest sphere of all. The question may be asked : supposing there are men whose understanding of the universe is like Tung Chung-shu's and who in their deeds have as objective the completing of what Heaven has not completed, what is the sphere in which those men are living ? Are they or are they not in the sphere of the transcendent ?

Our answer to this question is that these men's sphere is near to the transcendent, but strictly speaking it is only the moral sphere. This is because " Heaven ", as understood by them, is a Heaven which can be pleased and angry, can award punishments and rewards. If we may coin a harsh-sounding term, their Heaven is a universe-man. Their Heaven is a man on an extended scale, is a great human person, that is a " great man ", and the relation of this person to man is a social one. Tung Chung-shu says : " Besides, Heaven is man's grandfather, so that man is in the same class of being as Heaven." (Chapter on " The Producer of Man is Heaven.") This theory of man as supporting Heaven and completing what Heaven has not completed is exactly like grandsons following after their grandfather and completing what he failed to complete. If men act with such an understanding, then their sphere of living is near to the highest, but strictly speaking it is only the moral sphere.

At this point we should do well to consider the difference between religion and philosophy. Religious people use images, philosophically-minded people use pure thought. Religion is the product of the imagination, philosophy the product of abstract thinking. Religious thinking is near to ordinary people's thinking, whilst philosophical thinking goes counter to such. As has been said in the *Hsin Yüan Jen*, the ordinary man's thoughts, speaking generally, are pictorial in nature ; and speaking strictly, he can only grasp an image, he cannot think abstractly. He is only confusedly conscious that beyond man's sphere or above it, beyond or above society, there is a something, but what that something is he cannot get at all clear or know with any precision, using as he does pictorial ideas in thinking of it. He takes this something to be a god, a supreme ruler, or a paradise, a heavenly mansion. His pictorial ideas of " God " are products of his imagination and are, for the most part, inferences by analogy from man's own nature. For instance, since men have knowledge, many religions regard God as having knowledge, though there is this difference, that he is omniscient. Since men have power, many religions regard God as having power, though with this difference that he is omnipotent. Since men have a will, many religions regard God as having a will, though with this difference that his will is perfectly good. The heavenly mansion imagined is inferred by analogy from certain conditions in this world. Since this world and the things in it are concrete, the beings in the heavenly place are also concrete, with this difference, that whereas in this world nobody is perfect, in this heavenly place everybody is perfect. In this world there is both misery and joy, in this heavenly place there is only joy. As is said by Buddhists, " it is the world of the uttermost joy." The process which ordinary people regard as the one by which the world came into existence, follows by analogy from the actual process by which a craftsman creates utensils. God is like a craftsman, and the world is like a utensil which he has created. Thus God is like a human being extended to an unlimited degree, and the heavenly place is like an ideal world. All this is the result of man speaking from the human standpoint and using a pictorial idea in imagining that " something ".

What most men infer to be religion very often has in it something of art and something of philosophy. Religious rites and hymns and music belong to the category of art. That part of a religion's theology which gives men to know comes in the category of philosophy. Only that part of the theology which cannot give man to know but only to believe is really and truly in the category of religion. What we here call religion is only this part. Tung Chung-shu's theory of " Heaven " is from the human standpoint.

He uses pictorial ideas, so that what he gets is that man and Heaven belong to the same class of being. He really ought to say that Heaven and man belong to the same class because the nature of the Heaven he describes is derived by analogy from the nature of man. If a man's understanding of Heaven is in accordance with Tung Chung-shu's interpretation, his sphere of living is not a very high one, and according to the point of view of this book his philosophy is not in accordance with the criterion of attaining to the sublime. In the Han era the emphasis was on the actual and the practical, and the sphere as exemplified by the scholars of that era was on the whole not a very high one. That is not because these two emphases disable a man from reaching the highest sphere. But, because that age's understanding of the universe was inadequate, their philosophy failed to rise above shapes and features. Hence their sphere in which they lived failed to reach the sphere of the abstract and ferry over into the beyond.

As for the discussions in which their predecessors engaged about the highest sphere of living, these the Han Scholars for the most part were unable to appreciate. Take, for instance, the discussion in Chapter I about what Confucius had to say on his own sphere of living. " At forty, I had no doubts," which K'ung An-kuo explained as " having no hesitations of doubt " : " at fifty, I was conscious of the decrees of Heaven," which K'ung An-kuo explained as, " I knew the beginnings and endings of decrees of Heaven " : " at sixty, I was already obedient to these decrees," which Cheng K'ang-ch'en explained as " hearing the words and knowing their subtle significance " : " at seventy, I just followed my heart's desire without overstepping the boundary," which Ma Yung explained as, " in following the heart's desire in no respect transgressing the law (of righteousness)." (Vide Ho Yen's *Collected Commentaries on the Lun Yü.*) [1] Take also Mencius' " great morale ".[2] Tung Chung-shu's explanation is as follows : " The Yang represents Heaven's forbearingness, the Yin Heaven's exigency, the Mean Heaven's utility, concord Heaven's merit. Grasp hold of the Tao of Heaven and Earth and expand it with concord. The result for all living things is that *ch'i* being essential is welcomed and nourished. Mencius said, ' I am very skilful at nourishing my *hao jan chih ch'i* '." (Chapter on Following the Tao of Heaven.) Tung

---

[1] These expositions take the words at their face value and no more. (E. R. H.)

[2] Cf. Chapter I, great morale, *hao jan chih ch'i.*

Chung-shu's position was that the nourishing of the *hao jan chih ch'i* was a nourishing of the harmonized *ch'i* of Heaven and Earth. He did indeed inherit Mencius' ideas ; but it may well be said that in regard to Mencius' sphere of living he had no understanding.

The Han scholars were rich in religious faith. They used a religious disposition to pay honour to the Confucianist school and to Confucius. Confucius in the pre-Ch'in era was the first to create a particular school of thought, so that inevitably he occupies a very important position in history. But his position was only that of a teacher. On the other hand, the Han scholars held that he was not merely a teacher. Tung Chung-shu, along with the author of the *Kung Yang Chuan*,[1] held that Confucius received a charge from Heaven to become king. Although actually it was Ch'in Shih Huang Ti (the First Emperor) who took the place of the Chou overlord, yet Confucius was the one who received the charge from Heaven ; and this was why he wrote the *Spring and Autumn Annals* entrusting the kingship to Lu State and establishing institutions for a new dynasty. This was an exceptionally strange thesis to advance; but at a later date in the *Wei* (Weft) *Books* it was maintained that Confucius was not only the true king of a particular age, but that he was in addition a god. In the *Wei Book* on the *Spring and Autumn Annals*, it was maintained that Confucius was " the son of the Black God (*Ti*) ". Thus Confucius advanced from being a king to being a god. Some people in later generations gave to the Confucianist system the name of the Confucian religion. This name may rightly be given to the Confucian system as interpreted by some of the Han scholars for whom Confucius was the founder of a religion.

Afterwards, when the movement known as the Ancient Text School started, the adherents of that school cleared away the Yin-Yang school's elements which were mixed in with the Confucianist tenets. These elements in their turn were mixed in with Taoist teaching and so became a Taoist religion. In this way Confucius's position went back to being that of a teacher, and Lao Tzŭ became the founder of a religion.

Later this indigenous religion came to blows with the foreign religion of Buddhism. It must, however, be understood that although these Taoist devotees sailed under the Lao-Chuang flag, yet they had not accepted the Lao-Chuang philosophy.

---

[1] One of the three amplifications of Confucius's *Spring and Autumn Annals*. Its date of production was some time early in the Han era. (E. R. H.)

Hence the philosophical side of the Taoist religion in those later days was inferior to the Buddhist philosophy, so that Taoist religion only spread among the lower ranks of society. The majority of those in China who accept cultural nurture do not believe in any particular religion. This is because in philosophy they can get what we describe as ' attainment of the sublime and performance of the common task'. Philosophy which transcends shapes and features enables them in the midst of daily life " to reach the sphere of the abstract and ferry over into the beyond ". For this reason they have no need for " God " or a " heavenly mansion ". " Without abandoning the common affairs of daily life, they go directly to what was before the heavens." This is the accomplishment which did not begin to come until a large number of wise men had given their strength to developing this philosophy.

CHAPTER VII

THE MYSTICAL SCHOOL

The people of the Wei and Chin era (third and fourth centuries) came to have a much more discerning recognition of what transcends shapes and features. Indeed, we may say that their recognition of the transcendent was more thorough than that we find in the *Lao Tzŭ* and *Chuang Tzŭ Books* and in the *Yi Amplifications* and the *Chung Yung*. In the foregoing chapters we have on occasion quoted the words, " the mystery of all mysteries." This was the subject of the Wei-Chin men's inquiries. They took pleasure in this subject, and as we have said in Chapter V they gave the name of the " Three Mystical Books " to the *Lao Tzŭ* and *Chuang Tzŭ Books* and the *Yi Amplifications*. To discussions of " the mystery of all mysteries ", they gave the name of " mystical conversations ", to inquiries in this field the name of *hsüan hsüeh* (mystical studies). With regard to this vogue which originated in their days and is known in history as the Mystical Vogue, they may rightly be said to have been wholly mystics, nothing but mystics.

They were convinced that a philosophy of the transcendent enabled men to " reach the sphere of the abstract and ferry over into the beyond ". In the *Shih Shuo Hsin Yü* there is a reference to Hsiang Hsiu's commentary on the *Chuang Tzŭ Book* : " minute analysis of the depths, the flourishing of a vogue for mysticism." (*Wen Hsüeh Chapter.*) In the *Critique of the Seven Worthies of the Bamboo Grove* there is the statement : " Hsiang Hsiu produced this type of reasoning, and those who read him got a sense of transcendence stirred, as if they had passed from this dusty world and had caught a glimpse of an absolute indifferentiability, and now understood that beyond the world of the senses there are the sages of mystic wisdom and spiritual power who were able to discard the world of man and go beyond the world of things." (Vide Liu Hsiao-piao's *Commentary on the Shih Shuo Hsin Yü.*) Hsiang Hsiu [1] praised the *Chuang Tzŭ Book*, saying : " Although those who revert to greed and the officials who are busy over their careers for the time being are immersed in these supererogatory delights and this flood of tasty experiences, they still have empty moments and feelings of self-fulfilment. How much more do

---

[1] Third century A.D. (E. R. H.)

those who dally along the years to a great age and so go on and on in pure continuance, the dusty world left behind and they back in the bosom of the Indifferentiable ! (Preface to the *Chuang Tzŭ Commentary*.) The sphere to which reference is made here is the highest of all. The function of mysticism is to enable men to possess this kind of sphere.

The Mystic School was the descendant of the Lao-Chuang school of philosophy. Lao Tzŭ and Chuang Tzŭ (as the reader will remember) came under the influence of the Logicians and then surpassed them. The same applies to the Mystical School's way of thinking. The study of logic flourished in the Wei-Chin era. Take the statement in the *Shih Shuo Hsin Yü* : " Hsieh An, when he was young, invited Juan Yu to expound the *White Horse Discussion* [1] and make a dialectical essay for his edification. At the time Hsieh did not immediately understand Juan's words. So Juan sighed saying : ' Not only is it impossible to find a man who can speak on it, it is impossible even to find one who understands it.' (*Wen Hsüeh Chapter*). Again, Ssu-ma Fu asked Hsieh Hsüan : ' Why is it that among Hui Tzŭ's five cartloads of books there is not a word on the mystical ? ' Hsieh replied : ' The reason must be that the best of his sayings have not been handed down.' " (*Wen Hsüeh Chapter*.) To say that Hui Tzŭ had not a word on the mystical is wrong ; nevertheless the two passages serve to show the interest some Wei-Chin men had in the Logicians, as also their high esteem for Hui Shih and Kung-sun Lung.[2]

The Wei-Chin men's thought sprang from the Logicians, so that, in their dialectical conversations on the mystical, the principles they discussed were known as name-principles, viz. logical principles. Their skill consisted in " a capacity for distinguishing terms and analysing logical principles ". (Kuo Hsiang's *Commentary on the T'ien Hsia Chapter* of the *Chuang Tzŭ*.) In Chapter III, we saw the kind of work which the Logicians did, for instance Kung-sun Lung's, " A white horse is not a horse," and " hardness and whiteness are entirely separate ". All that was a distinguishing of terms and an analysing of logical principles. It meant analysing logical principles by means of differentiation

---

[1] Cf. Chapter III, p. 53 *et seq.*
[2] With regard to *ming li* (logical principles), in the *Wen Hsüeh Chapter* there is the statement " Chief Secretary Wang made a highly systematic statement of five hundred words, a statement which he himself described as ' a remarkable presentation of logical principles '.' In Liu Hsiao-piao's commentary on this chapter he quoted from a biography of Hsieh Hsüan in which he is described as having a capacity for philosophical conversation and being skilled in logical principles.

of terms and paying no attention to facts, as was demonstrated in the words quoted in Chapter III, " concentrating on terms without regard for feeling."

Again, in the *Shih Shuo Hsin Yü* (*Wen Hsüeh Chapter*), we find : " A visitor asked Yo Kuang, " What does it mean that the general notion (*chih*) of ' arriving ' is not true to fact ? " Yo did not analyse the sentence, but directly touched the table with the handle of a deer's-tail fly-whisk saying : ' Has it arrived or has it not ? ' The visitor answered, ' It has arrived.' Yo then picked up the whisk again and asked : ' If there was an arrival, how can that be removed ? ' " The sentence about a *chih* is taken from the *T'ien Hsia Chapter* in *Chuang Tzŭ*, where it is attributed to the Dialecticians generally. This refers to the Kung-sun Lung group among the Dialecticians in particular. (vid. c. III.) Now, to touch a table with a fly-whisk is ordinarily regarded as an arrival on the table. But if the arrival is really an arrival, then it is impossible for that event to be removed.[1] If it could, then the arrival was not a real arrival. Here by means of the term " arrival " we analyse out the principle of arrival. By means of the principle of arrival we criticize the fact of arrival. This is an illustration of the meaning of the words, " the discrimination of terms and the analysing out of principles."

Liu Hsiao-piao, in his comment on this passage, says as follows : " A boat concealed to view moves imperceptibly, to pass a man shoulder to shoulder is to pass him irrevocably.[2] A moment of time can never be held up : in a flash something has happened and something has ceased to happen. Therefore the shadow of a flying bird shows no movement to it : the wheel of a chariot never touches the ground.[3] The logical consequence to this is that if we assume that the removal (from the table) was not a removal, then surely there could have been no arrival at it ; and (*pari passu*), if we assume that the arrival was not an arrival, then surely there could be no removal. But then (we have also to realize that) there is no difference between the earlier and later stages in an arriving : the term " arrival " indicates the process of something happening. And there is no difference between the earlier and later stages in a removal :

---

[1] i.e. return to the *status quo ante*. (E. R. H.)

[2] Cf. the English proverb " a miss is as good as a mile " with its meaning that however closely the target is missed, it is utterly and irredeemably missed for that particular shot. (E. R. H.)

[3] A reference to two of the Dialecticians' conundrums : cf. *Chuang Tzŭ Book*, *T'ien Hsia Chapter*. (E. R. H.)

the term " removal " indicates the process of something ceasing to happen. To conclude, in all the world there is no such thing as a removal, so that the notion of " removal ", to be sure, is invalid. Since that is so, then surely the notion of " arrival " is not true to fact. The main idea there, as for the whole passage, is that events and things never for one moment cease from change. Every moment marks one indivisible coming-into-being-plus-ceasing-to-be. The shadow of a flying bird at any particular moment of time is not the shadow of the bird at the moment before. That shadow perished with the moment in which it came to birth. The shadow of the succeeding moment is a new-born shadow. If we link the two moments together, then we see movement ; but if we take them separately, then there is no movement. And in the case of the wheel, never touching the ground, the principle involved is the same. Thus, what is described as a removal is a number of momentary removings, each preceding one linking with its successor. With regard to " an arrival ", this also is a number of momentary arrivings each preceding one linking with its successor. Because the earlier and later stages of arriving appear to be alike, the conclusion is drawn that there is, as it were, one integrated arrival and the term " arrival " stands. But the truth is that because the earlier and later stages of removing are only, as it were, alike, and because what is spoken of as one integrated removal is only as it were, the conclusion to be drawn is that the term " removal " does not stand. Then, concentrating on the coming-into-being-plus-ceasing-to-be, all in a moment of time, we see that there is actually no such thing as " removal " ; and, that being so, there is also no such thing as " arrival ".

This, then, is " discriminating terms and analysing out principles ". In the Hsiang-Kuo exegesis of the last section in the *T'ien Hsia Chapter*, the statement is made that the Dialecticians' conundrums about taking a one-foot-long stick and halving it and never reaching nothing and about linked wheels being separable, these " bear no relation to the government of the country, in fact come under the heading of useless argument. But since young aristocrats must have some amusement when they are tired with the words of the Scriptures, then if they can discriminate terms and analyse out logical principles as an expression of their esprit (*ch'i*) and intellectual discipline, and if this serves to prevent wenching in future generations, this form of amusement is much better than other kinds." Hsiang Hsiu and Kuo Hsiang went further than the Logicians and, " after they had caught the fish, they forgot the traps," so that they appear to be opposed to differentiating terms and analysing logical principles. Actually they were not opposed. What they objected to was doing this and nothing more. They were themselves particularly clever at differentiating terms and analysing logical principles. Their commentary on the *Chuang Tzŭ Book* is a model of that kind of work.

Wang Pi (226–249 A.D.), as well as Hsiang Hsiu and Kuo Hsiang, was clever in analysing logical principles ; and this was the reason why their interpretations of the *Lao Tzŭ* and *Chuang Tzŭ Books* were very different from those in the *Huai Nan Book*. The statement in the *Lao Tzŭ Book* (c. 40), " The Tao produces the One," was expounded by Wang Pi as follows : " All creatures and all forms have their source in the One. How does it come about that there is the One ? It comes from non-being. From non-being there is the One. So the One can be said to be non-being. Since we already call it the One, there is speech about it. Since there is the One plus speech about it, then there is not one but two (entities). There being one and there being two, one plus two make three. By the passage from non-being to being, the process of reckoning is completed. To go beyond this is to get beyond the province of the Tao." Wang Pi also said, " The One is the beginning of calculation and the starting point of things." (Exegesis of c. 39.) The exact meaning of this passage for the moment we need not consider. But what Wang Pi calls the Tao, non-being, being, and the One is completely different from Huai Nan's meaning for these terms. This can be seen at a glance. If we go through Wang Pi's explanations, we find that these four concepts are all only formal concepts, not positive concepts. Also, " There is the Tao," and " There is being ", these are formal propositions, not positive ones.

Although the Mystical School inherited the tradition of the Lao-Chuang philosophy, yet most of the members of this school regarded Confucius as the greatest sage, and Lao Tan and Chuang Chou [1] as not equal to him. For example, the *Shih Shuo Hsin Yü* makes the statement : " Wang Pi in his young days went to Pei Hui. Hui asked him how it was that, since non-being is the groundstock of all things, Confucius would not speak on this,

---

[1] The writers of the Mystical School regarded Lao Tan as the author of the *Lao Tzŭ Book* and Chuang Chou as the author of the whole of the *Chuang Tzŭ Book*. (E. R. H.)

whilst Lao Tan expanded the idea without stopping. Wang Pi's answer was : ' The Sage [i.e. Confucius] identified himself with non-being and realized that it could not be made the subject of instruction, with the result that he felt bound to deal with being. Lao Tan and Chuang Chou were not yet completely outside the sphere of being, with the result that they constantly spoke of their own insufficiency.' " (*Wen Hsüeh Chapter.*) Wang Pi's meaning was that in Lao Tan's thought there was a contrast between being and non-being. From being he gained a view of non-being, and this was why he constantly spoke of non-being. In Confucius's thought the antithesis between being and non-being was completely synthesized. Confucius, being already identified with non-being, proceeded from a state of non-being to deal with being. Hence his constant occupation with being. If we use the criterion of attainment to the sublime and concern for the common, we must say that the reason why Lao Tan was not concerned with the common was because his sublime was not the highest of all. Confucius's sublime, on the other hand, was the highest of all, and therefore he was concerned with the common.

Hsiang Hsiu and Kuo Hsiang were the greatest of all the expositors of Chuang Chou, and at the same time the greatest of his critics. The probability is that a part of the commentary which is under the name of Kuo Hsiang came from Hsiang Hsiu's commentary, and so here we speak of it as the *Hsiang-Kuo Commentary.* In the preface to this book there is the following statement : " Chuang Chou may be said to have had knowledge of fundamentals, with the result that he did not conceal the wildness of his statements. These did not meet the requirements of daily life, his writings being merely subjective soliloquies. If a statement cannot meet the requirements of daily life, it follows that although the statement may be right, it is nevertheless useless ; as also in the case of a statement which goes counter to events and things, it may be lofty but it is not practical. There is certainly a gap between such a man and the man who is in a state of inward silence and quietude, from which something emerges without any volition on his part. The former may rightly be said to have knowledge about the mind in a state of inaction. The sage being in a state of inaction, he responds to immediate stimulus, and the response varies according to times and seasons. Therefore he refrains from much speaking. The result is that he is identified (*t'i*) with (the world process of) transformation, that he survives for ten thousand ages and is undifferentiable from all creation. Surely he must be very different from Chuang Chou, who made dialogues which were really arguing with himself and have nothing to do with life ! Therefore, although the *Chuang Tzŭ Book* is not one of the Sacred Scriptures, yet it is the best of the philosophical works ; although Chuang Chou did not identify himself with world transformation, yet his words are perfect. His theories give an understanding of the structure of Heaven-and-Earth, and an introduction to the order in the natures of all things. They make intelligible the changes in life and death, and so make clear the Tao of sageness within and kingliness without. Above he knew that there was no creator of the world ; below he knew that everything created itself." Here we have a critique of Chuang Chou, one which is divisible into two parts. The one is that Hsiang Hsiu and Kuo Hsiang regarded Chuang Chou's sphere of living as not equal to Confucius's sphere. They allowed that he had knowledge of fundamentals and of the state of inaction in the mind, but though he had this knowledge, he was unable to embody it in life and action. Thus he did not conceal the wildness of his statements, but made dialogues arguing with himself about it and about.

Their point is that when a sage identifies himself with the world process of transformation, he not only has knowledge of the state of inaction in the mind, but his mind is actually in a state of inaction. This they described as a state of interior silence and quietude from which at the right time the right action emerges without any volition. The conclusion they drew was that this kind of action is only in response to the actual, varying according to times and seasons ; and therefore he does not argue with himself about it and about : indeed he refrains from much speaking. To put this critique into the terminology of my *Hsin Yüan Jen*, Chuang Chou's sphere of living consisted in knowing Heaven, Confucius's sphere of living consisted in identification with Heaven. Examine the sentences above which contain the word *t'i* (to identify oneself with) in the particular context of identification with the process of transformation : there can be no question that the meaning is that of identification with Heaven. Chuang Chou only knew about this kind of identification ; he was unable to actualize it. Thus, although his sphere of living was a transcendent one, yet his sphere was one of knowing and not of doing.

Let us now take the second division in the Hsiang-Kuo critique. This was that Chuang Chou's wild statements cannot meet the requirements of daily life. They also criticized him for arguing with himself, for making dialectical excursions into " the world beyond ". This denotes that he was apart from the events of daily life and sought elsewhere " a realm of mystical indifferentiability ", " a pavilion of unintelligibility." And this is why his words, however right they may be, are yet of no use, however lofty are yet ineffectual ; and although he spoke of sageness within and kingliness without, yet he laid excessive emphasis on the sageness and too little emphasis on the kingliness. In this respect, therefore, the critique is one of Chuang Chou's philosophy as reaching to the height of sublimity but not concerned with the common task.

These being two grounds on which Hsiang Hsiu and Kuo Hsiang criticized Chuang Chou, they maintained that there was a gap between him and the sage man, and that his words were not good enough to be part of the Scriptures but only sufficient to make him the greatest of the philosophers. That is equivalent to saying that his sphere of living and the value of his work were below those of the sage man.

Lao Tan and Chuang Chou " had knowledge of non-being ", whilst Confucius identified himself with non-being. In this respect Confucius was on a higher level. Whilst Lao Tan and Chuang Chou could only wander in the world beyond, the sage could also wander freely in this world. There is a difference between being in this world and being outside of it. Although this difference is great, yet Lao Tan and Chuang Chou were one with the sage " in revealing the Tao of sageness within and kingliness without ". Hence in the Mystic School there were those who maintained that at bottom the three men were not different. In the *Shih Shuo Hsin Yü* there is the statement : " Juan Hsiu being a man of high reputation, when Wang Yen met him he asked him the following question : ' Are the teachings of Lao Tan and Chuang Chou the same as, or different from, the spiritual culture of the sages ? ' The reply given was : ' Are there not similarities ? ' " (*Wen Hsüeh Chapter.*) Juan Hsiu's meaning was that we cannot say that they are completely similar, nor can we say that they are completely different, and that is why he answered : " Are there not similarities ? ", the meaning being that they are at bottom similar.

Wang Pi, Hsiang Hsiu, and Kuo Hsiang all thought that the

pre-Ch'in Taoists had their defects, and in following after those earlier thinkers they did actually correct their faults. In the special terminology we are using, the early Taoists were not in accord with the double criterion of attaining to the sublime and having concern for the common. Hence the correction of their faults entailed bringing their theories into accord with this criterion. Wang Pi's main correction was the theory that the sages had delight and anger, sorrow and joy. Ho Yen wrote a *Discussion on the Sages being without Delight and Anger, Sorrow and Joy*, and, although the work is not extant, we have the main outline of it. It is in effect that the early Taoists maintained that they transmuted emotions by means of reason, or that " they subjected emotions to reason ". According to Chuang Chou's theory, the emotions have their rise in failure to understand the nature of things. The sages have complete understanding in respect to the nature of things, and so " sorrow and joy cannot enter into them ". (*Yang Sheng Chu Chapter.*) For them not to enter is for them not to exist, so that the sages were without emotions, though not in the insensible way of decayed wood and dead ashes. Rather their emotions are imbued and transmuted by their understanding of things : in other words they have their emotions transmuted by means of reason. Wang Pi regarded this as impossible of achievement. His theory was, " Intelligence can manage to search out the most recondite matters, but it has not the capacity for ejecting the nature which men naturally have." Again, " Where the sage is vitally superior to ordinary men is in his spirit-like intelligence and where he is like ordinary men is in having the five emotions. The result of this vitality of spirit-like intelligence in the sage is a capacity for identification with the harmony of the universe, so that he is imbued with non-being. The result of his having the five emotions like other men is that he is not able to do without emotion in responding to things. On the other hand, in responding though he experiences emotion, he is not caught in the toils of emotion." (*San Kuo Chih, Biography of Chung Hui, Pei Sung Chih's Commentary.*) For the early Taoists there were only two alternatives : either a man had emotions and was caught in their toils, or he had no emotions and so was not caught in their toils. For Wang Pi there was a third alternative, namely, that it is possible for a man to have emotions and yet not be caught in their toils. This is one correction that Wang Pi made of the early Taoists' position. In this he resolved the antithesis between having emotions and not having emotions. This antithesis is on the same footing as the antithesis between the sublime and the common.

The Hsiang-Kuo correction of the early Taoists consists in its most important aspect in resolving the antithesis between being and non-being, between Heaven and man, and making a synthesis of the antithetical states of being in the world and being outside of it.

With regard to being and non-being, the early Taoists' position, as we saw in Chapter IV, was that "all creatures were produced by being, and being was produced by non-being"; and it may rightly be said that the term "non-being" is the shortened appellation for "the unnameable" and non-being is not equivalent to the cipher o. In the *Chuang Tzŭ Book, Keng Sang Chu Chapter*, we find: "There is birth, there is death; there is issuing forth, there is entering; and that which one passes in entering in and issuing forth is the Gate of Heaven. The Gate of Heaven is non-being, and all things emerge from non-being." The Hsiang-Kuo exegesis here is, "Death and life, issuing forth and entering in,[1] all this comes in a flash of itself and is not the act of a creator. There are the processes of gathering together and scattering abroad, hiding and revealing, with the result that there are the names 'to issue forth' and 'to enter in'. These are only names, since in the last resort there is no issuing forth or entering in. That being so, where is the Gate? If we take non-being to be the Gate, non-being is nothing, and therefore there is no gate." And again, "This is not to say that non-being can become being; for if non-being can become being, how is it non-being?" And again, "once there is non-being, then forthwith there is nothing. If this nothing is finally nothing, then it is self-evident that being comes of itself in a flash." According to this exegesis with its "being produced from non-being", the position is that being is not caused by anything extraneous to itself. This theory of spontaneous generation only emphasizes that being was not the act of any creator, it does not maintain that there was a time when there was no being and then suddenly being was produced from nothing. On the *Chih Pe Yu Chapter*, in the *Chuang Tzŭ Book*, there is this exegesis: "Not only is it impossible that non-being should be transformed into being, but also it is impossible that being should be transformed into non-being. This is why being in itself, although it goes through a thousand changes and ten

---

[1] Chuang Tzŭ's idea was that man "issued forth" from non-being and at death "entered" again into non-being, like a man gone back home.

thousand transformations, yet cannot become non-being. Since it cannot become non-being, therefore from the past to the present there never has been a time when there was no being ; and from this it follows that being exists for ever."

Being has always continued to exist and was not produced from non-being. Things are produced of themselves in a flash and do not need any antecedent creation. To quote again from an exegesis of the *Chih Pe Yu Chapter*, " What is there which can be antecedent to things ? We regard the Yin and the Yang as antecedent to things, but the Yin and the Yang also come in the category of things. So the question is also asked what that is which is antecedent to the Yin and the Yang. We regard that which is so-of-itself as antecedent ; but that only means that everything is so-of-itself. We regard the ultimate Tao as antecedent, but this Tao is the ultimate non-being. Non-being being nothing, how can it be antecedent ? That being so, then what is there which can have been antecedent to things ? Yet there are things without end, and it is evident that the so-ness of things is naturally so, not because something made them so."

This then is the main meaning in Hsiang Hsiu and Kuo Hsiang, the eradication of any idea of a creator. And this applies equally to " God " and any kind of *ch'i* (gas, etc.) which is supposed to have created the world. From their point of view, this conclusion is inevadible ; and not only this, even the formal idea of the early Taoists also is eradicated. And after all these ideas have been eradicated, we see that, " the creating of things has no lord, everything creates itself; and, since each creates itself, there is nothing on which it depends. This is the truth about Heaven-and-Earth." (Exegesis on the *Ch'i Wu Lun Chapter*.)

If there was no " that by which things came into existence ", then the idea of " the Tao " amounts to the nothingness of the cipher 0. And if that be so, then to say that the Tao produced all things is to say that each and all came of themselves, and to say that all things possess some (quality) which they derived from the Tao, that is to say that they derived it from themselves. This is the exact meaning of the exegesis on the *Ta Tsung Shih Chapter* where it is stated that " the Tao is capable of nothing : to say that anything is derived from the Tao means that it comes of itself." This meaning also comes in the following : " All that they obtain is not obtained from the Tao without, nor does it come by any act of volition. In the last resort it is self-derived and self-transforming." Thus, according to this theory there exists actually only the " being " of the early Taoists and not their " non-being ". And their statement that, " being was produced by non-being," can only be said to amount to this, that there is nothing which produced being. In this way the contrast between being and non-being is resolved. There was one, P'ei K'uei of the Chin Dynasty era, who wrote a dialectical essay entitled " The Exaltation of Being ", and the Hsiang-Kuo theory may rightly be called exaltation of being.

We now deal with the early Taoists' contrast between " Heaven " and " man ". In the *Chuang Tzŭ Book, Ch'iu Hsüeh Chapter*, we find " Heaven is the inward, man the outward " ; and again, " A cow and a horse having four feet, come in the category of Heaven : the bridling of a horse's head and the putting a rope through a cow's nose, this is in the category of man." Thus, the one comes under what we call the natural or spontaneous, the other comes under what we call the artificial or deliberate. In the case of spontaneous activity, the activity is effected without knowledge of how it is and what it is ; hence the action is inaction (*wu wei*). In the case of deliberate activity it is with conscious purpose, and therefore the action is action (*yu wei*). Where the artificial takes the place of the natural, this is spoken of as " man destroying Heaven ". To the early Taoists this destroying of Heaven was the root of all man's miseries.

The *Hsiang-Kuo Commentary* deals with this contrast. On this passage the exegesis is as follows : " As for man's (daily) life, can it do without the service of a cow or the riding of a horse ? And as for this service and this riding, can a man do without putting a rope through the nose of the one and tying a halter round the neck of the other ? Cows and horses do not refuse to be noosed and haltered, and this lot which is dispensed to them by Heaven is surely right. If this be a right dispensation by Heaven, then in spite of its coming within the sphere of man's business its origin is in Heaven." This looks as if, when the *Hsiang-Kuo Commentary* speaks of the lot dispensed by Heaven, the term has the meaning of the natural. Again, in the *Jen Chien Shih Chapter, Chuang Tzŭ Book* : " Throughout the world, there are two disciplines, one the appointed lot, the other justice. The child's love of its parents is its appointed lot : it is impossible for this love to be loosed from its heart." On this the Hsiang-Kuo exegesis is, " it is knitted naturally together and cannot break free." In the *Ta Tsung Shih Chapter*, there is, " but the reaching of this extreme is a matter of lot," for which the Hsiang-Kuo exegesis is, " this is a reference to the naturalness of things with nothing causing them." On the basis of these statements what Hsiang Hsiu and Kuo Hsiang meant by " lot dispensed by Heaven " was " being naturally so ". A bird builds a nest : this comes from the bird being naturally so ; and the same is the case with a man building a house, and even, one may suppose, with the building of a skyscraper in New York.

From this point of view what has been called " artificial " is also the natural. To quote again from the *Ta Tsung Shih Chapter* : " To know that everything which Heaven or man does is in both cases naturally so." For this the Hsiang-Kuo exegesis is as follows : " With a thousand men congregated together without any one man as their lord, the result is either anarchy or dispersion. Therefore, if there were many worthy men present, there could not be many leaders, and if there were no worthy men present, there could not be any leaders. This is the Tao of Heaven and of man, and must be the height of rightness." The organization of a state and nation, this is a human tao, and also Heaven's Tao. It fits in with the above, " all that Heaven or man does is naturally so." If this be the case, then the contrast between Heaven and man is resolved.

From this point of view then, what the early Taoists called action (*yu wei*) may also be called inaction (*wu wei*). In the exegesis of the *Tao of Heaven Chapter* there is this comment : " The result is that where the higher and the lower are made complementary to each other, the sovereign remains still whilst the minister is active ; where past and present are made comparable, Yao and Shun were in a state of *wu wei* (inaction), and T'ang and Wu had to take action (with a view to becoming emperor). That being so, each used his own nature and the natural trend of events is mysteriously expressed ; that is, the higher and the lower, the past and the present, all represent inaction, and there is really no such thing as (artificial deliberate) action." Thus according to the new theory put forth by the *Hsiang-Kuo Commentary*, inaction is not just doing nothing. If " it fits in with the lot dispensed by Heaven ", then any individual man's actions, however numerous, or any society's organization, however complex, are " the mysterious expression of natural trend ". All are *wu wei*, not *yu wei*.

In the Hsiang-Kuo system the expression " Heaven " also is a general term for all things, as is expressly stated in an exegesis of the *Ch'i Wu Lun Chapter*, whilst in the exegesis of the *Sao Yao Yu Chapter* we find : " This ' Heaven-and-Earth ' is the general term for all things."

In my *Hsin Li Hsüeh* this " Heaven ", or alternatively " Heaven-and-Earth ", is what is called " the Great Whole ". The whole Heaven is " the sphere of the mysterious ", and all things " are self-transforming in the mysterious sphere " (vide Preface to the *Chuang Tzŭ Commentary*), and each " is itself and naturally so ". Among these things, although they are useful to each other, yet one thing does not exist for the sake of another, nor does it derive its existence from another. This is stated as : " in spite of them exactly complementing each other, yet there being no dependence of one on the other." Hence, " all things, although as a total they constitute Heaven, yet not one but also reveals itself." (Exegesis on the *Ch'i Wu Lun Chapter*.) Although the myriad things make up Heaven, yet not one of them but has its individual existence and is also the outcome of self-transformation. This then is " the truth about Heaven-and-Earth ".

In the Early Taoists, the Tao occupied the important position ; in the Hsiang-Kuo system, Heaven occupied the important position. Heaven is the Great Whole, and the sage is one who identifies himself with the Great Whole. In the exegesis of the *Ta Tsung Shih Chapter* there is this : " The sage wanders along the road of transformation, swims freely in the stream of daily renewal. There are ten thousand things being transformed in ten thousand ways, and the sage is in process of transformation with them. These transformations are without end, and the sage is transformed with them without end." And again, " (the sage) is in no way differentiable from things, and in no way not one with transformations. The result is that (for the sage) there is no outward or inward, no death or life, but identification with Heaven and Earth and with the Great Transformation, for there can be no loss attached to this. This is becoming one with Heaven, becoming one with transformation ; and this oneness is something which cannot be expressed, something which cannot be thought. In the exegesis on the *Ch'i Wu Lun Chapter*, there is the statement : " By means of words, oneness is expressed, but the oneness is not the expression ; that is, the expression plus the oneness expressed makes two ; for oneness being one, the expression of it makes two. Also, " The result is that he who takes oneness as oneness is not different from them (i.e. ordinary people) ; and he who forgets oneness makes no expression of it, so that he has oneness as a matter of course."

The Great Whole transcends shapes and features, and the man who identifies himself with the Great Whole wanders in spirit beyond the confines of shapes and features. This wandering, however, does not entail being a " contemplative in the midst of the hills and woods ". In the *Sao Yao Yu Chapter*, Hsü Yu and his fellow hermits are praised and Yao and Shun are depreciated. As is said : " When Yao offered the empire to Hsü Yu, the latter replied : ' Take your sovereignty easily, for my part I have no use for an empire.' " Also, " Even the dust and refuse, the chaff and the husks (of a spirit man) could form a Yao and a Shun." And again, " Yao ruled the empire and gave peace to this side of the ocean. Having paid a visit to the four wise men of the Miao Ku Yi mountain, on his return to his capital he was deeply mortified, and the empire no longer existed for him." Hsü Yu and the other hermits were men who wandered outside the world, whilst Yao and Shun were men who wandered within it. To this passage the Hsiang-Kuo exegesis gave a new interpretation by its praises of Yao and Shun and depreciation of Hsü Yu and their fellows. Thus we find the following : " Those who are self-confident stand in contrast to things ; but those who are in accord with them do not stand in contrast to them. Therefore there was nothing in the empire with which Yao stood in contrast, whilst Hsü Yu was only on a level with Chi and Hsieh (two ministers of that time). How do I come to say that they are so ? For those who are indifferentiable from creation the result is that all the tribes of creatures cannot divorce themselves from them. Hence, with no deliberate mind they make a profound response to them ; submitting themselves to the stimulus from them, drifting like an unmoored boat, floating hither and thither with no self-volition. Therefore there is nothing they do which is not in accord with the people, no place to which they go where they are not sovereign over all. With this (quality) making them sovereign, they are as a matter of course as exalted as Heaven. This indeed is the virtue of the true sovereign. Supposing a man standing out violently in contrast on the summit of a mountain, if he had no private feelings about guarding himself to himself, or about guarding the one-sided predilections of some school of thought, how could he thus stand out alone ? This kind of man is therefore just a thing among the common ruck of things, no more than an outside officer of Yao's." Each individual thing guards its own predilections, so that there is no thing which is not in a position of contrast to other things. The man who submits himself to things, he " reaches the centre of the circle " ; the man who guards no personal predilections, " goes along with all creation." By that is meant that in fact he transcends them all. He comes into a position which is not in contrast to them. Hence he is not a creature among the common ruck of creatures, nor is he in contrast to other men in the world. He has no deliberate mind ; hence he " responds to all creatures and is not caught in their toils ". The same commentary also says : " Although the sage may occupy the chief position in a court, yet in his mind he is in no different case from being among the hills and woods. How can he be understood by the world ? The world sees him as filling the imperial chariot, as having the imperial seal attached to his girdle, and so this is taken to be enough to trammel his mind. The world sees him passing by mountains and rivers, administering the affairs of the people, and so this is taken to be enough to weary his spirit. How can they know that the man who is perfect in perfection cannot suffer any loss ? " He cannot suffer any loss because he responds to the world but is not trammelled by it, because he responds to (the stimulus of) all creatures but is not caught in their toils.

Although the sphere of the sage is so exalted, yet his actions may be completely ordinary. As the Hsiang-Kuo exegesis has it in the *Sao Yao Yu Chapter* : " He whose footsteps carry him furthest of all comes nearer and nearer (to men and things) ; and he who reaches to the highest (sphere of living) is down among the lower ranks of men." And again, " If in uncompromising fashion he exalts himself alone to the highest and does not put himself on an equality with the common ruck of men, this is to be a hermit of the hills and valleys and not to be one who is unconditioned." And again, " Some people speak of being lost in contemplation among the hills and woods, describing this as *wu wei*. This is the reason why the teachings of Lao Tzŭ and Chuang Tzŭ are abandoned by men of affairs and these men confine themselves to *yu wei* and do not turn back (to *wu wei*)."

This being the new Hsiang-Kuo interpretation, the distinction between being outside the world and being inside does not exist for the sage man. This is stated in the exegesis of the *Ta Tsung Shih Chapter* : " Carrying reason to its highest point, the without and the within are indistinguishable. There is no case where wandering in the without is carried to perfection in which the

F

without and the within are still distinguishable ; there is no case where the without and the within are still distinguishable in which the wandering in the without is carried to perfection. Therefore the sage man constantly wanders in the without in order that he may enlarge the sphere of the within, has no deliberate mind in order that he may submit himself to all creation. And the result of this is that although (the sage) works his body all day, the essential spirit is not affected ; although he deals with every kind of business, he remains just what he is." This is quite true. He who really can wander in the without can do no other than make it indistinguishable from the within ; and he who can make the without indistinguishable from the within is sure to be able to wander in the without. A sage man has no private mind in following the natural course of things. Having no private mind, he makes no distinctions : submitting himself to all creatures, he wanders in the without. Hsiang Hsiu and Kuo Hsiang regarded this as " the main meaning in Chuang Chou's writings ". They held that if this be understood, " then the truth of wandering in the without and extending the sphere of the within becomes self-evident, and Chuang Chou's book is therefore to advocate ferrying over to the ordinary and thatching over this world which we see." (Exegesis of the *Ta Tsung Shih Chapter*.) Thus the Hsiang-Kuo Commentary was a special effort to turn the early Taoists' original theories of the solitary and the contemplative life into being a philosophy of this world and the ordinary beings in it, into being a philosophy which combines in one what is without this world and what is within it. This effort must be accounted a success. And yet it is in some respects open to criticism. The nature of the criticism will be explained in a later passage.

In the Wei-Chin era (third to sixth century) the Buddhist religion had already been for some time in China and had come to have great authority over men's minds. In the Buddhist system of thought there is the antithesis between " the eternally so, i.e. immutable reality (*ching jo*, Bhūtatathatā) and production-annihilation, i.e. the temporal (*sheng mei*, utpadanirodha) ; the contrast between permanence and change, between nirvana and life-plus-death. Thinkers of those days regarded the first contrast as the Taoist contrast between non-being and being, the second as the Taoist contrast between immutability and mutability, and the third as the Taoist contrast between *wu wei* and *yu wei*. One section of the exponents of Buddhism used all these Taoist concepts, and because of this, although the subject of their talk was Buddhism, the kind of Buddhism which they talked might be described as a branch of the Mystic School. Thus Sheng Chao was this kind of Buddhist teacher, a very outstanding one, whilst his *Discussion on the Immutability of Things* and his *Discussion on No real Unreality* are representative examples of this kind of Buddhist exposition. Wang Pi, Hsiang Hsiu, and Kuo Hsiang attempted to deal with the contrasts in Taoist philosophy, and Sheng Chao attempted to resolve the antitheses in Buddhist philosophy. His *Discussion on the Immutability of Things* is a resolution of the antithesis between immutability and mutability, and his *Discussion on No real Unreality* is a resolution of the antithesis between being and non-being ; whilst his *Discussion on Pan-jo (Real Knowledge, prajña) being no Knowledge* was a resolution of the antithesis between real knowledge and ordinary knowledge, as also of the antithesis between *wu wei* and *yu wei*.

In his *Discussion on the Immutability of Things*, Sheng Chao said : " Most men's idea of mutability is that things in the past have not come down to the present. The result is that they say that there is mutability and no immutability. That things of the past do not come down to the present is my idea of immutability ; and the result is that I say that there is immutability and no mutability. That there is mutability and no immutability is because the things of the past do not come down to the present ; that there is immutability and no mutability is because things of the past do not vanish away [i.e. become as if they had not existed]." And again, " Turn your attention to past things in relation to the past. In this respect they do not become null and void [i.e. their having happened cannot be cancelled out]. Turn your attention to them in relation to the present. In this respect they do not exist. For them not to exist in the present is to show that they have not come down to the present. They having existed in that past, the result is that we know that they do not become null and void. Turn your attention now to the present. The present cannot recede into the past. This is to say that past things of their nature are in the past and do not recede from the present into the past ; and that present things of their nature are in the present and do not come down from the past to the present." And again, " If this be so, then it is clear that things do not go backwards and forwards (in time among themselves). Since there is no slightest sign of things going backwards and forwards, the conclusion surely is that it is impossible that things should be mutable. There is nothing paradoxical in peaks revolving and mountains falling and yet being for ever immutable, in rivers competing as to the expanse they cover and not flowing away, in wandering airs going back and forth and yet not moving anywhere, in the sun and moon maintaining their courses in the sky and yet not revolving."

Above we have quoted Liu Hsiao-piao's commentary on *Shih Shuo Hsin Yü* to the effect that in speaking of reaching, there is a first reaching and a second reaching, and so with going away, there is a first going away and a second going away. What Sheng Chao is dealing with here is a similar idea. The " first reaching " and " first going away " do not come down from the past to the present. The " second reaching " and the " second going away " do not recede from the present to the past. Any event or thing at any particular moment of time of its nature is only that particular event and thing at that particular moment. That particular event or thing at any other moment of time is actually another thing altogether, and is not a continuation of the thing at the earlier moment of time. Thus, in the *Discussion on the Immutability of Things*, " Fan Chih, having become a monk in his early years, returned home when his hair was white. On seeing him, the neighbours exclaimed at a man of the past being still alive. Fan Chih said : ' I look like the man of the past, but I am not he.' " The later Fan Chih was only apparently the former Fan Chih. The former Fan Chih belonged to the past and had not come down from the past to the present. The later Fan Chih belonged to the later time and did not " recede from the present to the past ". " When we say that what has gone before not necessarily is gone altogether but abides eternally, this is because it is not mutable. When we say that the going away not necessarily is going away altogether, this means it does not recede from the present to the past, and this is because it does not come down to the present. Because things of the past do come down into the present, therefore they do not gallop in the time between the past and the present ; because things of the past do not go away altogether, therefore each of their natures abides in its own one space of time." Now, that in the past certain events and things have happened, this is a historical fact ; and this fact not only continues to exist but also has its abiding effect. In the *Discussion on the Immutability of Things* we find this statement : " With regard to the Buddha, his achieved merit flows along through ten thousand ages and thus abides continuously : his teaching spreads over a hundred æons and remains as strong as ever. A mound borrows its completion from the first basketful of earth, the completion of a journey depends on the first step taken. And the cause of this result is that accomplishment cannot be eradicated. Because the accomplished deed is ineradicable, therefore the past is not being transformed ; and because it is not being transformed, therefore it does not change ; and because it does not change, therefore it clearly remains untouched by time." The illustrations are of men piling up a hill, in which case every basketful of earth is the accomplishment of one basketful of earth ; and of a man taking a journey, in which case each step of the way is the accomplishment of one step. Thus the final mass of the hill depends on the first basketful of earth and the final reaching of the destination depends on the first step taken. The accomplishment of this first basketful and this first step is a thing of the past and is untransformable and so, if untransformable, then obviously not subject to change.

Ordinary people have the idea that if events and things are to be regarded as immutable, then the necessary conclusion is that the events and things of to-day are the events and things of yesterday. What they call immutability is the antithesis of mutability. Also, ordinary people have the idea that if events and things are to be regarded as mutable, then the necessary conclusion is that the events and things of yesterday change and become the events and things of to-day. What they call mutability is antithetical to immutability. As a matter of fact the events and things of to-day are not the events and things of yesterday, neither are they the events and things of yesterday in a changed form. The mutable is mutable in appearance and " immutable in reality " : going away is " going away in appearance and lasting on in reality ". Mutability is only in appearance mutability and is not antithetical to immutability. Going away is only in appearance going away and is not antithetical to lasting on. As the *Discussion on the Immutability of Things* says : " When we search for immutability, surely we do not find it by leaving mutability out of account. We must seek immutability in things mutable. Because we seek immutability in things mutable, therefore, although they are mutable, yet they are for ever immutable. Because we do not leave mutability out of account, therefore immutability is not divorced from mutability." Thus immutability and mutability do not involve an antithesis. In this way the antithesis which is popularly supposed to exist between mutability and immutability is resolved. We may also say that the solution is a synthesis.

Sheng Chao's *Discussion on No Real Unreality* has the statement : " All things have that in them which makes them not be something,[1] have that in them which makes them not be nothing. Because of the first characteristic, the result is that although they seem to be something, yet actually they are nothing ; because of the second characteristic, the result is that although they seem to be nothing, yet actually they are not nothing." All things without exception are the products of causation. Supposing what appears to be something is really something, then it will exist for all time and surely does not owe its existence to causation. Supposing that which appears to be nothing ; then if that nothing is really nothing it will not exist for all time, and surely it will not owe its non-existence to causation. If what is something be not something of itself but owes its existence to causation, the result would be the knowledge that that something is (in the last resort) not really something. Since that is so, although it may appear to be something, it would not be logical to designate it as something. With regard to nothing, if that should be really nothing, then there would be no disturbance of event, and that may logically be designated as nothing. If all creatures were nothing, then nothing would come about. If something comes about, then it cannot be altogether nothing. Since there is causation, this something which comes about through causation cannot be altogether nothing." Again, " That being so, then all things have that in them which makes them not something, and so they cannot be something, and at the same time have that in them which makes them not nothing, and so they cannot be nothing. What then ? If we want to affirm that they are something, then that something is not a real kind of something. And if we want to affirm that they are nothing, then they have happened with their individual features. Now, happening with individual features is not altogether nothing, and to be an unreal kind of something is not really something. That being so, the theory of no real unreality is thus clear. This was why in the *Fang Kuang Sutra* (Prajñâpâramitâ, vid. the first chapter on " Emitting Light "), there is the statement : " All things are false appellations

---

[1] In this paragraph and the succeeding ones dealing with Sheng Chao's views, the Chinese for something is *yu* and for nothing is *wu*, the two terms which above had the meaning of " being " and " non-being ". (E. R. H.)

and are not real. For instance, with the deva, it is not that there is no deva, but that a deva is not a real human being." All things come into existence through causation. If they are separated from their causes, they perish. They are just like the deva. In this respect, " all things have that in them which makes them not something." But although the deva is not really a man, yet a deva does really exist. Although all creatures exist in a state of production-annihilation, yet these creatures in this state all do have their existence. From this point of view it needs to be said that what is called unreality is both unreal and yet not unreal. " All things have that in them which makes them not nothing."

The popular view about nothing is that it means nothing being there, whilst the popular view of something is that it means that there really and truly is something there. As a matter of fact, there are some things which are there, but they are not real. In regard to these two popular ideas, that means that there is neither something nor nothing there. We may also say that it means both something and nothing are there. In the words of the *Discussion on No Real Unreality*, " If something is not real, and nothing is not equivalent to there being no trace of existence, then although something and nothing are different names, what they designate is the same." According to this line of argument, the antithesis in the popular mind is resolved, and we may say that a synthesis is made of something and nothing.

Sheng Chao defined *pan jo* as sage knowledge. According to this theory, if we give a wide enough meaning to knowledge, sage knowledge is also one kind of knowledge. On the other hand, this kind of knowledge is not the same as ordinary knowledge. To know necessarily entails having something which is known. What is known is then what is designated in modern speech as the object of knowledge. The object of sage knowledge is what is designated as absolute truth. But absolute truth cannot possibly be made the object of knowledge. This is because knowledge entails knowing the what of its object. Absolute truth has no what, and therefore it is impossible that it should be an object of knowledge. In the *Discussion on Pan Jo being not Knowledge*, there is the statement : " Knowledge consists in knowing what is known. Certain qualities (*hsiang*) are selected as its object, and thereby there is the name ' knowledge '. Absolute truth in the nature of the case has no qualities ; so how can there come to be knowledge of real knowledge ? " The qualities of a thing are the answer to the question of what that thing is. For knowledge to know what a thing is, is to select a quality for its object. Since absolute truth is about what is qualityless, therefore it cannot be an object of ordinary knowledge, and therefore cannot be known.

From another point of view, knowing and what is known are complementary. To know necessarily entails something known, and for something to be known necessarily entails knowing. The *Discussion on Pan Jo being not Knowledge* states : " Knowing and what is known go together in existing and go together in not existing." Also, " The what is known having given birth to knowledge, knowledge gives birth to what is known. The two having been born together, this birth entails causation. Since causation is not real, then what is not real is not absolute truth." An object of knowledge comes to be because it is known, and knowing comes to be because there is something known. Hence the object of knowledge is born of causation. That which is born of causation is not real, and that which is not real is not absolute truth. Hence absolute truth cannot be an object of knowledge.

On the other hand, *pan jo* is directly concerned with knowledge of absolute truth. This kind of knowledge uses as its object the very things which cannot be objects of knowledge. Hence this kind of knowledge is not the same as what is ordinarily supposed to be knowledge. As the *Discussion on Pan Jo not being Knowledge* says, " Hence real knowledge as a direct vision of absolute truth does not make use of objects of knowledge. This being so, how does this knowledge know ? " For this reason it is legitimate to describe the *pan jo* kind of knowledge as not knowledge. " The sage man by means of the *pan jo* throws light on absolute truth which is qualityless." (*Ibid.*) Also, " He is one who is calm and absorbed, having no knowledge and so knowing everything." To be without knowledge and so knowing everything is to have the knowledge which is not knowledge.

Nevertheless, what is designated as absolute truth does not exist apart from the sphere of events and things. Absolute truth represents the real condition of events and things. This is what Buddhists described as " the real quality (*shih hsiang*) of all things ". Since all things come into existence through causation, they are as illusory, just as a deva is. What they are is an illusion. Their qualities are not real qualities. *Pan jo* is the knowledge of the real quality. Since the real quality cannot be the object of knowledge, therefore *pan jo* is not knowledge. Sheng Chao, in his reply to a letter from Liu Yi-min, has the following : " With regard to the birth of knowledge, its limit is reached within the sphere of qualities. Since things have no real qualities, how can the sage's knowledge be knowledge ? " And then in the *Discussion on Pan Jo being not Knowledge* he says about sage knowledge that it is knowledge of that which is qualityless, and that the sage man has this kind of knowledge so that he also has " the illumination of not-knowledge ".

The illuminations of not-knowledge are in relation to the real essence of things. Hence, sage knowledge is not divorced from things. Not to be divorced from things is what is meant by the expression, " *ying hui* " or " *fu hui* ", namely to deal with events and things. The sage having the *pan jo* knowledge which is not-knowledge, that is described as " emptying the mind ". The sage also has " the illumination of not-knowledge ", and that is described as " having a real illumination ". " Emptiness does not fail to illuminate, and illumination does not fail to empty." " So then sage knowledge has a complete purview of essentials, and yet is not knowledge." His spirit has the function of dealing with things, and yet does not deliberate about them. Because it does not deliberate, therefore it has the capacity of being at home in the beyond. Because the sage has knowledge which is not knowledge, therefore he has the capacity of throwing a mysterious light on what is beyond the sphere of things. Although his knowledge is outside the sphere of things, yet at no time does he fail to deal with things. Although his spirit is in the beyond, yet it is all the time in the world." (*Discussion on Pan Jo being not Knowledge.*) " Hence in illuminating the qualityless, the sage does not lose the power of dealing with things. In his observation of change he is not in opposition to the qualityless." (*Ibid.*) " Hence the sage man is like a cavity, with his mind dwelling always on not-knowledge. He thus lives in the realm of change and utility and yet abides in the sphere of *wu wei* ; is within the walls of the nameable and yet out in the open country of what goes beyond speech. He being silent and alone, empty and all open, his state of being cannot be clothed in language." (*Reply to Liu Yi-min.*) Here the realm of change and utility and confinement within the walls of the nameable refer to the sage's deeds ; the abiding in the sphere of *wu wei* and the open country of what goes beyond speech refers to the sphere in which the sage lives.

In the *Discussion on Pan Jo being not-Knowledge*, we find :
" Therefore the *Pao Chi Sutra* says that the *Mahâratnakûta Sutra*
says : ' With no deliberate purpose and yet acting." And the
Fang Kuang Sutra says : ' Without interference with the ultimate
enlightenment all things are consolidated.' Hence, in spite of all
the multifarious effects springing from sageness, there is oneness,
no more and no less. This is why it is possible for *pan jo* to be
empty and yet illuminating, for absolute truth to be not-known
and yet known, for there to be a myriad happenings and yet
immutability, for the responsiveness of the sage to be expressed
in inaction and yet in action. This then is that he does not know
and yet of his very nature knows, is inactive and yet of his very
nature active."

Statements of this kind resolve the antithesis between inaction
and action, as also they make a synthesis of them.

The sphere in which this kind of sage whom Sheng Chao and
Wang Pi, Hsiang Hsiu and Kuo Hsiang portray lives is one of the
abstract and the beyond, whilst his actions " deal with the dusty
world ". (*Lao Tzŭ.*) This is a synthesis of the sublime and of the
common ; and this was what the original Taoists and original
Buddhists lacked and what the Mystic School most of all wished
to remedy.

Nevertheless, the synthesis which they succeeded in making
is open to criticism. In the *Tsai Yu Chapter* in the *Chuang Tzŭ
Book* there is the statement : " Things are not worth dealing
with, and yet one cannot help but deal with them." The Mystic
School, with their emphasis on " responding to the world ",
apparently were of the same mind. When they maintained that
the sages may respond to the world, their meaning was that the
sages also have the capacity to respond to the world. As we find
in Wang Pi's *Four Chapter Commentary on Lao Tzŭ* : " He modifies
his light but does not affect his self ; he mixes with the dusty
world, but does not do so at the expense of his integrity." This
amounts to saying that although the sage man may respond to
the world and follow its customs, yet that is no handicap to his
being a sage. As the *Hsiang-Kuo Commentary* on the *Ta Tsung
Shih Chapter* puts it, " He who wanders in the other world is
dependent on this world ; he who is divorced from men is in
accord with their common ways ; he who possesses the world
of men has no use for the world of men. Hence, discard all
creatures, and the result will be that you are in the middle of the
herd ; give yourself up to contemplative forgetting of the world,

and the result will be that you respond to its common affairs. The more you discard it, the more you gain it." This is nothing more than saying that only the man who lives in the sphere of the sublime has the supreme capacity of responding to the demands of the world. It does not say with regard to the sage man that for him to wander in the beyond is the same as depending on this world, that to be in accord with the common ways of men is the same as being divorced from men.

Let us take Sheng Chao's words on the sage man, namely that " he dwells in the realm of change and utility and yet abides in the sphere of *wu wei*, is confined within the walls of the nameable and yet is out in the open country of what is beyond speech ". This only says that the sage man's living in the realm of utility is no handicap to his dwelling in the sphere of *wu wei*. He still does not identify the two realms or spheres, still does not make confinement within the walls of the nameable one with being in the open country of what is beyond speech. Thus the Mystic School with their supreme desire to synthesize the antithesis between the sublime and the common, yet according to their own statements regarded them as two courses, not one course. In regard to what they said, there is need for a word which goes further. The mission of the Inner-light School was to say that word.

CHAPTER VIII

THE INNER-LIGHT SCHOOL (CH'AN TSUNG) OF BUDDHISM

The source of the Inner-light School of Buddhism may be traced back to Tao Sheng (*d.* 434). Tao Sheng and Sheng Chao were men of the same generation and had the same teacher. Tao Sheng laid down : " the thesis of good deeds receiving no recompense," " the thesis of sudden enlightenment for achieving Buddhahood," and " the thesis of making clear the Buddha nature in every man ". These theses of his were the bases in theory of the Inner-light School in the T'ang era (618-907).

Tao Sheng's writings have for the most part not survived, and his detailed argument on the thesis of good deeds receiving no recompense is to-day undiscoverable. But his contemporary, Hui Yüan, wrote a *Discussion Illustrating Recompense*, in which he maintained the same thesis, and what he says may well have been influenced by Tao Sheng. According to Hui Yüan's statements, what is called recompense is what is induced by the mind. If in the mind there is a greedy love of anything [cp. concupiscence], then immediately there is a clamping and attachment ; and if there is clamping and attachment, then what a man does is creaturely activity (*yu wei*) ; and if there is creaturely activity, then there is the creation of a cause in what Buddhists call the " revolving wheel of life and death " ; and if there is a cause, then there is an effect ; and this effect is the recompense. In this discussion of recompense Hui Yüan says : " The radical ignorance of a man obscures the light of his mind, with the result that feeling and thought become clamped on external objects : the greedy love saturates the nature, with the result that the Four Elements cohere and make his body. If the body coheres, then there is a boundary fixed between the I and the not-I. If feeling be clamped, then there is an agent of good and evil. If there be a boundary between the I and the not-I, then the body is regarded as belonging to the I, and thus cannot be forgotten. For there to be an agent of good and evil entails greedy love of life and the self bound on the Wheel. Thus he is willing to sleep ' in the Great Dream ', be blinded by delusion. Doubt is hugged to the breast through the long night, and there is nothing but attachment. The result is that failure and success push each other aside and blessing and calamity follow on each other's heels. Evil piles up and divine punishment comes of itself : sin comes to a head and hell is the punishment. This is the unavoidable fate without any shadow of doubt " (*Hung Ming Chi*, chüan 5). The sage man in his response to things acts without a deliberate mind. Hence although he responds to things, there is no clamping or attachment. That being so, then although his response appears to be creaturely activity it actually is not : that is, it is *wu wei*. Hence, although there is action on his part, yet it does not create a cause in the Buddhist wheel of cause and effect ; and, there being no cause, there is no effect. In Hui Yüan's discussion we find : " (The sage man) takes everything as it comes and goes on in the natural round of events, and whether there is cohesion or dispersal (of the Four Elements), he holds nothing to be the I. For him, all things are part of the Great Dream, and although he dwells with being, he is identified with non-being. How can he make compartments in what comes to him ? How can he be attached to anything by the tie of greedy love ? " " It is as if the not-I and the I together are the gainers and in the mind there is no antithesis between the two. That being so, when swords are in play, he is absorbed in the mystic significance of it ; when the battle is on, he meets the situation without revulsion : when he kills, it is not only that the killing does no harm to his spirit, but yet more the killing is not a killing." He is " the one who is as he is ", and " although his merit covers the world, there is no reward. How can there be punishment of sin for such a one ? " (*op. cit.*). Thus the sage man, although he takes action, does not bring about a cause, and since where there is no cause there is no effect, even if he kill a man, the killing is not a killing—his daily existence is in the midst of being, but he is identified with non-being. Thus, in spite of his activity, he is free from the bond of causation.

We now come to Tao Sheng's " thesis of sudden enlightenment for the achievement of Buddhahood ". This is to be found in Hsieh Lin-yün's *Enquiry into the Ultimate*. " Although the sage man dwells in the midst of being, yet he is identified with non-being." That is to say that the sage man's sphere of living is that of identification with non-being. As Liu Yi-min said in his letter to Sheng Chao, " The sage's mind is in the indifferentiable, in the silence of the beyond : his exercise of reason carries him to the ultimate and he is identified with non-being." And, " although his daily life is spent in the midst of the nameable, he is far away amid the unnameable " (*Chao Lun*). Hsieh Lin-yün (*op. cit.*) also said : " (The sage) is one with non-being and has complete enlightenment.   His exercise of reason carries him home to the One Ultimate." Now, as we have seen, non-being is qualityless, and to be qualityless is the real quality of all things, and knowledge of the real quality of all things is *pan jo*. On the other hand, what is without quality cannot be an object of knowledge, so that *pan jo* is the knowledge which is not knowledge. To have the knowledge of the real quality of all things is in fact to be one with it.   This is the same as " his exercise of reason carries him to the ultimate and he is identified with non-being ", and is the same as being one with non-being and having complete enlightenment, with his exercise of reason carrying him home to the One Ultimate.   His enlightenment being complete and he being one with non-being, he has an all-embracing vision of all creation.   And it follows from this, that when he is one with non-being, then at the same time he has complete enlightenment. The state of identification with non-being is what is called *nirvana*. *Nirvana* and *pan jo* are two aspects of one and the same state of affairs. *Nirvana* is the sphere in which the man with *pan jo* lives. *Pan jo* is the knowledge pertaining to the man who has obtained *nirvana*.   To obtain *nirvana* is to obtain *pan jo* : to obtain *pan jo* is to obtain *nirvana*.

Identification with non-being is something which once it is done it is done.   Hence with *nirvana* and *pan jo*, once they are obtained they are obtained.   The man who is engaged in spiritual cultivation cannot on one day become identified with one part of non-being and the next day become identified with another part.   Non-being cannot be divided into parts.   When a man identifies himself with non-being, he is completely identified : when he is not identified he is completely not identified.   With *nirvana* and *pan jo* it is the same.   Either a man has them, or he has them not.   This is what is meant by " a sudden enlightenment and becoming Buddha ".   The sudden enlightenment is equivalent to obtaining *pan jo*, becoming Buddha is equivalent to obtaining *nirvana*.   As Hsieh Lin-yün says (*op. cit.*) : " There is a Buddhist scholar with a new thesis who regards tranquil enlightenment as an exquisite mystery, one which does not allow of step by step attainment.   Step by step teaching is for the foolishly ignorant, but one indivisible enlightenment gets the true idea."   The Buddhist scholar referred to here is Tao Sheng.

What in the last resort is this " *wu* " which we translate as " non-being " ? With regard to this, there are two interpretations. One is that it is not anything at all, a final nil, nullity as against all that is, even null in relation to its own nullity. It is without any quality whatever, and therefore cannot be defined as a something. The sage's mind is one with this nullity, hence the statement that the sage man's mind is like empty space. The other interpretation is that *wu* denotes the mind, the mind which brings all things into existence.[1] Without the mind as the origin there would not be anything at all. When the mind is at work, things come into apparent existence. When the mind is not at work, things do not come into existence.[2] The existence or non-existence of things depends on the working or non-working of the mind. The real quality of things is the " original mind " in all living beings. This original is known as " the intrinsic nature " (*hsing*), or as it is sometimes put " the Buddha-nature ". To have a vision of the real quality of all things is equivalent to being enlightened in one's own mind and getting a vision of one's own nature. Tao Sheng put this as follows : " To turn one's back on delusion is to attain to the ultimate ; to attain to the ultimate is to attain to the origin." (Quoted by the *Collected Commentary on the Nieh Pang Sutra*.)

Sheng Chao adopted the first interpretation, Tao Sheng with his theory of the Buddha-nature apparently adopted the second. Later in the Inner-light School there were two tendencies. One tendency was in the direction of the first interpretation with the slogan " not mind, not Buddha ". The other tendency was in the direction of the second interpretation with the slogan " being mind, being Buddha ". To use the criterion of this book, the second interpretation is inferior to the first with its complete transcendence of shapes and features.

The Inner-light School, without respect to whether it accepted the first or the second interpretation of "*wu*", laid stress on five points. These were : (1) the First Principle is inexpressible ; (2) spiritual cultivation cannot be cultivated ; (3) in the last resort nothing is attained ; (4) there is not anything very much in the Buddhist philosophy ; (5) (the simple tasks of) carrying

---

[1] The force of this statement can only be appreciated if it be clearly understood that, to the Buddhist, the relation between the mind and things is like that between a piece of water and a wave. The wave does not exist apart from the water and is only a temporary form of its appearance. (F. Y. L.)

[2] Thus the Chinese term (*sheng*), which is translatable as bringing into existence, does not denote an act of production, such as is commonly meant when a carpenter produces a table.

water and chopping wood in all respects represent the mysterious Tao.

The First Principle is inexpressible because what it attempts to express is " beyond thought and the conscious mind " (*vide Sheng Chao's Works*). According to one tradition of the Inner-light School : " The body is like the sacred bodhi tree, the mind like a clearly reflecting mirror. At all times be diligent in cleansing the mirror. Do not let dust settle on it " (*vide* a hymn by Shen Hsiu, *d.* 716). In opposition to this there is Hui Neng's (*d.* 713) hymn with : " There is actually no bodhi tree, actually no mirror. Actually there is nothing at all where the dust can settle " (*vide Sermons of the Six Patriarchs*). The first two sentences in the Shen Hsiu quotation make an affirmation of a sort about what the term " First Principle " attempts to express, and thereby Shen Hsiu gave quality to what is qualityless. The last two sentences in the hymn are concerned with emphasizing that in order to reach what the " First Principle " attempts to express, there is need for the use of spiritual cultivation. The first two sentences of Hui Neng's hymn refer to the fact that in regard to what the " First Principle " attempts to express, nothing can be expressed. The last two sentences refer to the fact that in order to reach to what the " First Principle " attempts to express, there must not be any spiritual cultivation. This does not mean that there must be no cultivation, but that it must be cultivation by means of non-cultivation. The adherents of the Inner-light School for the most part maintained that not to disclose the First Principle was the right way of stating it. That is " statement by non-statement ". They also maintained that not to cultivate spiritual cultivation was the right way to cultivate it. That is, cultivation by non-cultivation.[1]

Hui Neng's famous disciple, Huai Jang (677–744), in the record of his sayings appears as saying : " Ma Tsu (*d.* 788) [i.e. Tao Yi] lived in the Ch'uan Fa Monastery on the Nan Yo (South Holy Mountain). He occupied a solitary hut in which all alone he practised meditation (*tso ch'an* [2]) and paid no attention to those who came to visit him. The Teacher [i.e. Huai Jang] one day kept grinding bricks in front of the hut, but Ma Tsu paid no attention. This having gone on for a long time, Ma Tsu at

[1] Shen Hsiu and Hui Neng are representative of doctrinal differences which had a geographical counterpart, Shen Hsiu being famous as the representative of the North, Hui Neng as the representative of the South. (F. Y. L.)

[2] Sitting in meditation. " Meditation " is hardly strong enough for the Chinese word *ch'an*, which emphasizes being lost in meditation. (E. R. H.)

length asked the Teacher what he was doing. He replied that he was grinding to make a mirror. Ma Tsu asked him how bricks could make a mirror. The Teacher replied that if grinding bricks could not make a mirror, how was it possible for *tso ch'an* to make a Buddha." (*Record of the Sayings of Ancient Worthies*, Chüan 1.) To say that *tso ch'an* could not make a Buddha was as much as to say that spiritual cultivation cannot be cultivated. Again (from the *Record of Ma Tsu's Sayings*), " The question was asked in what way spiritual cultivation could be cultivated. The Teacher [i.e. Ma Tsu] answered : ' Spiritual cultivation does not belong to the class of the cultivatable. If it be maintained that it can be obtained by cultivation, then, when it has been cultivated, it can also be lost as in the case of the *śrāvaka* (ordinary adherents). If we maintain that it is not cultivatable, then it is like the common man.' "

The method of obtaining spiritual cultivation is neither cultivating it, nor not cultivating it ; it is cultivation by non-cultivation.

To do a cultivation by cultivation is an activity of the deliberate mind and that involves creaturely activity. Creaturely activity belongs to the category of production-annihilation, and so where there is a completion there is likewise a decay. As Huang Po [i.e. Hsi Yün, *d.* 847) said, " Supposing that through innumerable æons a man has practised the six *Pāramitās*, has done good and attained the Buddha's wisdom, this also is not finally lasting. Why is this so ? The reason is because it is in causation. When the force of the cause is exhausted, he reverts to the permanent." And again he says : " All deeds are essentially permanent. All forces have their final day. They are like a dart discharged through the air : when its strength is exhausted, it turns and falls to the ground. They are all connected with the wheel of life-and-death. To cultivate in this fashion is to misunderstand the Buddha's idea and entails much fruitless labour. How vastly wrong is this ! " (*Records of Sayings of Ancient Worthies*, Chüan 3.) Cultivation with a deliberate purpose is creaturely activity : it is only one thing among other things and does not transcend them. What does transcend all things is what the Inner-light School described as " ceasing to be the boon-companion of things ". The lay monk P'ang Sun asked Ma Tsu : " What kind of a man is he who is not the boon-companion of things ? " Ma Tsu replied : " Wait until at one draught you can drink up all the water in the West River and I will tell you."

(*Records of Sayings of Ancient Worthies*, Chüan 1.) That which is not being a boon companion with things, is inexpressible, because what the expression expresses is itself a thing, so that at once there is a lapse into being the boon companion of things. Ma Tsu's reference to the condition of drinking up all the water in the West River was merely a way of saying that he could not answer the question. But this in itself was the answer. This is the way to express the inexpressible. If you want to express that which is not companionship with things, you have to use expressions which do not express it. If you want to obtain it, you have to use the cultivation which does not cultivate it.

Since the cultivation of spiritual cultivation is a form of creaturely activity, the ensuing actions, being within the Wheel, give birth to cause which means the creation of an inevadable recompense. As Huang Po put it, " If you do not understand having no deliberate mind, then you are attached to objects, and that is a state of devil-obstruction (*mo chang*). Even though you do something with a view to the Pure Land and to serving the Buddha, that also is action producing effect [i.e. Karma], and that is a state of Buddha-obstruction. The reason is that all these things obstruct the mind. Thus you will be controlled by causation and will have no freedom in going and coming [i.e. in dying and living]. Actually there is no such thing as bodhi wisdom. What the Buddha talked about in that connection was an adaptation of means to the end of men, like pretending yellow leaves are gold coins in order to stop the children crying. Therefore there is no such thing as *anuttarabodhi* (complete enlightenment). If you understand this, what is the use of being driven hither and thither (in your search) ? The only thing to be done is to get rid of your old karma, according as opportunity offers, and not to create a new karma from which will flow new calamities." (*Record of Sayings of Ancient Worthies*, Chüan 2.) Thus, to avoid creating a new karma involves avoiding spiritual cultivation. That being so, the true cultivation is to not cultivate. Hence this kind of cultivation is the cultivation of non-cultivating.

To avoid creating a new karma is not to refrain from doing anything at all, but to have no deliberate mind in whatever one does. As Ma Tsu put it, " The intrinsic nature of man is already enough. Not to be clamped to either good or evil, this is all that a man engaged in spiritual cultivation needs to do. To cleave to the good and to eschew evil, and to regard all things as unreal and to enter into contemplation, all these are creaturely activities.

And it is worse still if you are feverishly active over externals. The more you do that, the further you are from the true course." Further he said : " In a sutra there is the statement, ' It is only by the combination of various things that the body is produced.' When the body gets going, it is only these things which get going : when it fades out of existence, it is only these things which fade out. This getting going should not be taken as referring to the getting going of an ego, nor the fading out to the fading out of an ego (because the ego is unreal). When (you see that) earlier thoughts and later thoughts and thoughts in between are momentary thoughts independent of each other and do silently fade away, this is what is called *sagari samādhi* (the vision of all things in a Buddha-meditation)." (*Record of Sayings of Ancient Worthies*, Chüan 1.) Not to be clamped to either good or evil is to have no deliberate mind. Not to be clamped is to be detached and not to stay put, and this amounts to not being chained to feeling. In the *Record of Sayings of Pai Ch'ang* [i.e. Huai Hai] we find a questioner asking : " How is it that with feeling there is no Buddha-nature and without feeling there is the Buddha-nature ? " The Teacher's reply was " to go from being a mortal man to being a Buddha, this is a foolish clinging to the Buddha : to pass from being a mortal man to being in hell, this is a foolish clinging to one's mortality. You have only to let your mind be contaminated by concupiscence in relation to mortality or Buddhahood and this is what is designated as having feeling and not having the Buddha-nature. As the term expresses it, ' with feeling there is no Buddha-nature.' And now with regard to mortality and Buddhahood together with all things whether in the category of being or non-being, you need only to have a mind which does not deliberately select and reject, and to have no thought about having no such deliberate mind. This is what is designated as ' having no feeling and having the Buddha-nature '. To be unchained to feeling is what is meant by being without feeling. It does not mean not having any feeling at all, like a piece of wood or a stone, like the empty air or a yellow flower and the blue-green bamboo." There is also the statement : " If you tread the ladder which the Buddha trod, you are without feeling and have the Buddha-nature. If you do not tread the ladder which the Buddha trod, then you have feeling and have not the Buddha-nature." (*Record of Sayings of Ancient Worthies*, Chüan 1.)

To be without a deliberate mind is to have no thoughts. In

the Sermons of the Sixth Patriarch or the *T'an Scripture* [1] there is the statement by Hui Neng : " With regard to the teaching of our school from the founders down to the present, we have established no thought (*wu nien*), no object (*wu hsiang*) and no attachment (*wu ch'u*) as of fundamental importance. This ' no object ' means that there is an object there but it is not a real one. This ' no thought ' means that there is thought there but it is a momentary thought which silently fades away. This ' no attachment ' means that in the midst of a momentary thought a man does not think of the object before (his consciousness)." Again, " In regard to things, a momentary thought does not stay put : that is to say that the man's mind is not enchained [i.e. is free]." And again, " This is to regard not staying put as of fundamental importance. Here what is denoted as being without thought does not mean not thinking of anything, nor of an expelling of any and every kind of thought." As is said (*op. cit.*), " If you do not think of anything, then the truth itself becomes a chain." As Shen Hui (a disciple of Hui Neng) said, " Where the *śrāvaka* (ordinary adherents) cultivate unreality and stay put in unreality, the very unreality enchains them : where they cultivate contemplation and stay put in it, the very contemplation enchains them : where they cultivate stillness, and stay put in it, the very stillness enchains them : where they cultivate the silence of the beyond and stay put in it, the very silence of the beyond enchains them." (*vide Shen Hui's Literary Remains*, Chüan 1.) Not to think of anything at all is thus the cultivation of unreality. The " having no thought (*wu nien*) " is to avoid contamination in one's mind from the objects before one's consciousness, is always to be detached from these objects." (*vide T'an Scripture.*) To avoid contamination from things is equivalent to one's momentary thoughts not staying put by those things, and this is the meaning of " not staying put ". This also is equivalent to " there being an object, but it not being a real one ", and this is the meaning of the expression " no object ". Hence, where the *T'an Scripture* speaks of " no thought, no object, and no attachment ", it is really only saying " no thought ". As the *T'an Scripture* puts it, " If one's former thoughts be attached to their objects, this is misery : if

---

[1] T'an refers to the platform on which a teacher stood and addressed his disciples. " Scripture " is a translation of *ching*, the word used by the early Buddhists only to denote a sutra translated from the Sanskrit. . But *ching* was also the word universally used to denote any authoritative writing whether Confucianist or Taoist. We have here an instance of the Inner-light School using it as the designation for the recorded sayings of a great teacher. Thus *T'an Scripture* is the Inner-light School Scripture in which is recorded the platform teaching of the Sixth Patriarch, Hui Neng. (F. Y. L.)

one's later thoughts be detached from their objects, this is complete salvation (*bodhi*)." And this is the meaning of " good deeds receiving no recompense " and of " a sudden enlightenment and achieving Buddhahood ".

Lin Chi [i.e. Yi Hsüan, *d.* 720] said : " The men of to-day who engage in spiritual cultivation fail to achieve their ends. What is their fault ? Their fault is not having faith in themselves [i.e. in their own inner light]. If you are lacking in faith, then you are in a vastly undirected condition, absorbed by all the topsy-turvy changes in your surroundings, subject to the revolutions in those surroundings, unable to achieve freedom. If you succeed in stopping the mind as it dashes hither and thither, searching for this and that, then you are not different from the Patriarchs and the Buddha. Do you wish to know who are the Patriarchs and the Buddha ? All you who are before me listening to my teaching are the Patriarchs and the Buddha." (*Record of the Sayings of Ancient Worthies*, Chüan 4.) Also there is the passage, " You people who are engaged in spiritual cultivation, who wish to achieve the Buddha doctrine, for you there is no place for using effort. The only way is to do the ordinary things and nothing special, to relieve your bowels and to pass water, to wear clothes and to eat, when tired to lie down, as a simple fellow to laugh at yourself over these matters—though indeed the wise man understands (their significance) ! " (*Ibid.*) The man engaged in special cultivation needs to have adequate faith in himself and to discard everything else. There is no need to exert oneself in special spiritual cultivation outside the common round of daily living, but only whilst in the midst of the common round of daily living, to be conscious of no object and to have no thought. This, then, is the striving in non-striving, the cultivating in non-cultivating.

Lin Chi also said : " There are times when I eliminate the man but not his surroundings (*ching*), times when I eliminate his surroundings but not the man, times when I eliminate both, and times when I eliminate neither." " Man " is the subject which knows in regard to knowledge, his *ching* is what is known in regard to knowledge. According to a tradition of the Inner-light School, there is the incident of Abott Hui Ming approaching Hui Neng, the Sixth Patriarch, and begging for the doctrine. The Patriarch replied : " For the time being concentrate your mind, but do not think about either good or evil." The Abott having said that he was now thus prepared, the Patriarch said : " Having no thought about good and no thought about evil, just at this very moment give me the real features of the Abbot Ming, before his father and mother brought him into the world." The Abbot, under the impact of these words, was silently identified (with non-being). Then he did formal obeisance and said : " It is like a man drinking water, knowing in himself whether it is cold or warm." (*T'an Scripture*.)

Before his parents brought him into the world there was no Abbot Ming, a subject, neither was there an object in contrast to him as subject. The force of the Patriarch's request was to eliminate subject and object. When a man as a subject and its object are eliminated, then he is one with " non-being ", and is to be described as having silent identification with non-being ; and by that is meant that not merely the man knows there is non-being but that he is actually identified with non-being.

Silent identification with non-being is the same as what is described as sudden enlightenment. So also what is described as, " when one single thought is in accord (with the truth), at once you have the ultimate wisdom of the Buddha." (*Recorded Sayings of Shen Hui*.) This enlightenment is not the same as what is ordinarily called knowledge, where there is the contrast between the knower and the known ; for in a state of enlightenment there is no contrast between the man who is enlightened and that about which he is enlightened. Because there is no object of enlightenment, therefore we may rightly say that enlightenment is not knowledge. But enlightenment also is not lack of knowledge in the ordinary sense. It is neither the one nor the other but what is described as the knowledge which is not knowledge.

In the *Recorded Sayings of Chao Chou* [i.e. Ts'ung Nien] we find : " The Teacher asked Nan Ch'üan [i.e. P'u Yüan, *d*. 830] what the Tao was like. Ch'üan replied : ' The ordinary mind is the Tao.' The Teacher then asked whether the Tao can be something aimed at. The reply was : ' When you delineate the Tao, it is not the Tao.' The Teacher than asked, ' If you do not delineate the Tao, how do you know the Tao as the Tao ? ' The reply was : ' The Tao is not classifiable as either knowledge or not knowledge. Knowledge is illusory consciousness, not-knowledge is blind unconsciousness. If you really comprehend the indubitable Tao, it is like a wide open emptiness ; so how can distinctions be forced in it between right and wrong ? ' " (*Recorded Sayings of Ancient Worthies*, Chüan 13). Shu Chou [i.e. Ching Yüan, *d*. 1120] said : " My late teacher [i.e. Fa Yin] at thirty-five became a monk, and being in Cheng Tu submitted himself to learning the truths of the Buddhist Idealist (*Wei Shih*) School.   On one occasion he heard a lecture as follows : ' For a bodhisattva entering on vision of the Tao, knowledge and truth become indifferentiable, as also objects and the spirit (of the bodhisattva) become a unity ; and thus there ceases to be a distinction between the experiencer and the thing experienced.   There were heretics who criticized this on the ground that if there is no distinction between the experiencer and the thing experienced, there can be nothing that the experiencer experiences.   At that time no one was able to answer them, and all the lecturers ceased to ring the bell and beat the drum [i.e. to come out and lecture].   They went back home discarding their robes.   Afterwards Hsüan Ch'üan saved this doctrine by telling people that the indifferentiability of knowledge and truth and the uniting of object and the spirit (of the man) was like a man drinking water and knowing in himself whether it is cold or warm.   The next day Fa Yin was meditating on the fact that this is quite right ; water is either cold or warm ; but the question is what is knowing in one's self.   Becoming immersed in doubts, he asked the lecturer, saying that he could not understand the truth of knowing in oneself.   The lecturer was unable to answer his question.   Later Fa Yin came to Fou Tu Mountain and met Yüan Ch'ien.   He saw that he had penetrated the arcana of the truth, for all that he said was relevant to the issues in Fa Yin's mind.   So he stayed there for a year.   He was instructed to consider the saying : ' Śākyamuni had secret teachings, but Mahākāśyapa did not keep the secret.' One day Yüan Ch'ien said to Fa Yin : ' Why did you not come earlier ?   I am too old.   You can go to the monk Shui Tuan (d. 1072) at the Pai Yün Monastery.'   My former teacher then went to the Pai Yün Monastery, and one day on going into the hall of discussion, was greatly enlightened on the saying that Śākyamuni had secret teachings, but Mahākāśyapa did not keep the secret. ' Inevitably so, inevitably so (he said).   Knowledge and truth are indifferentiable : the object and the spirit are a unity, like a man drinking water and knowing in himself whether it is cold or warm.   This word indeed is the truth.'   He wrote a poem in praise of this. ' In front of the mountain there is a patch of fallow field.   With arms respectfully crossed I repeatedly asked the old greybeard teacher about the many times this field had been sold and bought back again.   The answer was that this was because they liked the fir trees and bamboos which

entice the fresh winds.' The monk Shui Tuan nodded his head."
(*Record of Sayings of Ancient Worthies*, Chüan 32.)

The truth is an object of knowledge, an object to the spirit.
Knowledge and spirit represent the knower, and the truth and the
object represent what he knows. Thus the indifferentiability of
knowledge and truth and the unifying of the object and the
spirit represent the merging of the knower and what he knows,
so that there is no distinction between them. Now, a man whilst
seeing no distinction here, is still conscious that there is no
distinction, and this is what is described as drinking water and
knowing in one's self that it is cold or warm. As Nan Ch'üan
said : " The Tao is not classifiable as either knowledge or not-
knowledge." Thus with the Tao there cannot be the distinction
which is ordinarily made between the knower and what he knows.
Therefore knowledge is designated as illusory consciousness.
In other words, the Tao is not classifiable as knowledge. And
yet, in relation to the non-distinction between knower and what
he knows, and the enlightenment which comes thereby, men are
not unselfconscious. If they were unselfconscious, then they
would be in " a brutish state of primitive ignorance, a state of
stupid empty-headedness ". This was why the statement was
made that not-knowledge is not blind unselfconsciousness and why
it was affirmed that the Tao is not classifiable as not-knowledge.

The Inner-light School constantly symbolized enlightenment
as " the bottom of the tub falling out ", the image being of the
contents of a tub being in a moment all gone. So when a man
obtains the enlightenment of the Tao, every kind of problem
which he has is solved in a moment. These solutions are not
positive solutions but an understanding in the midst of the
enlightenment that these problems are basically not problems
at all. This is why the statement was made that after the enlightenment the Tao thus obtained is " the indubitable Tao ".

What is obtained through enlightenment is not any positive
kind of knowledge, just as in the last resort it is not an attainment
of any sort. As Shu Chou said on one occasion : " If at the
present moment you comprehend this, where is that which you
could not comprehend before?" [1]

The conclusion to be drawn is that the thing about which
you were deluded before is the same thing about which you are
now enlightened, and the thing about which you are now
enlightened is the same thing about which you were formerly

---

[1] A rhetorical question signifying that it is nowhere at all. (E. R. H.)

deluded. (Cp. *Record of Sayings of Ancient Worthies*, Chüan 32.) The Inner-light School were continually referring to the question whether a mountain is a mountain or a river is a river. In the state of delusion a mountain is a mountain and a river is a river, and when a man arrives at a state of enlightenment a mountain is still a mountain and a river still a river. Thus, with regard to " the patch of fallow land in front of the mountain ", and " the many times it has been sold and bought back ", what was sold and what was bought back was just that patch of land, no more than what the monks had in the beginning. If you should want to get more out of the patch than what it is, that would be a case of " riding an ass and searching for it ", and if, after realizing what you are riding on you should think you have got something new [i.e. not there before you realized it] that would be a case of " riding an ass and being unwilling to dismount ". As Shu Chou put it, " there are only two diseases (of the mind), one riding an ass and searching for it, the other riding an ass and being unwilling to dismount. You say that if a man be riding an ass and at the same time searching for it, he is so silly that he should be punished. It is indeed a very serious disease. I tell you, do not search for the ass. An intelligent man will immediately understand my meaning, and thus the error of searching for the ass will be immediately eliminated, and the deluded state of his mind cease to exist. Having found the ass but being unwilling to dismount, this disease is the hardest to heal. What I say to you is, do not ride : you yourself are the ass, and everything is the ass. Why do you go on riding ? If you do, you cannot expel your disease. If you do not ride [i.e. if you and the ass are one], the worlds in all directions are as a great space open to view. With these two diseases in one moment expelled, nothing remains infecting your mind. This is what it is to be a man of (real) spiritual cultivation ; and there is nothing more that you need to do." (*Record of Sayings of Ancient Worthies*, Chüan 32.)

Before the enlightenment comes, there is no spiritual cultivation which can be deliberately cultivated. After the enlightenment has taken place, there is no further Buddhahood to be achieved. In *Huang Po's Recorded Sayings*, there is the statement : " A questioner asked where the Buddha was just at the moment of enlightenment. The Teacher said : ' (If there be enlightenment), speech and silence, movement and stillness, every sight and every sound is a buddha state of affairs. Where ever could you go to find the Buddha ? You do not put a head on top of a head or a mouth alongside of a mouth.' " (*Record of Sayings of Ancient Worthies*, Chüan 3.) Not only is there no form of buddhahood which can be achieved, but also there is no form of enlightenment which can be obtained. As Ma Tsu put it : " We speak of enlightenment as contrasting with delusion. Since delusion is unreal, then enlightenment also cannot stand." (*Record of Sayings of Ancient Worthies*, Chüan 1.) This is what is called " an obtaining which is not an obtaining ", and also " in the last resort nothing obtained ".

The conclusion is that the sage's daily life does not differ from the ordinary man's. The ordinary man, as the Inner-light School were continually saying, wears clothes, eats his food, relieves his bowels and makes water ; and the sage also acts in the ordinary way. In the *Second Instalment of the Light-Transmitting Record*, there is a conversation which Hui Yüan [*d.* 1176], of the Lin Yin Temple, had with the Emperor Hsiao Tsung, of the Sung Dynasty. The Teacher said : " Formerly there was one Kuei Sheng, an Inner-light Teacher in Yeh District, who had a disciple. The disciple went to Hangchow to the Shih Fang Fang Hsüeh Monastery there. Having made an enigmatic poem he communicated it to the people there. ' In a deep pool of the Fang Hsüeh there was a turtle-nosed serpent. A queer thing when you come to think of it ! Who pulled out the head of the serpent ? ' " The Emperor said : " Another sentence is needed." The Teacher said : " The poem was made with only three sentences." The Emperor asked why only three sentences, and the Teacher answered : "His idea was that he wanted to wait (for someone else to finish the poem)." Later an old monk of the Ta Sui Temple, by name Yüan Ching (d. 1135), after reading over the three sentences, added his own words, saying : " In a deep pool of the Fang Hsüeh there was a turtle-nosed serpent." (*Second Instalment of the Light-Transmitting Record*.) After the pulling out of the head of the serpent, there was still the turtle-nosed serpent of the Fang Hsüeh pool there. This is what is meant by the expression " in the last resort nothing gained ".

With regard to the main tenets in the Inner-light teaching, if the veil of the paradoxes be pierced, they actually are clear and simple. As Shu Chou said, " My late teacher said that the practice of Inner-light is to be described as the gold-and-ordure method. Before it is comprehended, it is like gold ; after it is comprehended, it is like ordure." (*Record of Sayings of Ancient Worthies*, Chüan 32.) In other words, once the veil of the paradox is pierced, there is nothing fantastic or secret in it. Hence, the teachers in this school constantly said : " Śākyamuni had secret teachings, but Mahākāśyapa did not keep the secret." Yün Chu [i.e. Tao Yin, d. 901] said : " If you do not understand, then it is a secret of Śākyamuni's : if you do understand, it is Mahākāśyapa not keeping the secret." What constitutes the secret is the fact that the mass of people do not understand. As Fo Kuo [d. 1135] said : " What Mahākāśyapa did not keep secret, that was the real secret in Śākyamuni's sayings. When a saying is not kept secret, it is a secret : when it is a secret, it is not kept a secret." The secret which is not kept a secret is what is called an open secret.

The cosmological and psychological theories of the original Buddhism were regarded by the Inner-light School as " arguments which are the ordure of nonsense ". (*Pai Ch'ang's Sayings, vide Ancient Worthies*, ch. 2.) They were also described as "useless furniture" by Yo Shan [i.e. Wei Yen, d. 834] (*Sayings in the Light-Transmitting Record*, ch. 14). These nonsense arguments were, so they felt, only fit to be thrown away, as furniture which is actually of no use. Then, after all these have been cleared away, what remains in the Buddhist teaching is only a few open secrets. As Lin Chi said, " In Huang Po's place I three times asked about the main tenets of Buddhism. Three times I was beaten. Afterwards in Ta Yü's place I was suddenly enlightened and said : ' At bottom there was not anything very much in Huang Po's Buddhism.' " (*Ancient Worthies*, ch. 4.) As a matter of fact, not merely Huang Po's Buddhism had not much to it, Buddhism itself had not much. This appears in the *Light-Transmitting Record*, ch. 11, where there is a different version of Lin Chi's words, namely that Buddhism has not much to it.

The meaning of passing from delusion to enlightenment is one of leaving one's mortal humanity behind and entering into sagehood. After that has come about, the sage's manner of life is no different from that of the ordinary man. That is to say, " the ordinary mind is the Tao." The sage's mind is the ordinary mind. This is described as leaving sagehood behind and entering into mortal humanity. To leave sagehood behind and enter mortal humanity is spoken of as a " falling into ". But " falling into " may also be described both as a falling from sagehood and as a rising above sagehood. (Cp. *Ts'ao Shan's Recorded Sayings.*) This rising above sagehood is what is described as " over beyond the top of a hundred-foot bamboo-cane rising yet another step ".

Nan Ch'üan made the statement : " After coming to understand the other side, you come back and live on this side." (*Ancient Worthies*, ch. 12.) In the *Ts'ao T'ung Record*, there is also a quotation from Nan Ch'üan : " Having first passed over to the other side to learn something, to come back and live on this side." To go to the other side is to leave mortal humanity behind and enter on sagehood ; while to come back and live on this side is to leave sagehood behind and enter on mortal humanity.

Because for the sage to do what the ordinary man does is to leave sagehood behind and enter on mortal humanity, therefore, although what he does is what the ordinary man does, yet the significance of his doing of it is not the same as the ordinary man's doing of it. As Pai Ch'ang said : " That which before enlightenment comes is called lust and anger, after the enlightenment is called buddha-wisdom. The result is that a man is not different from what he was before, only what he does is different." (*Ancient Worthies*, ch. 1.) Huang Po said : " But to have the mind unattached to all and sundry things, this is to have perfect wisdom. It means to go daily back and forth, to sit and sleep, to speak every kind of word, but not to make a creaturely activity of it. In that case the words one speaks and the glances one directs represent perfect wisdom." (*Ancient Worthies*, ch. 2.) As the lay monk P'an Yün's hymn said : " The power to work miracles and to function divinely is in carrying water and chopping firewood." If ordinary people carry water and chop wood, that is nothing more than carrying water and chopping wood. If the sage does it, then it is in the nature of a miraculous deed and something divinely useful.

Because in this fashion he is different, therefore, although the sage man does what the ordinary man does, yet his deeds are not subject to recompense within the compass of the Wheel. As Huang Po put it : " When a questioner asked whether mowing grass and chopping down trees, digging out the earth and ploughing new soil, had the quality of sin, his reply was : ' One cannot say for certain whether these are sin, nor can one say for certain that they are not sin. Whether there is sin or not depends on the man. If he be contaminated by all and sundry things, and if the mind be embedded in selecting and rejecting, and he cannot go beyond the Three Sentences, this man for certain has sin. If he go beyond the Three Sentences, and his mind be empty like empty space and he even does not think of the empty space, this man for certain has no sin.' " Again, " According to the transmitted teaching of the Inner-light School the mind is empty like empty space and does not retain one single thing, not even consciousness of emptiness. Where then can sin come in and abide ? " (*Ancient Worthies*, ch. 1.) Although the sage does all the ordinary things, he is not attached to them, nor is he caught in their toils. Huang Po said : " To eat rice all day and yet not swallow a grain, to walk all day and yet not tread an inch of the earth ; and in that state to have no sense of an object either in relation to the not-I or in relation to the I ; and all day long to be not separated from all sorts of things but not to be deluded by them, this is to be named the liberated man, the man who is at ease in himself." (*Ancient Worthies*, ch. 3.) Yün Men [i.e. Wen Yen] also said : " To have discussed affairs all day and yet have nothing come across your lips or teeth, nor to have spoken a single word : to have eaten rice and worn clothes all day and yet not have run against a grain of rice or to have touched a thread of silk." (*Ancient Worthies*, ch. 16.)

According to this view the sage is this kind of man, one at ease in himself, one who is liberated. As the *Record of T'ung Shan's Sayings* [i.e. Lang Ch'ieh, *d.* 869] puts it : " The Teacher on one occasion was fording a river with one Mi, and he asked Mi what sort of action crossing a river was. The reply was that it was (an action in which) the water did not wet the feet. The Teacher said : ' Most reverend Sir, you have declared it.' Mi asked him how he would describe it, and the Teacher replied : ' The feet are not wet by water.' " The significance of this is that one should do things without getting attached to them, without getting caught in their toils.

This is the outcome of the cultivation of non-cultivation. While this cultivation is going on, there is need that the momentary thoughts should be detached from their objects, that the objects should become not-objects. When the cultivation is completed, these thoughts are also detached from their objects and the objects have become not-objects. On the other hand, although during the earlier stage this desired state of mind is only achieved through conscious effort, in the second stage this state of mind requires no effort, but is so entirely naturally. This happens, not because the man engaged in this cultivation has nourished a habit of this kind and therefore does not need to exert any conscious effort, but because the man at the moment of achievement is suddenly enlightened and is identified with non-being. This is the reason why he need not exert any effort but can be like that entirely naturally. The sphere in which the sage lives is one which is described as having " neither subject nor object eliminated ". In this sphere a mountain is still a mountain and a river still a river, but the man is not one who has left mortal humanity behind him and entered on sagehood. That, according to Pai Ch'ang, means that he is not a different man from what he was before, but that he lives and moves in a different place. Strictly speaking he ought to have said that he is a different man from what he was before, but lives and moves in the same place. That is, he leaves sagehood behind and enters into mortal humanity. So although there are still subject and object, to him it is as if there were no subject and no object. To eliminate both subject and object, this is the process of leaving mortal humanity behind and entering into sagehood. To eliminate neither subject nor object, this is the sphere of the man who leaves sagehood behind and enters into the sphere of mortal humanity.

In Chapter VII we stated that the Mystic School maintained that the sage also responded to the call of affairs and to the demands of the world, and that this meant that the sage was not handicapped by doing this. What Sheng Chao said [cp. c. 7] was : " Living in the world of active functioning and yet residing in the world of *wu wei*." This meant that to do the one is not incompatible with doing the other. But to speak like this is to make the sage's mysterious aloofness and his response to affairs and this world two different courses. It is not to make them one and the same course. If we follow the lead of the Inner-light School, then response to affairs and the world is, as far as the sage is concerned, of the nature of the Mysterious Tao. To live in the world of active functioning is the same as to reside in the world of *wu wei* ; and to maintain this is to see that there are not two courses but only one course.

Thus the Inner-light School took a step beyond other schools in synthesizing the antithesis between the sublime and the common. On the other hand, if to carry water and chop wood are of the nature of the Mysterious Tao, then why should it still be necessary for a man engaged in spiritual cultivation to abandon his family and become a monk ? Why should not the service of father or of sovereign also be of the nature of the Mysterious Tao ? Here also there was need for a further word. The mission of the Neo-Confucianist School of the Sung and Ming eras was to say that word.

CHAPTER IX

THE NEO-CONFUCIANIST PHILOSOPHY

Chang Tsai's *Ting Wan* [1] (*Correcting the Ignorant*) is a Neo-Confucianist product of the greatest importance. In it we find " the *Ch'ien* (i.e. Heaven) is called Father, the *K'un* (i.e. Earth) is called Mother. (As a man) I am so insignificant that in a muddled kind of way I dwell between them. Therefore in regard to what fills the area which is Heaven and Earth [2] I am part of its body, in regard to what directs the movements of Heaven and Earth, I am part of its nature (*hsing*). All men are my brothers from the same womb, all things my companions." Also : " To honour men of great age is to pay due respect to their [i.e. Heaven and Earth's] elders : to be tenderly kind to orphans and the weak is to give due care to their young people. The sages are men who are identified with them [i.e. Heaven and Earth], the worthies are their fine flower." Also : " To have understanding of their transforming power is to be able to hand down what they do, to plumb the depths of their divinity is to maintain their purpose." Also : " Wealth and honour, heavenly grace and favour, may be given to me to enrich my life : poverty and low estate, grief and sorrow, may be given to you as the discipline required for accomplishment. While I am alive, I serve them obediently : when I am dead, I am at peace." (*Cheng Meng, To Enlighten Beginners, Ch'ien Ch'ang Chapter.*) Neo-Confucianists of the time and those after thought very highly of this essay. As Ch'eng Hao said, " I have the same idea as that expressed in the *Hsi Ming*, but it is only Tzŭ Hou [i.e. Chang Tsai] whose pen has the power to do justice to it. Other men are unable to achieve this, for from the days of Mencius down there has been nobody who reaches this level. Now that we have this expressed, much talking is saved." (*The Two Chengs' Literary Remains*, ch. 2a.)

Chang Tsai regarded *ch'i* (vital gas, etc.) as the basic element in all things. The entire body of *ch'i* he called " the Supreme Harmony ", or alternatively " the Tao ". As he put it : " What is called the Tao is the Supreme Harmony. Within it is contained

[1] Also known as the *Hsi Ming*.
[2] The question arises here in an acute form whether *t'ien* were more accurately translated as " the heavens " or " Heaven " and *ti* as " the earth " or " Earth ". The sense here for the most part requires " the heavens " and " the earth ", and yet his concept goes beyond the material. (E. R. H.)

the inherent natures of floating and sinking, rising and falling, moving and being still, with all of them affecting each other. These natures are what gave birth to the beginning of the mutual stimulation of conquering and being conquered, of declining and progressing." (*To Enlighten Beginners, T'ai Ho Chapter.*) To Chang Tsai within this *ch'i* is included the Yin and the Yang. The *ch'i* which has the Yin quality tends to be still, to be submerged and to fall, whilst the *ch'i* which has the Yang quality tends to move, to float on the surface, and to rise. *Ch'i* being like this, therefore " there are rising and falling, flying and dispersing which never cease ". Since in this there is mutual stimulation, therefore there is cohesion and dispersion continually going on. Where there is cohesion, there things come to be : where there is dispersion, there things revert back to being *ch'i*. " The cohesion of *ch'i* in the Great Emptiness is like water congealing and becoming ice, and its dispersion like ice melting and becoming water." (*Ibid.*)

Ch'ien and *K'un* are alternative names for Heaven and Earth. All men and all things are brought into existence by Heaven and Earth. Thus they may well be described as the father and mother of all men and all things, and men and things are alike in treating them as father and mother. Nevertheless, there is this respect in which men and things are different, namely that man, apart from his human body, possesses in addition " the nature of Heaven and Earth ". I, along with Heaven and Earth, am a cohering point of one and the same *ch'i*. Therefore I, along with Heaven and Earth and all things, am basically one body. " In regard to what fills the area of Heaven and Earth, I am part of its body." But the nature of Heaven and Earth signifies the directive force there. Since my nature is what I derive from the nature of Heaven and Earth, " in regard to what directs the movements of Heaven and Earth, I am part of its nature." Thus in regard to " my seven-foot tall body ",[1] in comparison with Heaven and Earth, I am a very insignificant object : in regard to the basis of my body and its mind and nature, I am one with Heaven and Earth and all things. To carry understanding to this point is to know that all men are my brothers from the same womb, all things my companions. As Chang Tsai said : " The nature is one fountain head of all things : the nature is not something I can take for my private edification. It is only a great man who can carry this tao to its limit. Therefore when he

---

[1] The Chinese *chih* (foot) equals roughly ten inches.

wants to establish himself, he is sure to establish all : in the matter of his knowledge, it is sure to be all-inclusive ; in the matter of his loving, to include every one : in the matter of his completion, to complete others. Those who obfuscate their nature have no idea how to obey our logic of humanity, and nothing can be done with them." (*To Enlighten Beginners, Ch'eng Ming Chapter.*)

It is not only the nature which is one fountain head of all things and which I cannot take for my private edification. The *ch'i* also is a fountain head which I cannot take for my private edification. The nature of man reveals a power to have conscious knowledge, and " the combination of this nature and conscious knowledge has a name, the mind ". (*T'ai Ho Chapter.*) Men have minds and thereby are able to have self-consciousness and understanding. Since the nature along with *ch'i* makes the source from which things come, the sage man is conscious of this and understands it. Therefore, when he wants to establish himself he is able also to establish others, to make his knowledge all-inclusive, to love all men alike, and to complete all while he is completing himself. This amounts to being able to give full development to his mind and to his human nature. Chang Tsai made the statement : " If a man enlarges his mind, then he is able to identify himself with all the things in the world. If there be any part of things with which he is not identified, then his mind has something beyond its range. The minds of ordinary people are restricted within the narrow range of what they hear and see. The sage gives full development to his human nature and does not pen his mind inside what he hears and sees. In his view of the whole world not one thing but is part of himself. This is how Mencius came to say that the full development of a man's mind was equivalent to comprehending his human nature and comprehending Heaven. Heaven is so vast that there is nothing beyond it ; and therefore the mind which has something beyond its range is inadequate for being united with the mind of Heaven." (*To Enlighten Beginners, Ta Hsin Chapter.*)

For there to be nothing beyond is the extremity of vastness, is to be the Great Whole. Since Heaven is so, the man who enlarges his mind unites it with the mind of Heaven, and therefore for him there is nothing beyond the range of his mind. For the man who unites his mind with the mind of Heaven everything he sets about, every movement he makes, is " in aid of the nourishing and transforming work of Heaven and Earth ". This is the ground of the statement in *Correcting the Ignorant*, that honouring men of great age is paying due respect to the elders of Heaven and Earth : being tenderly kind to orphans and the weak is giving due care to the young people of Heaven and Earth. Now, if the men of great age be taken as only the old men in one's society, and the young as only the young in one's society, then this honouring and caring are nothing more than moral acts. But the seniors in society are also Heaven's seniors, the young also Heaven's young ones. Now, the man who unites his mind with Heaven on the basis of his self-conscious understanding sets out to honour men of great age and to be kind to orphans and the weak. In so doing he is, just the same, honouring men of great age and being kind to orphans and the weak, but the significance of his actions is to treat Heaven's seniors as they should be treated and Heaven's young as they should be treated. In this respect, his actions transcend the moral. Thus, to the man whose mind is united with Heaven, the study of Nature and the making use of Nature in science are an understanding of the transforming work of Heaven and Earth, a plumbing of the depths of their divinity. To Heaven belongs the power of transforming, and when a man studies and comprehends this, this is a following on of the work which Heaven has not completed. The man whose mind is united with Heaven in doing these various things is thus like a filial son following on with his father's purposes, continuing his father's work. Hence the significance of it is that of serving Heaven. This kind of man on the basis of his self-conscious understanding does his duty in society, and it is all the same to him whether he is rich and of high station or poor and of low station, as also whether he come to a ripe old age or whether he die young. For every day that he is alive he has a day in which he can continue doing his duty in society : for every day that he is dead he rests in eternal peace. As was said above, " while I live, I obediently serve Heaven : when I am dead I am at peace."

This of which we have been speaking represents a particular attitude to life and also a particular method of spiritual cultivation. This method has been described in Chapter III as " accumulation of righteousness ". The Neo-Confucianists, in speaking of " the efforts necessary for achieving sageness " always have this method of cultivation in mind, so that they regarded themselves as in the true tradition of Mencius. The man whose mind is united with Heaven in all that he does, transcends the moral, and therefore the sphere in which he lives transcends the moral sphere. Likewise, he is not restricted to his social environment. On the contrary, for him there is no distinction between being in this world and being outside it. Thus the antithesis between the sublime and the common is synthesized. Since this principle is made clear in Chang Tsai's *Correcting the Ignorant*, here then is where the value of this work lies.

Ch'eng Hao said : " I have the same idea as is expressed in *Correcting the Ignorant*." This idea is the idea of making all things one body, an idea on which Ch'eng Hao himself spoke in the dictum of his which was later known as Comprehending humanheartedness (*jen*). There he said : " The learner needs first to comprehend *jen*. The *jen* man is indifferentiably one with all things. Righteousness, ritual courtesy, wisdom, and good faith, all these are *jen*. Get to comprehend this truth and cultivate it in sincerity and reverence : that is all that is required." Also : " This Tao has nothing in contrast to it : even the word great is inadequate to express it. The function of Heaven and Earth is my function." Mencius said : " There is everything in one's I." You must reflect and find that it is really so. Then it is a source of immense joy. If your reflecting does not reveal that it is really so, then there are two things which are still in contrast : even though you are trying to unite the I with the not-I, you have not yet achieved the unity of the self and the not-self. How then can joy be obtained ? In *Correcting the Ignorant* there is a perfect statement about this unity : " If you engage in spiritual cultivation with the idea which is there, surely there is nothing further requiring to be done." (*The Two Ch'engs' Literary Remains*, ch. 24.) The *jen* referred to in this passage is that special *jen* which the Neo-Confucianist associated with being united with all things. As Ch'eng Hao said : " A doctor should speak of paralysis in a man's arms or legs as non-*jen*, for thus the term *jen* acquires its greatest significance. The *jen* man takes Heaven and Earth and all things as one body with himself, as there being nothing which is not his self. Having recognized them as himself, there is no limit to which he cannot go. If there be not this relationship with the self, it follows of necessity that there is no connection between them. If the hand or the foot are not-*jen*, it means that the *ch'i* is not circulating freely and the parts are not properly connected with each other. Therefore to ' distribute all round and to bring salvation to all ', this is the function of the sage man." (*Op. cit.*, ch. 2a.)

Now we have stated above in Chapter IV that if we use the

Taoist method of discarding knowledge, the indifferentiable oneness is in regard to the intellect, and that if we use the Confucianist method of accumulating righteousness, the indifferentiable oneness is a oneness in regard to the emotions. The *jen* of becoming one body with all things to which Ch'eng Hao refers here is indeed an emotional oneness. The *jen* man is emotionally become one body, the " one body " being an inclusive term for everything that exists. This body is the Great Whole. This Great Whole is not a formal whole. Within this Great Whole, according to Ch'eng Hao's idea, everything has an inward connection with everything else. As Ch'eng Hao said : " The supreme virtue of Heaven and Earth is to give life." [1] He also said : " The tendencies in life are altogether admirable. This comes under the term ' *jen* '. *Jen* represents oneness with Heaven and Earth ; but men elect to minimize themselves. Why do they ever do this ? " (*Op. cit.*, ch. 11.) The tendencies in life in all things are the *jen* of Heaven and Earth. If there be an emotional oneness with all things, then this is the *jen* of the *jen* man. Since *jen* in this sense has as wide a scope as Heaven and Earth, we can see why the statement was made that *jen* represents oneness with Heaven and Earth.

Since the term *jen* has as wide a scope as Heaven and Earth, we have the statement about it : " that this Tao has nothing in contrast to it : even the term ' great ' is inadequate to express it." Any and every sort of thing is actually part of the life of Heaven and Earth, and everything comes within the scope of the *jen* of Heaven and Earth ; but it does not follow that any and every sort of thing is conscious of being so. For example, the great majority of men are not conscious that they are so. This is what is meant by men electing to minimize themselves. The sage man not only comes within the scope of the life of Heaven and Earth : he is also conscious that really and truly he is so. This is what is meant by reflecting and finding that he is really one with all things. This reflecting " is like turning a ray of light on one's self ", and here denotes the power of reflection in self-consciousness and understanding. Thus by means of reflection there comes the genuine consciousness of everything being in one's I. If reflection produces no real consciousness of this, then the distinction between the I and the not-I still remains. If I

---

[1] This is a quotation from the *Yi Amplifications*. In Chapter V we translated *sheng* as " *produce* ", here we say " *give life* ", as this seems to be Ch'eng Hao's interpretation of the term. (E. R. H.)

remain I, and Heaven and Earth remain Heaven and Earth, then unity is not achieved. The expression " comprehending the truth " is what is spoken of in my *Hsin Yüan Jen* as " knowing Heaven ". So also in relation to " cultivating this in sincerity and reverence ", this is equivalent to using a real mind and a real intention in devoting one's self to this truth. When this has continued for a long time, then it is possible to have the experience of being blended as one body with all things, or, as my *Hsin Yüan Jen* expresses it, " to be identified with Heaven."

Mencius' method of " nourishing the great morale " was that of accumulating righteousness. That means, as Mencius said, " something to be put into action." In other words, at all times accumulating it, not ceasing for a moment : as he said, " never forgetting." When this accumulating has gone on for a considerable time, then the great morale of itself comes into existence. It is impossible for it to be gained suddenly or for one to give artificial assistance to it to grow. This is the method of accumulating righteousness. Ch'eng Hao said that it was cultivated by sincerity and reverence, no more and no less, and asked what more could be needed. These expressions bear a close resemblance in meaning to those used by Mencius.

The man who has become really and truly a *jen* man is the sage, and the sage is one body with Heaven and Earth and all things. For him Heaven and Earth and all things are not something external to himself, nor is he in relation to them something internal. The contrast as between himself and others for him no longer exists. They are just in each other, and there is no distinction of external and internal between them. The sage man also responds to the world, and here again the distinction of being in this world and being outside it no longer exists. Ch'eng Hao, in a letter replying to one from Chang Tsai, makes the statement : " With regard to what I speak of as spiritual composure, in activity there is this composure : in stillness also. There is no anticipating and no retrospecting, no distinction of internal and external. If you take external things to be external and regard yourself as implicated in following them, then you are taking your nature [1] to be divided into two parts, external and internal. Further, if you regard your nature as able to follow after things outside, then whilst it is engaged outside, what is there

---

[1] In this letter there can be no question but that when he speaks of the nature (*hsing*) he is really thinking of the mind part of *hsing*. (E. R. H.)

inside you ? You may have a purpose to eliminate the enticements of the external, but you are then ignoring the fact that in
one's nature there is no distinction of external and internal. If
the internal and the external are to be taken as entirely separate,
then surely you are straight away disqualified from advocating
spiritual composure ! The constancy of Heaven and Earth
lies in the fact that there is mind in all things, but Heaven and
Earth have no mind. The constancy of the sage man lies in the
fact that his feeling is in accord with all things, but he himself
has no feeling,[1] with the result that in learning to be a man of
principled intelligence (*chun tzŭ*) there is nothing more important
than being open and impartial, than showing no favour to one
thing or the other, but responding spontaneously to everything
as it comes. The actual condition in men is to have a blind spot,
and this is the cause of their inability to achieve the Tao. The
trouble generally is that they are selfish and rely on the use of
their intellect. Since they are selfish, they are precluded from
making their actions to be spontaneous responses : since they
rely on the use of the intellect, they cannot regard their intuitions
as something entirely natural. As to regarding the external as
wrong and the internal as right, this is not so good as forgetting
that there is any external and internal. If you forget this
distinction, then you are in a limpid state with nothing to disturb
you. In that state you have spiritual composure. Having spiritual
composure, then you are clear-minded : being clear-minded,
what is there which can catch you in its toils when you respond
to things ? " (*Collected Papers*, ch. 3.) This letter of Ch'eng Hao's
later generations have entitled " the letter on the Composure of
the Nature ". The ideas expressed in this letter are in many respects
similar to those held by the Inner-light School. Take their
ideas and carry them to their logical conclusion, and what you
get is just what Ch'eng Hao had to say in this letter.

What the Neo-Confucianists took to be an antithesis between
the active and the still is what we have dealt with in previous
chapters where an antithesis was made between being in this
world and being outside it. Other-worldly people are the latter,
separating themselves from society and becoming mysteriously
remote, stillness being their guiding principle. This-worldly
people are the former, complying with the demands of practical

---

[1] The idea here is not that the sage is without feeling, but that his feeling is not
caught in the toils. This is because there is no selfish element in his feeling. (Cf.
Wang Pi's theory in Chapter 7.) (E. R. H.)

affairs, with activity as their guiding principle. Lao Tzŭ and Chuang Tzŭ, together with the original Buddhists, all made stillness their guiding principle. The earlier Neo-Confucianists also did so, as for example Chou Tun-yi, who said : " The sages fixed the principles of *jen* and *yi* (righteousness), and made stillness the guiding principle, thus establishing a standard for mankind." (*T'ai Chi T'u Shuo*.)   The later Neo-Confucianists in their statements about spheres of living no longer inculcated stillness but composure, in their statements about methods of spiritual cultivation no longer urged stillness but reverence. This was a very great change.   Activity and stillness are antithetical. Composure and reverence are not antithetical to activity, but represent a synthesis of stillness and activity. In regard to living, activity may be composed as stillness is composed, whilst, in regard to method, activity may be reverent as stillness is reverent.

The sage man is composed both in his activity and in his stillness, and for him there is no distinction between the external and internal. Because he is blended into one body with all things, and everything is in his I, and the function of Heaven and Earth are his function, therefore for him there is nothing external to him. The man to whom stillness is the guiding principle, regards the affairs of the world as externals, and sees in them forms of enticement which are calculated to throw his stillness into confusion. For the sage man, however, to whom there is nothing external and nothing internal, the result is that he is not concerned with eliminating external enticements. The scope of his mind is as wide as the scope of Heaven and Earth, and he, like Heaven and Earth, has no private predilections. His mind is like " the emptiness of a mirror and the evenness of a balance ".   When business comes to him, he follows the naturalness of his mind's intuitive response to the demand.

The sage man is not selfish, nor does he rely on the use of his intellect. This corresponds to what the Mystic School and the Inner-light School called " having no deliberate mind ". Whereas these two schools said that the sage man had no deliberate mind, what the Neo-Confucianists said was that, whilst Heaven and Earth have no mind, the sage man has a mind, though not a deliberate mind.   As Ch'eng Hao put it : " The constancy of Heaven and Earth lies in the fact that there is mind in all things, but Heaven and Earth have no mind.   The constancy of the sage man lies in the fact that his feeling is in

accord with all things, but he himself has no feeling." Ch'eng
Yi (Ch'eng Hao's younger brother) said : " Heaven and Earth
have no mind and yet they completely transform : the sage man
has a mind and yet is *wu wei*." Thus what the Mystic and Inner-
light Schools spoke of as having no deliberate mind amounted
to the sage man having a mind but having nothing contaminating
or enchaining it. In this respect there is a close resemblance
between those two schools and Ch'eng Hao's conviction.

Turning to his conviction, the sage man being open and
impartial with no private predilections and responding
spontaneously to things as they come, that responding is done
without a deliberate mind. This entails regarding his intuitions
as entirely natural. There is also a resemblance here with the
Inner-light School's theory about having thoughts and yet
having no thoughts and having objects and yet having no objects
of thought, and thus making *yu wei* (creaturely activity) equal to
wu wei (inactivity).

Having reached this point, we see clearly how Ch'eng Hao's
famous letter bears many resemblances to the ideas held by the
Inner-light School. None the less, this school thought people
ought to become monks and abandon the world. That is to say,
they still had a feeling of repulsion against external things and a
strong predilection for the realm of non-being. They still could
not forget the distinction of internal and external. In other
words, they had a sound idea, but failed to carry it to its logical
conclusion. They had not really thought the problem out, for
if a man can forget the distinction between external and internal,
then this world and the other world are not distinguishable.
Not only is carrying water and chopping wood the Tao
fraught with mystery, but " serving one's father and one's
sovereign " are also this Tao. That being so, then in terms of
such a man's sphere of living, it is impartial and has no private
predilections : it is in harmony with Heaven and Earth. And,
in terms of his actions, they are a response to things as they come
to him. He makes no selections between one thing and another :
nothing is not permissible. Whatever comes to him is good for
him, nothing is not good for him. Thus the antithesis between
the sublime and the common is at once synthesized.

In the past, Ch'eng Hao and Ch'eng Yi were called " the
Two Ch'engs ". The traditional view was that the two brothers
had very much the same ideas. As a matter of fact, Ch'eng Hao
had an affinity with Taoism and Inner-light Buddhism and was

the forerunner of the *Hsin Hsüeh* (Mind Doctrine) of the Neo-Confucianist philosophy. Ch'eng Yi laid emphasis on the " Tao " of the *Yi Amplifications*. He rediscovered what in European philosophy is called the world of ideas and became leader of the *Li Hsüeh* (Doctrine of the Principal or Ideal Pattern) School of the Neo-Confucianist philosophy.

Ch'eng Yi stated : " All the things in the world can be comprehended by means of the *Li*. If a thing exists, there must be a law (*tsê*) to it. That is, for each individual thing there must be a governing principle (*li*)." (*Literary Remains*, ch. 18.) Speaking strictly, what he ought to have said was that for each kind of thing there must be one *li*, for that was what he meant. In the Chinese language a large number is expressed by " ten thousand " or " a hundred ", and this applies in the case of *li*, of which the Neo-Confucianists spoke as ten thousand or a hundred *li*. As Ch'eng Yi said : " In an examination of the Tao we find the ten thousand *li* all there complete." (*Op. cit.*, ch. 15.) He also said : " In speaking of the divine *li* (plural) the ten thousand are all there complete and none are missing." (*Op. cit.*, ch. 18.) Now, since all the *li* are already and always there, it is impossible that at first there could have been no *li* and then afterwards there were. Nor could there first be *li* and then afterwards none. Ch'eng Yi said, " In speaking of the divine *li*, this or that *li* never ceases to be. It could not owe its preservation to a sage emperor Yao or its destruction to a villainous tyrant Chieh." Again : " With regard to the *li*, how can you think of them as being preserved or being destroyed, or being increased or decreased ? None of them can be missing, but all must be complete." (*Op. cit.*, ch. 2a.) And again : " There is here neither a shortage nor an overplus : it is only that men are unable to see them with their eyes." (*Op. cit.*, ch. 2a.) That is to say, they transcend shapes and features.

A *li* is not subject to change. As Ch'eng Yi said : " A *li* spread out across the world is one and the same *li* ; extended across the four seas it is exactly what it is. Even though it be tested in the light of Heaven and Earth and examined in relation to the Three Kings, it does not change." (*Op. cit.*, ch. 2a.) Likewise it does not move. As Ch'eng Yi said when declaring that the divine *li* are all there complete : " The relationship between father and son and sovereign and subject is an everlasting *li* which does not change : so how could it ever move ? " (*Op. cit.*, ch. 2a.)

Events and things are the actual instances of the *li*. Now, since the *li* always are what they are, it makes no difference whether men know or do not know that they are there, nor whether there is an actual instance of a *li* in existence or not. As Ch'eng Yi put it : " All the *li* are plainly there. There is no time at which we can say that Yao, in exhausting the possibilities in the tao of sovereignty, made additions to it, or that Shun, in exhausting the possibilities in the tao of sonship, made additions to it. Whether in the past or the present, the two tao retain their identities." (*Op. cit.*, ch. 2a.) Yao, in exhausting the possibilities of the tao of sovereignty, set up an actual instance of it, and Shun did the same with the tao of sonship. But the *li* of sovereignty or that of sonship is not increased in size by the existence of any actual instance, nor is it decreased in size by any lack of an instance. The *li* are always the same. This is the meaning of *li* not being preserved by a Yao nor destroyed by a Chieh.

The world of the *li*, as it is described, is " silent, empty, with no physical trace in it, and yet all of them are there in great profusion ". In other words, they transcend shapes and features and yet are plainly there.

In the *Hsi Tz'ŭ* of the *Yi Amplifications* there is the statement : " That which transcends shape is to be called the Tao, that which has shape is to be called a utensil." According to Ch'eng Yi's interpretation of this, the *li* belong to the first category, things to the second. That which transcends shapes is forever what it is. Since it is impossible that it could first not be and then afterwards be or vice versa, therefore it cannot be either produced or destroyed. It is not in the category of production-destruction. That which has shape is in that category, its production coming from a cohesion of *ch'i* and its destruction from a dispersion of *ch'i*. A thing's existence is caused by its having a *li* as its pattern and *ch'i* as its raw material. To use the Aristotelian terminology, a *li* is its formal cause, *ch'i* its material cause.

The systems of the *Li Hsüeh* School only became fully built up under Chu Hsi's influence (1122–1200). He made a clearer distinction between that which transcends shape and that which has shape. Thus he said : " That which transcends shapes being without shape or semblance of shape, is this or that *li*. That which has shape and factuality is this or that utensil." (*Yü Lei, Classified Recorded Sayings*, 95.) From the angle of what transcends shape, there must first be a certain *li*, before, from the angle of what has shape, there can be a particular kind of utensil. As

Chu Hsi put it : " The act of making that thing shows that there is that *li*. The production of a certain thing by Heaven and Earth shows that there is the *li* of that thing." (*Op. cit.*, ch. 101.) Also : " A squared brick has the *li* of squared bricks, a bamboo chair has the *li* of bamboo chairs." (*Op. cit.*, ch. 34.) There has to be that *li* before it is possible for there to be that kind of thing ; and once there is that kind of thing in existence, it follows necessarily there is the *li* of it. But it may be that although there is a *li* of something, that something is not actually in existence. As Chu Hsi said, in his answer to Liu Shu-wen : " If, we look at the *li*, although there are no corresponding things in existence, the *li* are there. But they alone are there, because the things have not yet come into existence." (*Collected Works*, ch. 46.)

The *li* of any class of things is its ideal pattern, the highest standard of that class of thing : standard here being what is called its *chi* (perfection point). As is found in the *Yü Lei* : " Every kind of thing has its own *chi*, namely perfection point, which is the *li*. Chiang Yüan-chin said : ' For instance, *jen* for a sovereign and reverence for a subject, these are the perfection points.' The Master [i.e. Chu Hsi] said : ' This is the perfection point for a particular event or thing, and, adding together all the *li* of Heaven and Earth and all things, this is the *T'ai Chi* (the Supreme Point of Perfection.' " (*Op. cit.*, 94.) The Supreme Point of Perfection is the sum total of all the *li*, and so also it is the highest standard of Heaven and Earth and all things.

The Supreme Point of Perfection is always what it is. As Chu Hsi put it : " It is important to realize that the *li* are not in the category of existence and non-existence. Thus before Heaven and Earth existed, they were already what they were and are." (*Answer to Yang Chih-jen, Collected Works*, 58.) Also we cannot ask where the *T'ai Chi* is. As Chu Hsi said : " The *T'ai Chi* has no place where it is, and having no form or body, cannot be deposited in any position." (*Yü Lei*, 94.) So also in regard to movement and stillness, " the *T'ai Chi* belongs to the category of *li*, how can it either move or be still ? It is things which either move or are still. The *T'ai Chi* having no material form cannot rightly be thought of as moving or being still." (*Vide* Cheng Tzŭ-shang's question and Chu Hsi's agreement, *Collected Works*, 56.) Further, the *T'ai Chi* has no power to create, for as Chu Hsi put it : " A *li* is in a purely ideal world without any trace of the material, so that it has no power to create." (*Yü Lei*, 1.)

Thus, the realm spoken of is one which transcends shapes and features, one which " man is unable to see ". But it does not follow that it is unreal. Chu Hsi always spoke of the *li* as real. By this he meant a *li* has a real subsistence.[1] Thus, " The *T'ai Chi* consists of the *li* (plural) of the Five Forces and the Yin and the Yang. All these are not unreal. If they were unreal, they would correspond to the Buddhists' idea of the nature of things." Also he said : " The Buddhists only see the rind and the covering, but the many *li* inside, these they fail to see. For them the relationship of sovereign and subject, and that of father and son are delusion (*maya*)." (*Yü Lei*, ch. 94.) And again : " The Buddhists' idea of the unreal is not wholly wrong, but behind the unreal there must be the *li*. If we only say that we are unreal, and we do not know there are the real *li*, that surely is inconclusive. For instance, a pool of clear water, clear to the last degree so that you see it as if there were no water : the Buddhists say that the pool is really empty. They have never touched with their hand and examined whether what is there is cool or warm. They do not know that there is real water there. The Buddhists' type of knowledge is like this." (*Op. cit.*, 126.)

Neither the Taoists nor the Buddhists had anything to say on the world of the *li*. They talked about what transcends shapes and features, but what they called transcending shapes and features was something which could not be put into speech and could not even be conceived. Hence they could only speak of non-being. The *li* transcend shapes and features, but they can be put into speech and be the object of thought. Speaking strictly, it is only the *li* which can be put into words and be the object of thought. The *li* are in very truth the objects of speech and thought. Speaking strictly, things also cannot be put into words or be made the object of thought. They can only be the object of sensation. In all truth the *li* are in the category of the nameable. Whilst things are not in that category, yet it is possible for them to have names. For instance, a thing is a concrete " this ", and nevertheless this " this " can have a name. We may rightly say that there is that which can neither be the object of sensation nor the object of thought and is therefore in the category of the unnameable. There is also that which can only be the object of thought and cannot be the object of sensation and is therefore in the category of the nameable, while there also are things which cannot be the object of thought and can only

---

[1] In Chinese philosophy there is no special term for " subsistence " as distinct from " existence ". The word *yu* (being) is used for both. (E. R. H.)

be the object of sensation, and it is possible for these to have
names.

The discovery of the world of the *li* enables men to attain
to an eternal, pure and ideal world, a world which can neither
be added to nor be subtracted from ; which cannot be produced
or perish, neither moves nor is still. As we have said, if there be
a certain class of thing in existence, there must be a certain *li*,
though if there be a certain *li* it does not necessarily follow that
there is a corresponding class of things in existence. Once men
have seen this world they know that what they formerly saw
was restricted to shapes and features, a state of affairs described
as " having the purview of a frog in a well ". This new vision
can " enlarge the mind with its sense of ten thousand pasts ". It
is a spiritual liberation of the highest kind.

The *li* cannot create, for they neither move nor are still.
That which can move and create is *ch'i*. *Ch'i* is the raw material
out of which the world was created. Chu Hsi said : " Within
the area of Heaven and Earth there is *li* and there is *ch'i*. *Li*
is the Tao which transcends shape : it is indispensable for the
production of things. *Ch'i* is a utensil which has shape : it is
the tool which produces things. Hence the coming into existence
of men and things must be endowed with *li* before they can have
their inherent natures : they must be endowed with *ch'i* before
they can have material form." (*Answer to Huang Tao-fu, Collected
Works*, 58.) There is also the statement : " I suspect that the
action of *ch'i* is dependent on *li*. When the time comes and the
ch'i coheres, there is a *li* there also. Because the *ch'i* can weld
itself together into a mass, thus creation takes place. *Li* has no
feeling, no intention, no power of planning or creating. The only
thing is that in the place where the *ch'i* has become massed
together, the *li* is there also." (*Yü Lei*, ch. 1.)

In the *Li Hsüeh* School's system, the position of *ch'i* is like the
position of *Tao* in the Taoists' system. Nevertheless, in this
respect the Cheng-Chu thesis had originated with Chang Tsai.
What they had to say about *ch'i* had a resemblance to Chang
Tsai's *ch'i*. He maintained that *ch'i* is like " the finest particle of
matter ", so that it is also a class of thing. Although Chu Hsi
did not clearly state whether the *ch'i* for him was these fine
particles, yet he made distinctions between the pure and the
impure, and between the sound and unsound *ch'i*. Hence *ch'i*
is for him still a class of thing, something which can be named
and is not unnameable ; not, therefore, transcending shapes and

features. In Chang Tsai's and the Cheng-Chu systems alike, the concept of *ch'i* is not a formal concept, but a positive one.

When *ch'i* has become massed together and made a thing, this thing must belong to a certain class. It is in that class because it is endowed with that *li* ; and this endowment is the inherent nature of that class of things. Hence the statement : " In the production of men and things, they must be endowed with a *li* before they can have their inherent natures." This is as necessarily true as that they must be endowed with *ch'i* before they can have bodies.

The species man has been endowed with a nature of consciousness and intelligence, as also a nature in which *jen* and righteousness and a sense for ritual and wisdom are constituent parts. This is why in man there are the manifestations of consciousness and intelligence, as also the manifestations of fellow-feeling, of shame over wickedness, of distinguishing right and wrong, of yielding and courtesy. This human nature of consciousness and intelligence and *jen* and the other virtues is called by the Neo-Confucianists " the pre-actual ". Actual consciousness and intelligence, together with fellow-feeling and the other manifestations, are called the actual. The former is " the inherent nature ", the latter " feeling ". What the *Li Hsüeh* School meant by " the mind " included both the pre-actual and the actual, as appears in the statement, " the mind contains inherent nature and feeling."

The mind of a man not only contains the *li* which have been noted above. It also contains the whole total of all the *li* there are. This is to say that in the mind of a man there is the whole of the *T'ai Chi*. And not only is this the case with men, it is also the case with everything. As Chu Hsi said : " Every single man has the *T'ai Chi*, and every single thing has the *T'ai Chi*." (*Yü Lei*, ch. 94.) Also : " For all things there is only one *T'ai Chi*, but every single thing has the *T'ai Chi*. (*Ibid.*) Also Chu Hsi was asked the question whether, that being so, the *T'ai Chi* was split into parts. His answer was : " At bottom there is only one *T'ai Chi*, but everything in the world is endowed with it and with the whole of it. Take for instance the moon in the sky. There is only one moon, but when it is dispersed in the rivers and the lakes and we see it in one place after another, we are not warranted in saying that the moon is split into parts." (*Ibid.*)

Although the whole and indivisible *T'ai Chi* is in every man and every thing, yet because the endowment of *ch'i* in every man and thing is different in respect to its purity or impurity and its being sound or unsound, therefore there are some who are conscious that they have the *T'ai Chi* and some who are not conscious that they have it. Things other than man are endowed with a *ch'i* which is impure and unsound. Hence these things are entirely unconscious that they have *li* and the *T'ai Chi*. The *ch'i* with which man is endowed is purer and sounder. Hence it is possible for men to be conscious that they are endowed with *li* and with the *T'ai Chi*. Nevertheless, although it is possible for them to be conscious of this, there is still the necessity that they should expend some effort before they are actually able to be conscious. According to Chu Hsi's theory, the effort needed is that which in the *Great Learning* is described as *Ke wu chih chih*, interpreted by Chu Hsi as meaning " the investigation of things and the extension of knowledge ".

In Chu Hsi's *Analytical Commentary on the Great Learning*, there is his supplementary amplification to the chapter on *Ke Wu*. In it we find the following : " the extension of knowledge consists in the investigation of things, and these words indicate the desire on my part to extend my knowledge, this consisting in the full study of the *li* in things. The spiritual intelligence in men's minds in every case has knowledge, and the things in the world in every case have their *li*. It is only because the *li* is not fully studied that knowledge is incomplete. Hence the initial teaching of the *Great Learning* is that the learner must be enabled to make a full study of the *li* in all things in the world, on the basis of the *li* which he already knows, continuing with this until the limit be reached. After a long expenditure of effort, suddenly one day everything will be linked together and intelligible, and thus everything both in its outward appearance and its inward significance, in its fineness and its coarseness, will be reached, and thus the whole substance of my mind and its great function will be clearly demonstrated." This is very like Plato's recollection theory according to which the soul of a man in regard to all ideas has in the beginning perfect knowledge, but owing to the trammels of the body the soul does not remember the knowledge it originally had. Philosophers or poets, either by means of a mystical inspiration or by their efforts in the fields of mathematics and science, are enabled to lift their souls above their bodies' limitations and recall the knowledge they originally had. When this happens, the philosophers and poets emerge from a cave and again see the light of the sun. Whilst they were in the cave, what they saw was nothing more than the shadows of things and the light of the candle. When they have emerged, then only are they able to see things as they really are and the real splendour of the sun and the moon. This is the parable which Plato gave in the *Republic* on the world of ideas. He thus illustrated a certain sphere of living, the sphere which Chu Hsi described as a sudden enlightenment in which all the *li* are comprehended and the substance and function of the mind are clearly demonstrated. The man who possesses this sphere is for Chu Hsi the sage man, for Plato the philosopher or the poet.

The man who possesses this sphere employs himself in being a sovereign or a subject, in being a father or a son, that is, in the daily duties of human relationships. Nevertheless, these affairs which engage him are for him always not merely affairs but actual instances of the eternally abiding *li*. Thus his sphere of living is the highest of all, whilst what he does is what most men do. In this way the antithesis between the sublime and the common is synthesized.

After Ch'eng Hao came Lu Hsiang-shan,[1] the leading spirit in the *Hsin Hsüeh* (Doctrine of the Mind) School of Neo-Confucianism, who may rightly be reckoned as the one who spoke the further word which the tenets of the Inner-light School called for. His philosophy and his method of spiritual cultivation are those of that school ; or at the very least are the nearest of all to them.

If we use the Inner-light method, we see that the Ch'eng-Chu School in their search went too far, as also in what they affirmed. Hsiang-shan put it, bluntly : " their teachings were not to the point." When in his youth, Hsiang-shan heard a man repeat some sayings of Ch'eng Yi's, " he felt as if he had received an injury." Another time he said to a man : " Why do Yi-chuan's[2] words bear no resemblance to Confucius' and Mencius' words ? " On another day he was reading an ancient book and came to the two characters *yü* and *chou*.[3] An expositor said : " The four points (of the compass) together with above and below, this is called *yü*, and the past, present and future are called *chou*." Suddenly he was enlightened and said : " All the business in

---

[1] He is better known as Lu Hsiang-shan though his real name was Lu Chiu-yüan. (E. R. H.)

[2] Yi-chuan was Ch'eng Yi's name as a teacher. (E. R. H.)

[3] *Yü* means space-universe, *chou* means time-universe. The two together begin to appear in early Han times. Later the combination has been used as one of the terms for denoting the universe. (E. R. H.)

the space-time universe comes within the scope of my duty : the scope of my duty includes all the business in the space-time universe." Also on one occasion he said : " The universe is my mind, and my mind is the universe." (*Collected Works*, ch. 33.) His enlightenment was the same as an Inner-light School enlightenment. From the time a man is enlightened in this fashion all he need to do is to have faith in himself and let everything else go. We find the same meaning in one of Ch'eng Hao's sayings, where he said : " After comprehending this truth, cultivate it with sincerity and reverence. There is no need for other precautions or efforts."

The learner needs first of all to have this enlightenment ; or as it is sometimes expressed, " to establish first what is most important." Hsiang-shan said : " Recently there have been people criticizing me, saying that apart from the single sentence emphasizing first establishing what is most important I have no other trick to offer. When I heard this I exclaimed : " To be sure ! " (*Op. cit.*, 34.) Also when a man has first established what is most important, he has faith in himself. The man who has faith in himself believes that " all things in their prolific variety are in the inch-space of the heart [i.e. the mind].[1] What the mind expresses in full fills up the gaps in the universe, and is no other than the *li* " (*ibid.*). Now to have faith in one's self is the same as to know that " the Tao fills the whole universe, and there is no space anywhere without it. Since The Four Beginnings and the Ten Thousand Virtues are what Heaven has vouchsafed, there is no need for man to labour at embellishing them. Only because a man is (morally) defective is he at odds with the Tao ". (*Op. cit.*, ch. 15.) If one knows that embellishment is unnecessary, he can stop embellishing. To know that one has a defect, it is only necessary to remedy it. This is what is meant by " letting everything else go ".

Hsiang-shan made the statement : " This *li* being in the universe, how was it there was anything to impede it ? It is you who have drowned and buried yourself and have shut yourself away from the light in the middle of a pit, and know nothing about anything that is high and far away. Destroy the pit, and break through the bars of your prison." Also he said : " Be courageous, be zealous, break open the net, burn the thorns in

---

[1] The " inch-space " is of course a reference to the heart. In Chinese traditional psychology the heart (*hsin*) was the seat of the mind. From Han times down the poetical variation " inch-space of the *hsin* " was common as a designation of the mind. (E. R. H.)

your path, wash away the mire." Also : " A hog or a chicken all day go to and fro with no purpose beyond. The Gordian knot must be cut, for to what end is there all this going to and fro ? " This is very much in Lin Chi's vein, namely, let everything else go.

Hsiang-shan took his own method to be one of simplification and Chu Hsi's method to be one of complication. In his *Recorded Sayings* we find : " I [i.e. the recorder] say that the old habits are not easy to do away with. But, if one habit can be done away with, a hundred habits can be done away with. From this, I say that the trouble with Chu Hsi is that he cannot do away with his habits. The Master said, " You cannot take him for comparison. His aim is to make things complicated." (*Collected Works*, ch. 35.) He also said : " The sage man's words are clear of themselves. For instance, ' at home a young man does his filial duty ; in society he does his duty as a junior.' Here clear directions are given you about your duty in the family and in society, the one filial, the other that of a junior, so what need is there for amplification and comment ? The learner loses his energy in all this amplifying and commenting. Hence the burden becomes heavier and heavier. When he comes to me, all I do is to decrease the burden." (*Collected Works*, 35.)

The method of simplification is one which lets everything else go. After that has been done, all that is left is my mind and I as a man. Hsiang-shan said : " I lift up my head and grasp at the Great Dipper, I turn my body round and am in the company of the North Star. With my head erect I look beyond the heavens : there is no such man as I am." Here the two expressions, " I as a man," and " such man as I am ", denote " the Great Man ". Hsiang-shan said : " There is the Great World, but you do not enjoy it. You just follow the small track. You do not want to be a great man, but to be like a small child. Alas, that this is so ! " Having reached this sphere, not only does the great man not need what is called the heavy burden of amplifications and expositions, but even the Six Scriptures he does not need. This is what is described as : " If in learning a man comprehends what is fundamental, the Six Scriptures are only his footnotes." (*Collected Works*, 34.)

If one has faith in one's self and lets everything else go, the Ten Thousand Virtues and the Four Beginnings are what one's nature most certainly possesses. The only need is for one to put them into practice. Hsiang-shan said : " If man's spiritual energies are devoted to externalities, then he will be without peace all through his life. You must collect yourself and be your own master. Get your spiritual energies collected within, then when there is call for fellow-felling, you will have fellow-feeling, when there is call for being ashamed of evil, you will be ashamed of evil. Who is there who can deceive you ? Who is there who can cheat you ? When you have a clear grasp of it and cultivate it without ceasing, how wonderful it is ! " (*Ibid.*) This injunction to collect your spiritual energies is in reference to paying attention to yourself, or in other words reflecting about yourself, what the Inner-light School called " turning the ray of light to shine upon the self ". Thus the ordinary man only pays attention to externalities, that is, devotes his spiritual energies to them, with the result that he has no peace. But when his energies are collected, when the light is turned inward, then he can be enlightened to the fact that the universe is his mind and his mind the universe. That being so, external things are no longer external. So that when he responds to external things, he is not without peace. The cause of this is that his mind is wide open and he has no private predilections. His response to things is that of being spontaneously in accord with things as they come. Hsiang-shan said : " In regard to things, do not be so attached to them. In my life, I have a skill in this direction, that is, in not being attached to things. Nothing can catch me in the toils. When I handle an affair, all the essentials [lit. pulse and bones and marrow of it] are within my control. But I myself am like a man at leisure with no affairs to occupy him. I am not caught in the toils." How exactly this resembles the Inner-light School's words, " All day eating rice and yet not one grain of rice touching (one's lips), all day wearing clothes and yet not putting on a thread of silk ! "

Judging by the above, we can see how Hsiang-shan's philosophy and method of spiritual cultivation has a distinct affinity with the Inner-light School's philosophy and method. There is indeed a simplicity and directness in it which cannot be denied. The Ch'eng-Chu School maintained that there was this affinity, though Hsiang-shan himself denied that this was so. This denial is also not wrong, because he affirmed that serving one's father and one's sovereign came within the scope of our inherent nature and that this was " the Tao which is fraught with mystery ". Because he added this further word, therefore his tenets are Neo-Confucianist and not those of the Inner-light School.

The last of the great teachers of the *Hsin-Hsüeh* School was Wang Yang-ming (A.D. 1473–1529). His philosophy and method of spiritual cultivation also emphasized faith in one's self and letting all else go. This faith in one's self is a belief in one's self as knowing good and knowing evil by means of an intuitive knowledge (*liang chih*). To let all else go is on the one hand to abstain from making any calculations and on the other hand to follow one's intuitions and act accordingly. In Yang-ming's *Questions on the Great Learning*, we find in the section where he deals with the Three Main Principles (*San Kang Ling*), the following statement : " The great man is one who regards Heaven and Earth and all things as one body. He sees the whole of the society of man as one family and the Middle Kingdom as one man. As for the man who emphasizes the division of one body from another and so distinguishes a you and a me, he is a man of no moral intelligence [lit. a small man]. The ability of the great man to regard Heaven and Earth and all things as one body does not come by conscious purpose. The *jen* (human-heartedness) of his mind is of its very nature united with Heaven and Earth and all things. Surely not only is the great man so ! Even the small man's mind is also the same, only he minimizes himself. The result of this is that if there be no beclouding of selfish lusts, then even a small man's mind has the human-hearted-ness of the one body, as is the case with the great man. Once there be the beclouding of selfish lusts, then even the great man's mind becomes divided and vulgarized like the small man's mind. The result is that those who are engaged in learning to be great men cast away these selfish lusts in order that they may reveal a shining virtue (*tê*) and recover the original condition of being one body with Heaven and Earth and all things. This they do, no more and no less. It is not true that they can add anything to this original nature. . . . To reveal a shining virtue is to establish the substance of the unity with Heaven and Earth. To love men is to extend this unity in functional action. The result is that the revealing of shining virtue cannot but consist in love of men, and so love of men be the means by which shining virtue is revealed. The attainment of the highest good is the highest standard for the revealing of shining virtue and the exercise of love for men. The nature with which Heaven has endowed man is perfectly good without spot or blemish. The light of this nature cannot be entirely dimmed. The expression of the highest good is the original substance of shining virtue, and is what I call intuitive knowledge. With this expression of the highest good it is intuitively known that the right is right, and the wrong is wrong, that less important matters are less important and the more important are more important. Whenever a stimulus comes, intuitive knowledge responds spontaneously. Circumstances may continually change, but there is always a constant mean. This represents the highest standard for men and the invariable law for all things, and it is incompatible with any intellectual calculating with a view to making it more or less. Should there be any such calculating of less and more, then it arises out of selfish intention and pettiness of knowledge and is not in the category of the highest good." (*Complete Works*, ch. 26.) Man's intuitive knowledge is then the expression of man's shining virtue. To follow in action the commands of one's intuitive knowledge, this is called to extend one's knowledge As for the idea that calculation in regard to this intuitive knowledge is the outcome of selfish purposes and pettiness of knowledge, this is what Ch'eng Hao in his letter *On the Composure of the Nature* called selfishness and relying on the intellect's sense of utility.

Since intuitive knowledge is an expression of man's shining virtue, therefore to extend this knowledge is the means by which men can get back to the original substance of shining virtue, namely the human-heartedness of being one body with Heaven and Earth and all things. As Yang-ming said : " The mind in men is a heavenly pool to which nothing is not vouchsafed. Speaking fundamentally, there is only one Heaven, and it is only through the obstruction of selfish lusts that this original unity with Heaven is lost. Thus, if every thought is used in extending intuitive knowledge, then the barriers and obstructions will be entirely cleared out of the way. Then the substance of Heaven will be recovered and there will be again the heavenly pool." (*Complete Works*, ch. 3.) Hsiang-shan said : " The universe has never fenced men apart from itself. It is men who themselves fence off the universe." The extension of intuitive knowledge is the means by which this fence is removed.

There is a conclusion to be drawn from this theory of intuitive knowledge and shining virtue and this virtue being the *jen* (human-heartedness) of being one body with Heaven and Earth and all things. This conclusion is that the revealing of shining virtue consists in the putting of *jen* into practice. This is why Yang-ming said that the revealing of this virtue consists in loving men, and loving men is the means by which virtue is revealed.

The extension of intuitive knowledge is that extension of it which comes with action. It is only by acting in obedience to the commands of intuitive knowledge that that knowledge can be completed. As Yang-ming said : " Knowledge and action are an indivisible whole." The *Record of Sayings for Exercising* has the following : " Ai said : ' For example, people to-day know quite well that to fathers one ought to be filial and to elder brothers one ought to discharge the duties of a younger brother, and yet they are incapable of being filial sons and good younger brothers. From this it follows that knowledge and action get put into separate compartments.' The Master said : ' This is the outcome of the divisive influence of selfish lusts. It is not in accordance with the basic nature of knowledge and action as one. There never has been a man who knew and yet did not put his knowledge into action. To know and fail to act is equivalent to not knowing. What the sages tried to do was to recover this basic nature. They did not want us to remain just as we are. . . . I have always said that knowledge affords the guiding purpose to action, and action is the practical side to knowledge. Knowledge is the initial step to action : action is the completing of knowledge. If this be understood, then we have only to think of knowledge, and action is there ; have only to think of action, and knowledge is there.' " (*Complete Works*, ch.1.) The basic nature of the human mind, at such times as it is not beclouded with selfish lusts, entails knowledge and action being one indivisible activity. Supposing when a man sees a child on the verge of falling into a well, that in his alarm he inevitably has a feeling of sympathy and obedience to this feeling as a spontaneous expression of his mind, without a doubt what he does is to rush forward and save the child. This purely spontaneous expression of the sympathetic mind by rushing forward is one indivisible activity, namely knowledge as the initial step to action plus action as the completing of the knowledge. But if at the time there should be a sense of hesitation, perhaps because of the fear that action will be difficult, or perhaps because of hatred for the child's father and mother, in both cases the result being doing nothing, then this is knowledge without action. This comes from selfishness and a use of the intellect, and the unity of knowledge and action is lost. There is also the knowledge that a man should be filial to his father. If the spontaneous expression of this knowledge be followed up, then there is sure to be filial conduct. If a man be prevented from acting so, then here there is a case of the mind being beclouded by selfish lusts. When this happens, the intuitive knowledge is there, but it is not carried to its conclusion, namely that of the completing action. The carrying of knowledge to its conclusion entails eliminating these becloudings and getting back to the basic nature of knowledge and action as one activity, and that is getting back to the substance of shining virtue.

In Wang Yang-ming's *Record of Sayings for Exercising*, we find a request for explanation of the Master's saying that the Buddhists do not attach themselves to objects but actually are attached by objects, whilst we Confucianists attach ourselves to objects but actually are not attached. The reply was : " The Buddhists are afraid of being trammelled by the father-son tie and so they run away, are afraid of being trammelled by the sovereign-subject tie and so they run away, are afraid of being trammelled by the husband-wife tie and so they run away. In all these respects, because first they are attached by the object, therefore afterwards they run away. With us Confucianists, having the tie of father and son, we deal with it by means of *jen*, having the tie of sovereign and subject, we deal with it by means of *yi* (justice), and having the tie of husband and wife, we deal with it by means of the sexes keeping their proper distance. Are we thereby attached by these objects ? " (*Complete Works*, ch. 3.) This then is a carrying of the Inner-light conviction to its logical conclusion. As Chapter VIII showed, the Inner-light position was that objects of knowledge should not be objects, thoughts not be thoughts. On that assumption, why should they not have taken such objects of knowledge as the father-and-son tie as not-objects, and thoughts on them as not-thoughts ? This is where the Inner-light School broke down and did not make a thorough solution to the problem. It is here that the *Hsin-Hsüeh* School on the one hand criticized the Inner-light School and on the other hand followed on from where they left off.

Intuitive knowledge is knowledge, and to complete that knowledge is to act. To be of one mind and one heart in completing what one knows by intuition is to be in a state of reverence. To be really conscious and comprehend the fact that intuitive knowledge is an expression of that shining virtue which is the unity of Heaven and Earth and all things, and to have one's whole mind and heart set on action in tune with what we thus know, this is to make a synthesis of the sublime and the common. Wang Yang-ming's metaphysic was not so good as Ch'eng Hao's

and Lu Hsiang-shan's metaphysic. To use the Inner-light
School's terminology, his metaphysic had a taste of " adulteration
from mud and water ". To use the terminology of this book, he
asserted too much about the actual. Nevertheless the emphasis
he laid on extending intuitive knowledge by action as a method
of spiritual cultivation was clearer and better defined than the
emphasis laid by Ch'eng Hao or Lu Hsiang-shan.

The Neo-Confucianists took these antitheses of the sublime
and the common, the internal and the external, the root and the
branch, the refined and the coarse, and synthesized them. As
Ch'eng Hao said : " To be faithful to one's daily round, to be
reverent to one's duties, and to be loyal to one's fellow-men,
these words touch bottom in regard to both things above and
things below ; and from the beginning (true) sages have had
no two ways of speaking on these matters." (*Literary Remains*,
ch. 18.) As Ch'eng Yi said : " Men in later ages have had a
theory that dealing with one's (Heaven-given) nature and
(Heaven-given) lot is a special kind of business. But to deal with
these matters and to discharge one's filial and younger-brotherly
duties, all comes under one category. Sprinkling and sweeping
floors, responding to demands and answering questions, are in
the same category as developing one's (Heaven-given) nature to
the highest and making the very best of one's (Heaven-given)
lot. There is no 'more important' and 'less important',
no fine and coarse. . . . That to-day those who in every way
discharge their filial and younger-brotherly duties are yet
unable to develop their nature to the highest and make the best
of their lot is due to their failure to understand." (*Ibid.*) These
acts, then, are what the sages were engaged in doing. Because they
were engaged in doing them, these acts were part of the perfect
Tao. It is like the saying : " If you go astray, you are of the
earth, earthy . . . ; if you understand, you are a sage " in things
above and things below, for they all come under one category,
not two categories. All these duties are part of the perfect Tao.
The Inner-light School failed to reach this conclusion, and it is
a more penetrating one.

These are the grounds on which the man who uses the Taoist
method and becomes a sage " stays where he is and rejoices in the
daily round ". " His mind is away in direct contact with Heaven
and Earth and all creation, with things above and things below
in complete accord." (Chu Hsi's comment on Tseng Tien's aim
in life : *vide Lun Yü*, Bk. xi.)

We have a poem of Ch'eng Hao's :

> These later years have brought me
>   Quietude of life.
> My eastern window reddens :
>   I awake.
>
> The world a vision is,
>   Stillness self-revealed.
> The seasons, fair to view,
>   To man akin.
>
> The Word doth pierce the corporeal world,
>   Itself without a form.
> Thought enters wind and cloud,
>   Changing with them.
>
> The pride and pomp of life
>   Brings me no vicious joy.
> Thus I am a man, no more,
>   And thus a hero amongst men.
>
> (*Ming T'ao Wen Chi*, ch. 1.)

This is the joy which the Taoists said came to Confucius and Yen Hui and which comes to the man who lives in the sphere of Heaven and Earth.

CHAPTER X

A NEW SYSTEM

The philosophy of the Sung and Ming eras had not directly received the baptism of the Logicians, with the result that what these philosophers said was unavoidably affected by shapes and features. In Chapter VI we pointed out that the elements of religion and primitive science were characteristic of the Yin-Yang School and that early Taoism came to be amalgamated with these elements. Thus was formed a Taoistic religion. The cosmology held by the earlier Neo-Confucianists was derived from this Taoistic religion. It is quite clear that Chou Tun-yi's *Diagram of the T'ai Chi* and Shao Yung's interpretation of the *Yi Scripture* were derived from that source, whilst Chang Tsai's theory about *ch'i* (vital gas, etc.) appears also to have its origin in it. In his *Correcting the Ignorant*, where he spoke of the *Ch'ien* representing the Father and the *K'un* representing the Mother, we see how unavoidably his thought was more or less pictorial. So with his " *ch'i* ", it was even more in the category of shapes and features. All his statements about *ch'i* were assertions about the actual.

The Ch'eng-Chu theory of *ch'i* was not so bound to shapes and features as Chang Tsai's theory was, but all the same it did not transcend shapes and features. On the other hand, what they meant by *li* was something fundamentally abstract ; although in this respect it seems as if they had not arrived at a complete understanding of the nature of the abstract. For instance, Chu Hsi said : " The fact that the Yin and Yang and the Five Forces do not get out of their order, this is *li*." This is to take an order of happening as a *li*. Now, although such an order may also be termed a *li*, yet an abstract *li* is not the order in any concrete set of things, but that by which an order is an order, or that by which a certain class of order is that class of order.

Chu Hsi has been described as a Taoist monk and Lu Hsiang-shan as a Buddhist monk. These words are not without reason. The *Li Hsüeh* School of Neo-Confucianism was influenced in many ways by Taoistic religion, just as the *Hsin Hsüeh* School was influenced by Buddhist religion of the Inner-light form. With regard to the latter, although there was this influence over them, yet what these thinkers emphasized was the Inner-light dictum,

" being mind, being Buddha," but not that of " not mind, not Buddha ". This shows that in their emphasis there was still a touch of the shapes-and-features point of view. This is particularly the case with Wang Yang-ming.

We are, therefore, in a position to say that the philosophy of the Sung and Ming Neo-Confucianists contained the defect which the Inner-light School designated as that of " the adulteration from mud and water ". Because of this these Neo-Confucianists were unable to use their philosophy as a means for reaching the position where they could attain to the sphere of the abstract and ferry over into the beyond. They made a synthesis of the antithesis between the sublime and the common, but the sublime in their synthesis was not perfectly sublime.

The thinkers of the Ch'ing era (1644-1911) were very much like the thinkers of Han times. They took no interest in abstract thinking. They could only imagine : they could not think in the proper sense of the term. Now, their interest in " Han Learning " is by no means inexplicable. In the development of the spirit of Chinese philosophy there came a counter-influence in two periods in its history, namely the Han and the Ch'ing. The thought of the latter epoch was limited to criticism or revision of the Neo-Confucianist philosophy. The revisions they made only drove Neo-Confucianism further from the sublime, whilst their criticisms made out that these theories were too mystical and too empty. From the point of view of this book, it was not that they were too mystical and empty but that they were not mystical and empty enough.

With regard to the *volte-face* in Han times, it was three or four hundred years before philosophy regained its true path. So also with the influence of the Ch'ing epoch. It is only now, after three to four hundred years, that philosophy is beginning to enter on its true path again. In this chapter, I propose to take my new *Li Hsüeh* [1] as the best illustration that I can give of new developments in the spirit of Chinese philosophy.

In the West the last fifty years has seen the most remarkable progress in the study of logic. Yet among Western philosophers there would seem to be few who have been able to utilize this advance in logic as a means for building up the new study of metaphysics, whilst there have been quite a number of logicians who have used this advance as a means for eliminating meta-physics altogether. Whilst they think they have thus eliminated

[1] Cf. Preface I.

metaphysics, really all that they have eliminated is the time-honoured metaphysics of Western philosophy, not metaphysics itself. It is impossible to eliminate metaphysics itself. Nevertheless after these present criticisms have got home, there are bound to be new metaphysical systems which will be very different from the old. The need here is for something not bound to the actual, for affirmations which are not bound by shapes and features but transcend them. Any new metaphysic must avoid assertions about the actual. In what it does have to say, it will say nothing positive. Now, in the history of Western philosophy there would seem to have been no such tradition in metaphysics, and Western philosophers apparently have not found it easy to comprehend how the nonsense which says something but really says nothing can constitute a metaphysic. In the history of Chinese philosophy, fortunately, such a tradition has been created, one built up by the pre-Ch'in Taoists, the Wei-Chin Mystics, and the T'ang Inner-light thinkers. The philosophy which I have called a new *Li Hsüeh* derives its inspiration from this tradition. With the help of the criticisms of metaphysics made by modern logic it sets up a metaphysic which is entirely divorced from the actual.

The new *Li Hsüeh* also derives from the *Li Hsüeh* of the Sung and Ming eras. Thus, in regard to its practical application it bears a resemblance to the Confucianists' concern for the common. In so far as it speaks of *li* it bears a resemblance to what the pre-Ch'in Logicians designated as " universals " (*chih*). At the same time it discovers a suitable position for what in Chinese philosophical language is known as the nameable. In its use of " *ch'i* " the meaning bears a resemblance to the early Taoists' Tao. As for the " unnameable ", as it is called in Chinese philosophy, it also has its proper place. In so far as it is the nonsense which appears to say something and really says nothing, it bears a resemblance to the Taoist, Mystic, and Inner-light Schools. Hence, in its devotion to the sublime it goes beyond the pre-Ch'in and Sung and Ming Confucianist philosophers. Thus it is the inheritor from every point of view of the best traditions in Chinese philosophy. At the same time it passes the test of the criticisms of metaphysics made by modern logic. Being entirely divorced from the actual, it may be described as " empty " (*k'ung*). Its emptiness, however, is only in the sense of the metaphysic having no positive content, not in the sense in which people speak of man's life or the world as empty. In this respect the meaning is different from that given to it by the Taoist,

Mystic, and Inner-light thinkers.   And finally, if I may be allowed to say so, although it is a continuation of the Neo-Confucianists, it is, if not an entirely new metaphysic, at the least an opening of a new road in metaphysical thinking.

In this metaphysical system there are four main concepts, namely *li* (principle or ideal form), *ch'i* (matter), *Tao Ti* (the Evolution of the Tao), and *Ta Ch'üan* (the Great Whole). These all come in the category of formal concepts and have no positive content. They are empty (*k'ung*) concepts. Also, in this new *Li Hsüeh* metaphysic there are four sets of main propositions which also are formal propositions. The four main concepts are derived from these four sets of propositions.

The first set is this : any and every thing (lit. event and thing, or event-thing) cannot but be a certain thing, and being such cannot but belong to a certain class of thing. If a certain class of thing is, then there is that by which that class of thing is that class of thing. To borrow an old expression in Chinese philosophy, " If there are things, there must be *tsê* (principles or laws)."

Let us illustrate this proposition that everything is a certain thing. Thus a mountain is a mountain, a river is a river. It is obviously all right to say " a mountain is a mountain ", or " a river is a river ". Being a certain thing, it follows directly that the thing in question belongs to a certain class of thing, for instance a mountain to the class " mountain ", a river to the class " river ". A metaphysic is not in a position to say in point of fact what classes there are in the actual world, but it is in a position to say that all things cannot but belong to one class or another.

A mountain is a mountain, and a river is a river. A mountain is not a not-mountain, nor a river a not-river. The reason why a mountain is a mountain and not a not-mountain is that a mountain possesses that by which a mountain is a mountain. The same applies to a river : the reason why a river is a river and not a not-river is that a river possesses that by which a river is a river. Here is the formal explanation of a mountain being a mountain or a river being a river. That by which a mountain is a mountain or a river a river is not possessed by this or that upstanding mass of mountain alone, or by this or that length of river alone. There can be no question that other mountains have that by which a mountain is a mountain, and other rivers that by which a river is a river. Other mountains are different from this particular upstanding mass of mountain, but they all equally possess that by which mountains are mountains. The same also applies to other rivers and this or that particular length of river. That which all mountains have in common is that by which mountains are mountains. That which all rivers have in common is that by which rivers are rivers. This is what the new *Li Hsüeh* designates as the *li* of mountains and the *li* of rivers. If there be a mountain, then there is a *li* to it ; and if there be a river, then there is a *li* to it. If there be a certain class of thing, then there is a certain *li* to that class. The *li* of any class of thing is nameable, and the things which belong to any class are things for which it is possible to have a name.

Let us look further into the statement that given there is a certain class of thing, there must be that by which that class of thing is that class of thing. We state it in the form of a proposition : " that there is a certain class of thing implies that there is that by which that class of thing is that class of thing." In this proposition what is implied cannot say more than that which affords the implication. Here, " there is a certain class of thing," is that which implies, and " there is that by which that class of thing is that class of thing ", is that which is implied. The word " is " in the second part of this proposition cannot mean more than the word " is " in the first part. The word " is " in the first part connotes what my new *Li Hsüeh* calls the actual be-ing, which means the existence in time and space. The word " is " in the second part connotes what the new *Li Hsüeh* calls the real be-ing, which means not existing in time and space, and yet not to be spoken of as being nothing. Actual " be-ing " is what Western philosophy has denoted as " existence " : " real be-ing " is what Western philosophy has denoted as " subsistence ".

From this proposition we can infer two other propositions. The one proposition is : " it is possible there is that by which a certain class of thing is that class of thing without there being that class of thing." The other proposition is : " there being that by which a certain class of thing is that class of thing is logically prior to the be-ing of the things in that class." Let us illustrate. " There is a mountain implies there is that by which mountains are mountains." In this proposition, if " there is a mountain " be true, then " there is that by which mountains are mountains " is also true. But if " there is that by which mountains are mountains " be true, it does not necessarily follow that " there is a mountain " is true. This is to say, given the existence of a mountain, then there must be that by which mountains are mountains, but given the subsistence of that by which mountains are mountains, it does not necessarily follow that there is a mountain in existence. That being so, that by which mountains are mountains can subsist without there being any mountains in existence.

I take a second illustration. " That there is a mountain implies there is that by which mountains are mountains." According to this proposition, if there are mountains, then there must first be that by which mountains are mountains. This is just like saying " that Mr. A. is a man implies that Mr. A. is an animal ", then his being a man must be preceded by his being an animal. In these two sentences, " first " and " preceded " refer to logical priority and not priority in time. That by which mountains are mountains is not in time, nor is it actual.

Speaking, then, from the point of view of knowledge, if there be no class of a certain kind of thing, we cannot know that there is that by which this class of thing is this class of thing. On the other hand, speaking from the point of view of logic, without there being that by which this class of thing is this class of thing, it is impossible that there should be this class of thing. Thus, we can infer from the non-subsistence of a certain *li* (principle or ideal form) that no such thing exists, but we cannot infer from the non-existence of the thing the non-subsistence of the *li*. For this reason we are warranted in saying there are more *li* than there are classes of things : that is, assuming that we can properly speak of the *li* (plural) as having a definite number, the number of the *li* is greater than the number of the classes of things.

The *li* taken as a whole are designated in the new *Li Hsüeh* as the *T'ai Chi*, or alternatively as the world of *li*. This world of *li*, logically speaking, has precedence of the actual world. As has been said, " it is empty, silent, without a sign and yet with all forms there " ; and, to use pictorial language, we may say that the variegation among them can be greater than is the case in the actual world. Thus, from a formal explanation of the actual we discover a new world, " a world which is pure and empty of actual content."

In the new *Li Hsüeh* metaphysic, the second set of main propositions is as follows. Things cannot but exist. Those things which exist cannot but be able to exist. Those things which are able to exist cannot but have that by which they are able to exist. To borrow an old expression in Chinese philosophy, " if there is *li*, there must be *ch'i* (matter)."

In the first set of these main propositions the subject of

consideration is classes of things. In the second set the subject of consideration is the individual thing. In the first set we saw that given there be a certain class of thing, then there must be that by which that class of thing is that class of thing, but it does not necessarily follow that if there be that by which a class of thing is that class of thing, there must be that class of thing in existence. We cannot infer the actual from the *li*. All the more we cannot derive the actual from the *li*. Neither can we from the *li* of existence infer existence. The *li* of existence is that by which existence is existence. Given that there is that by which existence is existence, it does not necessarily follow that there is existence. On the other hand, each individual thing is in existence. Starting with the individual thing as the subject of consideration, we make a formal explanation in relation to its existence. Thus, we get the propositions we have set forth above. Those things which can exist must have that by which they can exist, and this, according to the new *Li Hsüeh*, is what is called *ch'i*. Actual things in all cases belong to classes of things : that is to say, actual things actualize their *li*. A *li* cannot actualize itself. There must be a thing in existence before the *li* of it is actualized. Since things must have that by which they can exist before they do exist, therefore we maintain that " if there is *li* there must be *ch'i* ", by which we mean that if there be actualization of a *li* there must be the *ch'i* which actualizes the *li*.

The term *ch'i* may have a relative meaning and also an absolute meaning. Speaking of the relative meaning, it is possible for *ch'i* to be in reference to a certain class. For instance, we ask the question : what is that in an individual man by which he can exist ? The answer may be given that his blood and flesh and sinews and bones are that by which he is able to exist, and these constituent parts may be summed up in one word, *ch'i* in the relative sense. Blood and flesh and sinews and bones are things of certain classes, and they too must have that by which they can exist. We may say that a certain kind of organic element is that by which a man's blood and flesh and sinews and bones can exist. But this element is itself things of a certain class, and must have that by which it can exist. Thus, we can extend the inquiry until we arrive at something about which we cannot say what it is. This something is after all that by which all things can exist, and in itself is only a potentiality of existence. Because it is only a potentiality of existence, therefore we cannot ask what is that by which it can exist. This is what in the new *Li Hsüeh* is called the true, primordial *ch'i*. In thus speaking of *ch'i* as true and primordial the aim is to express an abstract meaning for the term *ch'i*. In my own terminology the term *ch'i* always has an absolute meaning.

The *ch'i* is the something about which we cannot say what it is. There are two reasons for this. One is that if we say what *ch'i* is, we are bound to say that the things which exist are the product of this whatever-it-is, and to say this is to make an assertion about the actual, and this whatever-it-is is *ipso facto* in the sphere of shapes and features. The second reason is that if we say that *ch'i* is anything definite, then what is called *ch'i*, *ipso facto*, becomes something which can exist and ceases to be that by which all things are able to exist. *Ch'i* is not a " what ". It is the unnameable, or to use the term used so often in this book, " non-being."

In the new *Li Hsüeh* metaphysic the third set of main propositions is as follows. Existence is a continuous process. All existences are existences of things. The existence of a thing is the process of actualization of a certain *li* by means of its *ch'i*. Existence viewed as a whole is the process of actualization of the *T'ai Chi* (the Supreme Point of Perfection) by means of the true primordial *ch'i*. All continuous processes taken as a whole are to be called " the Evolution of the Tao ". All processes imply change and movement, and the change and movement implied in all processes is to be called *Ch'ien Yüan* (the First Mover). To borrow an old expression in Chinese philosophy, " there is non-being, yet there is the *T'ai Chi* " ; and again, " the *Ch'ien Tao* transforms, and everything is true to its nature and destiny."

This set of propositions comes from a formal explanation of the actuality of things. Therefore we may draw the conclusion that these propositions are necessarily true in regard to everything. Existence is a continuous process, because to exist is itself a movement, is to do something. A movement must continue to move, otherwise it ceases to be a movement. Existence must continue to exist, otherwise it ceases to be existence. Continuation is the continuation of process. In actual fact, there is no such thing as just bare existence as such, and this is why all existences are existences of things. Whatever exists is a thing ; and since things being things must belong to one or more classes of things, it follows that they are the actualization of one or more *li*. That being so, that which actualizes one or more *li* is *ch'i*. Since the *ch'i* which actualizes a certain *li* becomes the things which

I

are in that class, and since there is no thing which does not exist, and no existence which is not the existence of a thing, and since there is no thing which is a thing and yet does not belong to a certain class, it follows that the existence of a thing is the process of actualizing a certain *li* by means of *ch'i*.

The actual is then the whole of things, whilst the *T'ai Chi* is the whole of the *li*. From this it follows that the existence of the actual is the process by which the primordial *ch'i* actualizes the *T'ai Chi* (Supreme Point of Perfection). Since all the processes taken together as a whole equal the Evolution of the Tao, this evolution is the process of this actualization.

Since all processes imply change and movement, and process is itself change and movement, then actualization of the *li* of change and movement by means of *ch'i* is prior in the logical sense to the actualization of the rest of the *li*. As a matter of fact, there is no bare process as such. All processes are processes of the actualization of the *li* of certain classes of things. For example, all the animals there are belong to one class of animal or another. Being an animal of a certain class implies being an animal. Speaking logically, in order to be an animal of a certain class, an animal must first be an animal. On the other hand, as a matter of fact, there is no animal which is not an animal of a certain class, that is to say, a mere animal as such does not exist. Although a mere animal as such does not exist, it is implied in an animal " being an animal of a certain class ". So the mere animal as such is logically prior to any class of animal. In pictorial thought when mention is made of priority, the reference is always to time. From this angle then, an animal which is prior to any class of animal is ancestor of all animals. But in our statements above we are not referring to priority in the sense of time, and when we speak of animals generally we are not thinking of the ancestor of the animals but only of " animal ".

Actually there is no such thing as bare process as such, but the bare process as such is implied in any sort of process. Logically speaking, it is prior to any sort of process. It is " the First Mover ". In pictorial thought " the First Mover " was the creator of all things, namely the being spoken of as God. But this First Mover is not God, nor is it a creator. It is only the change and movement implied in all sorts of process. Since this change and movement is change and movement, it follows that it is the actualization of the *li* of change and movement by means of *ch'i*. In my *Hsin Li Hsüeh* book, this is called " the changing and moving *ch'i* ", and later on it is spoken of as " *Ch'ien Yüan* " (the First Mover). This name of *Ch'ien Yüan* may appear to mean what in pictorial thought is thought of as the Creator, but in my thought it may be described as the pure activity of *ch'i*. By that is meant that what is actualized is no more than the *li* of change and movement and not yet the *li* of anything else. This " not yet " has only a logical significance, not an actual or temporal one. To speak of a *Ch'ien Yüan* is only to make a formal explanation of the actual. Hence, to speak of there being a *Ch'ien Yüan* does not entail any assertion about the actual. To speak of God or a Creator is in the nature of an assertion about the actual.

In the new *Li Hsüeh* metaphysic, the fourth set of main propositions is as follows. The sum total of beings is the Great Whole. The Great Whole is then the sum total of beings. To borrow an old expression in Chinese philosophy, " the One is the all, and the all is the One."

Since the Great Whole is another name for all that is, to say that the Great Whole is the sum total of beings is a tautological proposition. To this I reply that all things equally belong to the Great Whole, but what belongs to the Great Whole is not only things. The task of metaphysics is to make a formal explanation of everything actual. Once this grade of explanation is made, there is in addition the discovery of the world of *li*. The subject matter of metaphysics is all that is and at the beginning of its task the all is seen to be the all in the realm of the actual. When metaphysics is near to completing its task, the all is seen to be not only the all in the realm of the actual but also the all in the realm of the real.[1] There is that which has actual be-ing : there is that which only has real be-ing ; and all these taken together are what is called the Great Whole. Because all that is is included in it, therefore it is called the whole. This whole is not a sectional whole, not like China as a whole or mankind as a whole. Hence it is the Great Whole.

The Great Whole may also be called the universe. This which I call the universe is not the universe of physics or astronomy. That is the physical universe. The physical universe may be said to be a whole but it is only a sectional whole, it is not the supreme whole beyond which there is no other. What I mean by the universe is not the physical universe but the supreme whole.

[1] The real includes the actual. (F. Y. L.)

The Great Whole may be named the One. The pre-Ch'in philosophers, as also the Buddhists and Western philosophers, constantly spoke of the One. What they wished to express was not what was usually meant by oneness. Thus the term " Supreme Oneness " or " Great Oneness " was constantly on the lips of the pre-Chin philosophers, whilst the Buddhists spoke of the " Mysterious Oneness ". Western philosophers have constantly trusted to the first letter of the word for " one " being written with a capital. The new *Li Hsüeh* borrows the Buddhist saying, " the One is the all and the all is the One."

Although I borrow the Buddhists' words to express my meaning, yet my meaning is not the same as the Buddhists' meaning. The new *Li Hsüeh*, in speaking of the One as the all and the all as the One, makes no assertion that there are inner connections or internal relations [1] between things. What the new *Li Hsüeh* is asserting is merely a formal oneness. The One is only the general name for the all, so that although we speak of the One being the all and the all being the One, there is no assertion about the actual.

The four sets of propositions above are all analytical propositions, or, as we may say, formal propositions, and from these we get four formal concepts, one of *li*, one of *ch'i*, one of the Evolution of the Tao, and one of the Great Whole. From the new *Li Hsüeh* point of view the true task of metaphysics consists in proposing and expounding these four concepts.

Li and *ch'i* are concepts gained from speculative analysis in regard to things. The Evolution of the Tao and the Great Whole are concepts gained from speculative synthesis in regard to things. In Chapter V the statement was made that what the *Yi Amplifications* called the Tao was an unclear idea in relation to what we mean by *li*, and what the Taoists called the Tao was an unclear idea in relation to what we mean by *ch'i*. These ideas are open to criticism as unclear because what they call the Tao is in both cases capable of being analysed further. The " Tao " of the *Amplifications* and the " Tao " of the Taoists were both able to produce. Thus we are in a position to say that where there is something which is able to produce there must be that by which a producer is a producer, namely the *li* of a producer. The actual producer is an existent something, and it must have that by which

[1] Internal relations are those relations which idealist philosophers such as Bradley have emphasized. The inner connections are such connections as the Buddhists have emphasized. (F. Y. L.)

it is able to exist. This is the *ch'i* of those things which can produce. The Tao in the *Yi Amplifications* is akin to what we call *li*, but it is not purely *li*. What the Taoists called Tao is akin to *ch'i*, but it is not purely *ch'i*. This is why I say that these concepts are not pure concepts. What they represent is not " that which is prior to things ".[1] This priority is not in connection with time : it is a logical priority. *Li and ch'i* are both prior to things. Because *li* and *ch'i* represent the final result of speculative analysis in regard to things, it is impossible to go any further in regard to analysis. Therefore *li* and *ch'i* are prior to all things : nothing can be logically prior to them.

The concept of *li* bears a resemblance to the concept of " being " in Greek philosophy, notably in Plato and Aristotle, and in modern philosophy, notably in Hegel. The concept of *ch'i* also bears a resemblance to the concept of " non-being " in these philosophers. The concept of the Evolution of the Tao bears a resemblance to their concept of " becoming " or " change ". The concept of the Great Whole bears a resemblance to their concept of " the Absolute ". According to the theories of the Western tradition the task of metaphysics is also to propose and to expound these concepts. From my point of view the four concepts which I set up only bear a resemblance to Western traditional metaphysics with its four concepts. This is because the four concepts in the new *Li Hsüeh* are derived by the formal method, and therefore are entirely formal concepts. In them there is no positive element. In the Western tradition the four concepts are not necessarily derived by the formal method and do contain some positive elements ; and being so make assertions about the actual. That, however, which has no positive element contains no assertion about the actual.

Speaking strictly, the concept of the Great Whole and that which it attempts to represent do not correspond to each other. The concept of the Great Whole is a concept, and all concepts are in the realm of thought. But what this concept attempts to represent cannot be made an object of thought. Since the Great Whole equals all being, there can be nothing outside it ; as Hui Shih said : " the greatest has nothing beyond itself and is to be called the Great One." The Great Whole is just this Great One. If it were not and there were something outside, then the Great Whole is not a whole, and the one is a duality, in other words not one. If we take the Great Whole as an object of thought,

---

[1] An expression found in the *Chuang Tzŭ* Book. (E. R. H.)

then the Great Whole as an object of thought does not include the thought of it. That being so, then this Great Whole has something outside itself and is not the Great Whole. The conclusion is that the Great Whole cannot be thought. That being so, it cannot be expressed in words, because the Great Whole which is expressed in words does not include that expression. That being so, this Great Whole has something outside itself and is not the Great Whole. What cannot be the object of thought or put into words is something which cannot be comprehended. That does not necessarily mean that it is a " chaos ". All we say is that it is impossible for it to be the object of comprehension.

Continuing from this angle, the Evolution of the Tao also is something which cannot be thought or expressed because it is the whole of all forms of process. Thought and speech are themselves processes. The Evolution of Tao as an object of thought and expression does not include these processes. Any total of all forms of process which does not include these two processes is not the whole of all the forms of process and accordingly is not the Evolution of the Tao.

Ch'i also cannot be thought or expressed, but the reason why it is inexpressible is different from the reason why the Great Whole and the Evolution of the Tao are so. The reason for their being so is that it is impossible for them to be the objects of thought and speech, for if they are, then they are not the Great Whole and Evolution of the Tao. The reason why *ch'i* is not thinkable or expressible is that it is impossible for it to have a name. If we give it a general name, then we *ipso facto* make it some sort of thing and in accordance with its *li*. But it is not any sort of thing nor is it in accord with any *li*. This is why in my *Hsin Li Hsüeh* book it is maintained that though a name is given it, namely *ch'i*, this is to be taken as a proper name. Since metaphysics is not history, how can it have proper names? This is a very real difficulty. Hence our naming *ch'i* is done because we cannot help doing so, as was the case with Lao Tzŭ in naming his Tao.

It may be some one will say that the reason for the Ch'ing era scholars criticizing Neo-Confucianism was because it was an " empty kind of knowledge ". (*Vide* Ku Ting-ling's *Sayings.*) That was to say, it was not practical. Yen Hsi-chai said : " The sage man in coming forth undoubtedly would build up a work of peace in the cause of Heaven and Earth." The northern and southern Sung Neo-Confucianists at their most flourishing period " on the one hand did not achieve anything to help in the danger the country was in, and on the other hand did not produce any one who had the calibre of a prime minister or a general. Should an age of many sages and worthies be like that ? " (*Ts'un Hsüeh Pien, Criticism of Hsing and Li*.) By parity of reasoning, if the new *Li Hsüeh's* main concepts are all formal, then it is empty and not practical, and all the less can it give men positive knowledge about the actual. The Neo-Confucianists denied that they came near to mysticism or the Inner-light position. The new *Li Hsüeh* publicly confesses that it is near to mysticism and the Inner-light position. How can it fail then to be more impractical ?

All we then need to say is that what we are discussing is philosophy. We can only take philosophy as philosophy, and philosophy of its very nature is an " empty branch of know-ledge ". It is a form of study which enables men to achieve entry into the highest sphere of living. It is not concerned with increasing man's knowledge or ability concerning the actual. Lao Tzǔ made a distinction between the Tao and ordinary knowledge. A philosophical discussion or the study of philosophy belongs to the branch of the Tao, not to that of ordinary learning.

The mistakes in the former Chinese philosophers for the most part do not arise from their attention to the " empty branch of knowledge ", but from their failure to know themselves or from their failure to express clearly that what they studied was the " empty branch of knowledge ". Some of them were wrong in regarding the sage man as one who merely by virtue of his being a sage had the very highest form of knowledge with regard to the actual, or the ability of controlling practical affairs. Some of them may not have had this wrong idea, but the words they used to describe the sage gave people this wrong impression. For instance, the *Yi Amplifications* say : " The sage man makes an accord between Heaven and Earth and his virtue, between the sun and the moon and his intelligence, between the four seasons and his sense of order, between the manes and the spirits and his good and bad fortune." Or, as the *Chung Yung* put it : " The sage man is in a position to aid the transforming, nourishing processes of Heaven and Earth." Or, as the *Hsiang-Kuo Commentary* on the *Chuang Tzǔ Book* (*Sao Yao Yu Chapter*), says : " The minds of sage men explored the possibilities of the Yin and the Yang to their furthest point, exhausted the mysterious destinies of all things." Sheng Chao [1] in his *Essays* said about the sage man : " His knowledge has an exhaustive and mysterious purview, his divine powers have the utility of meeting all occasions." He also said : " The sage men's achievements are as sublime as Heaven and Earth and yet are not *jen*, they shine with the splendour of the sun and the moon and yet are obscure to view." Chu Hsi, in speaking of the effort entailed in the examination of things and the extension of knowledge, said : " With regard to the long expenditure of strength and then one day, in a flash, everything becoming linked up together, this is a revelation of the outside and the inside, of the refined and the coarse in all things, and my mind in its essence and its prime function becomes enlightened in every way." These words are apt to make the deep impression that the sage man is one who merely in virtue of his being a sage has nothing which he cannot know, has nothing which he cannot do. To learn to be a sage man is like what amongst Buddhists and Taoists was spoken of as learning to be a Buddha, learning to be an immortal. To learn up to a certain standard naturally entails having a certain numinous power. Ordinary people regard a sage man as bound to have the very greatest knowledge, the very greatest practical ability ; and amongst the Neo-Confucianists there were a number who thought so. Thus, amongst these scholars there were a number who regarded themselves as having expended the necessary effort " in dwelling in reverence and maintaining sincerity ", and so, in knowledge of the actual and in practical ability, as being themselves fully capable without any need of further learning. Thus they did not work for any further knowledge or ability. To be in that state of mind is inevitably to be without knowledge and without ability. " These men used such loose words in setting up a standard for the people, establishing a mind for Heaven and Earth, setting forth the achievement of peace for ten thousand generations, to intimidate and silence all men. When suddenly the country was in danger and the time came for them to pay their debt to their country, then their jaws dropped, and they were like men sitting in a mist." (Huang Li-chou's (A.D. 1610–95) Sayings, *Nang Lei Wen Ting, Later Collection*, ch. 3.) These men were quite useless, and this for the reason that they did not know that they had learnt an empty learning. If they had known that their learning was such, they

---

[1] Cf. Chapter 7, p. 147 *et seq.*

might have taken early measures to learn something else which was of some use, and so have avoided becoming useless.

In the new *Li Hsüeh* it is realized that it is concerned with philosophy and that philosophy of its very nature can do nothing more than exalt man's sphere of living, that philosophy is not qualified to give men positive knowledge in regard to the actual. Because this is so, it is also not qualified to give men the ability of controlling practical affairs. Philosophy has the power to enable men, in the midst of answering to the claims of humdrum affairs, to make the most of their inherent nature and achieve their highest destiny. It has this power also whilst an airman is engaged in taking a plane up into the air or a gunner is engaged in firing his gun. But it has no knowledge to give on how to discharge the humdrum duties, on how to control a plane or fire a gun. Thus, from this point of view philosophy is useless.

This being the position affirmed by the new *Li Hsüeh*, it is to be noted that of all the schools of thought mentioned in the foregoing chapters only two agree with it, namely the Inner-light School and the school of Wang Yang-ming. The former of the two understood and acknowledged that the sage man, in virtue only of his being a sage man, was not necessarily endowed with knowledge and ability. They said that what the sage man could do was to wear clothes and eat food, to relieve his bowels and make water. As they said, the Inner-light method is the gold-and-ordure method ; namely, when you do not understand it, it is like gold, when you do understand it, it is like ordure. Nevertheless, most people had the idea that the Inner-light School, in saying this, meant something deliberately paradoxical. Also, because this school had not entirely lost its religious quality therefore ordinary people also made the legend that the great teachers of this school had every kind of miraculous power. This is the reason why later generations have not understood or paid attention to the fact that this school had this philosophical position.

Wang Yang-ming had his " theory of eradicating the root and blocking the source ". As he said, " If theories of eradicating the root and blocking the source be not understood anywhere in the country, then for all those everywhere who are learning the way of sagehood, the longer they do it, the more difficult they find it. These men are sunk in animality and barbarism and yet thinking they are learning to be sages." Further : " To learn to be a sage consists in something extremely simple and extremely easy, something easy to know and easy to carry out, easy to learn and easy to be competent in. The reason for this is that, generally speaking, the way to become a sage is nothing more than restoring the original essence of the mind, which is common to all men, and leaving knowledge and skill out of account. (*Reply to Ku Tung-ch'iao, Recorded Sayings for Exercising*, ch. 2.)   Wang Yang-ming also said : " That by which pure gold is pure gold is the purity and not the weight : that by which a sage is a sage is his being perfect in the *li* (ideal pattern) of Heaven and not in his having any skill. The result is that all men can take on this learning by which their minds can become perfect in the *li* of Heaven, and thus they can become sages, just as with an ounce of gold in comparison with ten thousand pounds of it, although the weight is different, the purity is the same. That is why all men can become a Yao or a Shun." (*Op. cit.*, ch. 1.)

Although this statement is true, yet in one respect it does not go far enough.   Practical ability and sphere of living are two entirely different matters, nor do they necessarily have any connection with each other. To speak of a sage with great ability as ten thousand pounds of gold, of a sage without this ability as an ounce of gold, is as if ability and sphere were connected with each other to some extent.   In this respect, we may say that Wang Yang-ming did not wean himself entirely from the ordinary attitude of mind.

Positive knowledge and practical ability, this, as has been emphasized, is outside the purview of the new *Li Hsüeh*. Yet the concepts of *li* and *ch'i* can enable men's minds to wander in that which is prior (*ch'u*) to things and the concepts of the Evolution of the Tao and the Great Whole enable men's minds to wander in the wholeness of being. With the aid of these concepts, men can know Heaven, can serve Heaven, and can rejoice in Heaven to the point where they become identified with Heaven. With the help of these concepts the sphere in which men live can become different from the unselfconsciously natural, the utilitarian and the moral.

These four concepts are also " empty ". What they represent is what transcends shapes and features. Therefore the sphere we attain to with their aid is the sphere of the empty beyond. The men who are in this sphere are absorbed in the abstract and ferried over into the beyond.

Although these men have become thus ferried over into the beyond, yet the business in which they are engaged may be the discharge of the daily duties in human relations. They are mysteriously remote and yet not divorced from actual utility. They are in the beyond, and yet they are still engaged in " carrying water and chopping wood ", " in serving their fathers and serving their sovereign." And this does not merely mean that these humble offices are no barrier to their being in the beyond, but that in regard to their selves these offices are an absorption in the abstract, are a ferrying over into the beyond. The sphere in which they live is that of the sublime, but this sublime is one and the same as the common.

The men of this sphere are sage men. If philosophy can enable men to become sage men, then this is the usefulness of philosophy's uselessness. And should this coming to be a sage man be the reaching to the height of what it means to be a man, this is the usefulness of philosophy's uselessness. This kind of uselessness may rightly be called the highest form of usefulness.

As Shao Yung said in the Sung era : " The sage man is the perfection of humanity." Humanity's highest point is what Chuang Chou called " the perfect man ". A certain branch of knowledge or kind of ability may make a man an expert in a certain profession, for instance as a physician or an engineer. Philosophy cannot do that. It can only make a man a perfect man. The perfect man is not limited to any particular profession. Any man whose avocation is of use to society can become a perfect man. But nobody can devote himself to the profession of being a perfect man. Should he attempt to do that, he would at once become like a monk devoting himself to the profession of becoming a Buddha. Immediately he would fall between the two stools of the sublime and the common.

A sage man cannot merely by virtue of being a sage become a competent man of affairs. But he can by virtue alone of being a sage become a king. What is more, and speaking strictly, it is only a sage who is supremely suited to be a king. When I say " king ", I am thinking of the man who has the highest quality of leadership in a society. There is no need for such a leader to do anything very much himself. Indeed, he ought not to do anything much himself, in other words he should be *wu wei* (inactive), as the Taoists maintained. As the *Chuang Tzŭ Book* put it : " The man at the top must certainly be *wu wei* and so employ all men in society : the man below must certainly be *yu wei* (active) and so be employed for the whole of society." This does not mean that the supreme leader in his *wu wei* just does nothing, but that he gets all the talents in the country to do their best. And since the supreme leader does not do anything himself, there is no need for him to have any special professional knowledge and ability. And, should he have any such knowledge and ability, he ought not to exercise it ; and this because, if he does something, he *ipso facto* becomes inoperative in other ways. He should not be operative but set all the talents in the country to do their best. Let him do that, and he will do nothing, but everything will get done.

What the man who is the supreme leader needs is a mind which is open and impartial and all-embracive. It is only the man who lives in the transcendent sphere who can really be like this. He identifies himself with the Great Whole and can see things from the standpoint of the Great Whole. His mind is like the Great Whole in which all things follow their own course and do not conflict with each other. Thus his mind is all-embracing. In his sphere of living he is not on the same level with things, but is above them. Therefore he is the most suitable to be the supreme leader in society.

Hence the sage man, by virtue alone of his being a sage man, is best suited to be king. If then what philosophy deals with is the Tao by which men can become sage men, then the result is what early in this book was spoken of as sageness within and kingliness without. In spite of the highly mystical and " empty " nature of the new *Li Hsüeh*, yet it retains this feature, that it upholds sageness within and kingliness without, and, further, attempts to probe into the essential elements in this Tao.

INDEX

Abstract, the, 45–6
Abstract thinking, 59
Achievement, great, 91–2
Action and inaction, 142, 153–4
Action and knowledge, 198
Aim of Chinese philosophy, 3, 4
Amoral actions, 13, 14
Ancient Text school, 128
Argument, 48–9, 66
Axis of Tao, 67, 72

Being and non-being, 60 ff., 113–14, 139–141, 213
" Best," the, 14
Buddha, 1, 13
Buddha-nature, 159, 163
Buddhism, 128–9, 146–7, 188, 199 ; Ch'an school, 156 ff.

Causation, 150 ; the Sage and, 157
Chang Tsai, 175–7, 179, 181, 189–190, 202
Chao Chou, 166
Ch'en Ch'un, 11 n.
Ch'eng Hao, 175, 179–184, 193, 197, 199–201
Cheng K'ang-chen, 89, 127
Cheng Meng, 175–7
Ch'eng Yi, 16, 184–6, 192, 200
Ch'engs, the Two, 184
chi, 96, 187
ch'i, 23 n., 24, 27, 47, 79, 120, 121, 123 ; and Tao, 85–6, 113, 114, 118–19 ; varied meanings, 119 ; Chang Tsai and, 175–6 ; Neo-Confucianists and, 189–191, 202 ; new *Li Hsüeh* and, 204–5, 207 ff.
Chiang Yüan-chin, 187
Chieh Chuang Hsia, quoted, 40
Chien Ai Chung, quoted, 43
Chien Ai Shang, quoted, 40
Chien Pai Lun, 57
Chien Tsu T'u, 89
Ch'ien Yüan, 209–211
Chih (a universal), 52–3
chih (wisdom), 11, 18–19, 69 ; new *Li Hsüeh* and, 204
Ch'ing thinkers, 203
Ching Yüan, 166
Chou Tun-yi, 183, 202
Chu Hsi, 17, 25 n., 27, 106, 186–192, 200, 202, 216
Ch'ü Li, quoted, 18
Chuang Chou, 9, 32, 65–6, 70–1, 76, 134–8, 146, 219 ; Hsün Tzŭ on,

Chuang Tzŭ, 5–9, 10, 31–2, 48–51, 58, 60, 61, 63 ff., 113–14, 130, 132, 136, 139, 141 ff., 154, 219
chung, 17, 38
Chung Ni Yen Chü, 18
Chung Yung, 3 n., 13, 16, 82–3, 103 ff., 117, 122, 215
Classes and things, 205 ff.
Composure of the Nature, Letter on, 182–4, 197
Confucius, 10 ff., 30, 75, 79–80, 117, 127–8, 134–5, 137 ; *Chung Yung* on, 103
Consideration for others, 17
Correcting the Ignorant, 178–9, 202
Creation, mystics and, 140
Critique of the Seven Worthies of the Bamboo Grove, 120
Cultivation, spiritual, 160–2

Dialecticians, 48 ff., 66, 132
Distinctions, 68, 76, 78

Enlightenment, and realness, 108–9 ; sudden, 157–8, 163
Equilibrium and harmony, 107
Evolution of the Tao, 205
Existence, new *Li Hsüeh* and, 209–211 ; *see also* Subsistence
Experience, possible objects of, 45

Fa Yin, 166–7
Fate, Confucianist view of, 34–5
First Mover, see *Ch'ien Yüan*
First Principle, inexpressibility of, 159–160
" Five Constant Virtues," 11
Fo Kuo, 171
Forces, Five, *see Hsing*, Five
Forgetfulness, sitting in, 75–6
" Four Buds," 11
fu (returning), 98–9
Funerals, Mohists and, 40–1

God, 46, 126
" Great Man," 26–7
" Great Whole," 205

Han Fei Tzŭ, 30
Han K'ang-po, 85
Hao jan chih ch'i, 19 n., 23–7, 127–8
Harmony, and equilibrium, 107–8 ; Supreme, 175

221